Palgrave Teaching and Learning

Series Editor: **Sally Brown**

Coaching and Mentoring in Higher Education
Facilitating Work-Based Learning
Facilitating Workshops
For the Love of Learning
Fostering Self-Efficacy in Higher Education Students
Leading Dynamic Seminars
Learning, Teaching and Assessment in Higher Education
Live Online Learning
Masters Level Teaching, Learning and Assessment

Further titles are in preparation

Universities into the 21st Century

Series Editors: **Noel Entwistle and Roger King**

Becoming an Academic
Cultures and Change in Higher Education
Global Inequalities and Higher Education
Learning Development in Higher Education
Managing your Academic Career
Managing your Career in Higher Education Administration
Research and Teaching
Teaching Academic Writing in UK Higher Education
Teaching for Understanding at University
Understanding the International Student Experience
The University in the Global Age
Writing in the Disciplines

Palgrave Research Skills

Authoring a PhD
The Foundations of Research (2nd edn)
Getting to Grips with Doctoral Research
Getting Published
The Good Supervisor (2nd edn)
Maximizing the Impacts of University Research
PhD by Published Work
The PhD Viva
Planning Your Postgraduate Research
The Postgraduate Research Handbook (2nd edn)
The Professional Doctorate
Structuring Your Research Thesis

You may also be interested in:

Teaching Study Skills and Supporting Learning

For a complete listing of all our titles in this area please visit
www.palgrave.com/studyskills

Learning with the Labyrinth

Creating Reflective Space in Higher Education

Edited by

Jan Sellers
Bernard Moss

First published 2016 by
PALGRAVE

Palgrave in the UK is an imprint of Macmillan Publishers Limited, registered in England, company number 785998, of 4 Crinan Street, London, N1 9XW.

Palgrave is a global imprint of the above company and is represented throughout the world.

Palgrave® and Macmillan® are registered trademarks in the United States, the United Kingdom, Europe and other countries.

ISBN: 978–1–137–39383–8 paperback

This book is printed on paper suitable for recycling and made from fully managed and sustained forest sources. Logging, pulping and manufacturing processes are expected to conform to the environmental regulations of the country of origin.

A catalogue record for this book is available from the British Library.

A catalog record for this book is available from the Library of Congress.

Inside front cover:

The Canterbury Labyrinth (University of Kent, England) in heavy frost, with Canterbury Cathedral in the distance.

Photograph courtesy Jim Higham, University of Kent.

Printed and bound by CPI Group (UK) Ltd, Croydon, CR0 4YY

By the same authors:

Holloway, Margaret and Moss, Bernard (2010), *Spirituality and Social Work,* Basingstoke: Palgrave Macmillan

Moss, Bernard (2015), *Communication Skills in Health and Social Care* (3rd edn), London: Sage

Sewell, Ruth, Sellers, Jan and Williams, Di (eds) (2012), *Working with the Labyrinth: Paths for Exploration,* Glasgow: Wild Goose

Contents

List of figures and tables

Teaching resources to photocopy: diagrams by Jeff Saward, Labyrinthos

List of figures

List of tables

About the editors

▶ Jan Sellers

Dr Jan Sellers is a National Teaching Fellow (NTF), Fellow of the Higher Education Academy and Fellow of the Royal Society of Arts. Jan is a freelance lecturer, leading workshops and labyrinth events in educational, Quaker and community contexts. At the University of Kent, she founded the Student Learning Advisory Service, developing holistic approaches to student learning development and retention. Following her NTF award, Jan became Kent's first Creative Learning Fellow, playing a key role in 'Creative Campus' initiatives including Kent's labyrinth project and the installation of the Canterbury Labyrinth. She is co-editor of *Working with the Labyrinth: Paths for Exploration* (Glasgow: Wild Goose, 2012).

▶ Bernard Moss

Bernard Moss is Emeritus Professor of Social Work Education and Spirituality at Staffordshire University, UK, and a Principal Fellow and National Teaching Fellow of the Higher Education Academy, UK. Using his portable canvas labyrinth he leads staff and student workshops in higher education settings as well as in religious contexts. He was an invited contributor to *Inspiring Academics: Learning with the World's Great University Teachers* (2011, OUP). His publications include *Spirituality and Social Work* (2010, with Margaret Holloway, Palgrave Macmillan) and *Communication Skills in Health and Social Care* (2015, 3rd edn, Sage).

Both Jan and Bernard have trained with Veriditas as labyrinth facilitators (Jan to advanced level, in Chartres, France, 2013). Jan is a life member of the Labyrinth Society. She is also amongst the first four advanced facilitators who are now accredited to lead Veriditas-approved workshops.

Acknowledgements

We wish to acknowledge the many colleagues and friends whose labyrinth experiences and expertise have enriched our own journeys and have drawn us into deeper understanding of this fascinating artefact.

To our colleagues at Palgrave, past and present, during the production of this book, and to our reviewers, we extend our gratitude for their faith in this innovative project, and for their detailed feedback and suggestions, which have only served to make the book better. We thank Dr Gaie Burnet, Alex Irving and Jeff Saward for expert advice at challenging times, and Veriditas and the Labyrinth Society for the opportunities they have given, to learn, to network, ask questions and deepen our understanding. It is a rich and continuing journey. We are especially grateful to the contributors to this book, who have generously shared their teaching, learning and research and who have encouraged us, questioned us – and shown admirable patience. Thank you all!

To the amazingly rich and diverse network of UK National Teaching Fellows we owe more than we can ever say. Their inspiring commitment to excellence in learning and teaching has provided us with a framework and a goal for our own contribution; and without Sally Brown's wisdom, inspiration and generosity at the cutting edge of learning and teaching, we would all be immensely poorer.

Jan wishes to thank colleagues and students, past and present, at the University of Kent, whose vision and enthusiasm enabled the labyrinth project to take root on the Canterbury and Medway campuses – including, not least, the building of the Canterbury Labyrinth. To visit the University recently and find students creating a performance of *Romeo and Juliet* on the labyrinth – theatre in the round – was a sheer delight and bodes well for future innovation. On a personal note, working on a book such as this has been a real adventure. Jan would like to express her heartfelt appreciation for the support and encouragement given by her partner, Sue McCarthy, in the course of this fascinating journey.

Bernard wishes to thank his academic colleagues and students at Staffordshire University who have shared in his labyrinth workshops and have thereby helped him appreciate the unfolding riches of its rhythms; and to acknowledge the loving companionship of Sheila who has made every aspect of their journey together infinitely worthwhile.

Jan Sellers and Bernard Moss
October 2015

Series Editor's Preface

▷ **Palgrave Teaching and Learning**

I am delighted to include this highly original volume in the Palgrave Teaching and Learning series, designed for all who care about teaching and learning in higher education. The series has the express aim of providing useful, relevant, current and helpful guidance on key issues in learning and teaching in the tertiary/post-compulsory education sector. Texts in this series address a range of essential teaching and learning imperatives, with a deliberately international focus. This book is a particularly valuable contribution to the series in that it offers fresh perspectives on how to foster learning through a unique kind of reflective space for learning. The editors are both UK National Teaching Fellows, so are teachers of demonstrable excellence, committed to sharing good practice with others. Their contributing authors draw on international best practice to illustrate how creative spaces can be established and maintained in universities and colleges.

If you read this book from start to finish, by the end you will have learned a great deal not only about using labyrinths in higher education settings but also about yourself, with the process of reading in some ways emulating walking calmly and progressively through a labyrinth. If you dip in and out you will still gain valuable perspectives: after all the authors themselves say it is permissible (and even to be encouraged) to skip across boundaries. Working across and beyond disciplinary and institutional structures is, of course, what excellent educators often do best.

Sally Brown
August 2015

1 Introduction: The heart of learning

Jan Sellers

Above all, do not lose your desire to walk ... I have walked myself into my best thoughts

(Søren Kierkegaard, 1978, p. 214)

As a mature PhD student, I studied women's working lives. During that time, I played with and was inspired by the image of a patchwork quilt, using this to represent career development for those who work as part-time teachers in adult and continuing education (Sellers, 2001). The image spoke to me of something enduring, useful, often beautiful, built up from pieces; something you could see in sections, but never know the whole until, perhaps, the end of one's life. The complexity of the metaphor allowed for change and uncertainty, opportunities taken or relinquished, whilst recognising creativity (even if not, at the time, identified as such) and the strength required in building a career out of fragments.

Gradually, over the last eight years, I have made a transition to a different image, an image of a winding and convoluted path where, at any time, the walker can stand still, look back on their journey so far and look ahead, knowing that one foot in front of the other will bring them safely to the centre and the return to the outer world. Unlike a maze, a labyrinth commonly has just one path to the centre, and you can always see where you are as the 'walls' are low or non-existent. To walk a labyrinth is to experience, physically, the metaphor of journey. It is a potentially powerful and deeply peaceful experience, and as many have found, this narrow, meditative path may offer the opportunity for fresh insights, for time within – in touch with our inner selves – and for renewal.

Since 2007, I have explored ways of teaching and learning with labyrinths. The metaphor of journey, the path solitary or shared, is the journey of our lives and the many forms and stages that journey takes: as students, researchers, teachers, advisers and within our communities; our journey to

1

the present moment; the times when we look back at the path we have taken, and reflect on our way forward. The labyrinth offers a place of deep reflection, of calm and contemplation; a wellspring for creativity; a place to connect with our deepest selves. This is the heart of Higher Education: this is what teaching and learning is about. It is the inspiration for this book.

▶ Labyrinth or maze?

The confusion between maze and labyrinth in the English language is unhelpful and the two words still overlap today in common use. In the literature on mazes and labyrinths, however, a valuable distinction is made. A maze has many paths, high walls and dead ends: it is designed for confusion. A labyrinth commonly has just one path: *'there are no choices to be made, and the path inevitably leads to, and ends at, the centre ... once there, the walker must turn around and retrace the same path to return to the outside'* (Kern, 2000, p. 23). Kern describes the labyrinth as *'a symbol of wholeness, offering one clear path'* (2000, p. 306). The low walls (or 'fields'), sometimes just simple lines, are there purely to define the path, and the walker has an unobstructed view, giving a sense of safety absent from a maze. The illustration inside the front cover of this book shows the Canterbury Labyrinth in heavy frost: the path is paved with stone and the 'walls' are curves of grass.

Figure 1.1 shows a labyrinth pattern known as the 'classical labyrinth'. This design is some 4000 years old and has been discovered around the world, from petroglyphs (carved on rock faces) in Spain and India, to patterns on pottery, coins, Roman mosaics and much more (Kern, 2000; Saward, 2003a). Laid out on the ground, and large enough to walk on, this pattern may at first have been a dance (Kern, 2000) and in this form is also found in many parts of the world, as historic artefact, meditative walking space or both. To draw this pattern requires a simple technique, easy to learn and readily transmitted (see Jeff Saward's chapter). As patterns became more complex they were, of necessity, recorded on manuscript; such patterns contain much of interest to mathematicians as well as historians (McCague, 2007; Phillips, 2015). England has eight of Europe's remaining turf labyrinths, where the pattern is cut into the ground.

Over the centuries, the pattern developed and now takes many forms; the most common are the classical and medieval patterns illustrated throughout this book. The labyrinth is an international image: appearing in many faiths, cultures and communities, it does not belong to any single tradition and can be walked by people of all faiths and none. A major, international resurgence of interest in the labyrinth arose in the 1980s and 1990s,

Figure 1.1 A seven-circuit, classical labyrinth pattern.

Image by Jeff Saward, Labyrinthos.

initially in Europe and then further afield (for a comprehensive overview, see Kern, 2000, and Ferré and Saward, in Kern, 2000). In the USA, this led to the development of two non-profit organisations, both now with international programmes: Veriditas, founded by Revd Dr Lauren Artress (2006a, 2006b) and the Labyrinth Society (2011, 2015). These two organisations each have a different focus and both are well represented in contributions to this book. Veriditas specialises in training people to hold and facilitate labyrinth events: nearly half the contributors to this book have undertaken such training, which provides a helpful introduction and firm grounding from which to build. The Labyrinth Society has a wide community focus, substantial online resources, a research committee and an informal annual conference; this provides a key opportunity to find out about new research, to learn from experts in the field and to hear about new and developing initiatives. For more on the work of both organisations, see Kimberly Saward's chapter. The two organisations are jointly responsible for the comprehensive World-Wide Labyrinth Locator (WWLL, 2015), a valuable online resource for visitors and researchers.

Figure 1.2 Labyrinth walk held in a university theatre.

Cave of the Heart Conference, St. Mary's University, Twickenham. Photograph courtesy Jan Sellers.

As a result of these developments, three critical resources became widely available. First, the technique for drawing labyrinths became widely shared; once a labyrinth can be drawn on paper, the technique extends to drawing it on the ground. Second, fabric labyrinths were made that could be laid out on the floor, then packed up and stored. Third, as interest grew, more labyrinths began to be constructed, in private and public settings. These factors fostered access to labyrinth walking throughout the 1990s and continue to do so, through a hugely diverse range of permanent, portable and sometimes ephemeral labyrinths.

What is special about a labyrinth walk?

Søren Kierkegaard's letter to his sister-in-law Jette in 1847, quoted at the beginning of this chapter, reminds her – and us – of the value of walking (Kierkegaard, 1978). Walking, as an activity, is the subject of a growing body of literature ranging from health to spirituality.[1] As we have seen, a maze is about getting lost, where a labyrinth walk can be seen as a path of discovery. The labyrinth path, however, is a complex one, frequently turning back on itself, and concentration is required to follow it. This concentration, an absorbed focus, may serve to quieten the mind, as distractions are set aside. The convoluted path provides an opportunity to slow down, to be still, though moving; it offers a meditative, peaceful path and may lead to deep insights. Equally, it may simply be a pleasant walk: there are no guarantees, but there is a growing body of research exploring 'the labyrinth effect' (Rhodes and Rudebock, 2015), as discussed by John Rhodes in this volume. The following chapters offer many examples of how this experience, this quietness, may be part of a whole class or individual activity – including different ways of engaging with labyrinths, indoors or outdoors, at a desk, or on open land. The labyrinth also offers a creative, sometimes playful and often inspiring environment. Not all labyrinth activities are quiet, as illustrated through examples of performance and community engagement within this book. Short courses are available internationally for professional and personal development to build skills in planning and facilitating work with the labyrinth.

▷ The first university labyrinths

My focus here is on the resurgence of interest in the labyrinth in the twentieth and twenty-first centuries. The earliest example I have found in a university context was built at Stevenson College (University of California, Santa Cruz, USA) in 1972. This was a project initiated by (then) recent graduate, Barbara Horsting, 'as a study in symbolism ... it is patterned after labyrinths on ancient coins and mosaics, and it is impossible to lose your way' (*Santa Cruz Sentinel,* 1972, p. 1). The labyrinth included high walls, with a bridge and a slide for ease of departure – features which do not tend to appear in labyrinths today! Sadly this construction no longer exists.

Where fabric labyrinths are concerned, it appears that their earliest use in universities may have been in the early to mid-1990s arising from Veriditas initiatives (Attali, 1999). The construction of outdoor labyrinths at universities began to expand from the turn of the century (WWLL, 2015), the earliest examples from that date being as follows:

▷ 2000: Chadwick Arboretum, Ohio State University, USA
▷ 2000: University of Nottingham, UK
▷ 2000–2001: 'Farm in the City', Concordia University campus, St. Paul, Minnesota, USA
▷ 2001: Brescia University College, London, Ontario, Canada.

It has not proved possible to determine precisely how many labyrinths exist worldwide in higher education settings: projects come and go, and some initiatives undoubtedly exist with little or no external publicity or online presence, making them very difficult to trace. A conservative estimate suggests 140 or more at the time of writing (whether permanent, landscaped or portable fabric). This includes labyrinths at universities, at higher education colleges and specialist HEIs in Australia; Canada; Costa Rica; France; Germany; Hong Kong; India; Indonesia; Ireland; Japan; Myanmar; Norway; the Philippines; Taiwan; the UK and the USA. The number of university labyrinths continues to grow (and in fact has increased while this book was underway).[2]

In mainland Europe, striking examples include the lavender labyrinth at the University of Hohenheim, Germany, created in 2004, and the new stone and grass labyrinth at the Ecole Catholique d'Arts et Métiers de Lyon (ECAM Lyon), Graduate School of Engineering, France. This collaborative American/French project, led by artist Reginald Adams with international student participation (Adams, 2015), is probably the first contemporary university labyrinth in France.[3] Permanent labyrinths in the UK now include the Edinburgh Labyrinth (University of Edinburgh, 2004), the Canterbury Labyrinth (University of Kent, 2008) and most recently, the University of Bedfordshire (2014). For a list of universities and allied organisations with labyrinths in the UK, see Table 1.1 at the end of this chapter.

This book offers examples of work with the labyrinth in Australia, Canada, Finland, Ireland, Norway, the UK and the USA. We are conscious that there is exciting work developing with the labyrinth in a wider range of countries and cultures than we have been able to represent in this book. The choices that we have made reflect an important range of academic disciplines and practices which we hope will serve as a springboard to further enquiry and research. These demonstrate thoughtful and creative uses of the labyrinth, many of which are highly adaptable to different contexts. They are supported by practical and expert guidance on resources.

▶ Case study: The University of Kent and the Canterbury Labyrinth

To illustrate the introduction of labyrinths to universities, I turn now to the example I know best. To set the context: I joined the University of Kent in 1992 as a mature postgraduate student, and in 1993 took up a new post there, to develop a resource and guidance centre that later became the Student Learning Advisory Service, within the Unit for the Enhancement of Learning and Teaching (UELT). This was an exciting opportunity to work with academic departments and other colleagues, building student learning development and student retention initiatives. I am profoundly grateful to my colleagues at the University of Kent who share that vision and who pour their own enthusiasm and creative energy into student learning development. In 2005, I was awarded a National Teaching Fellowship (NTF), a turning point in my life that proved to be transformational. I had long been concerned about the rising pressure on staff and students across the sector, including increased levels of stress. With NTF funding, I embarked on an exploratory journey to look for joy and laughter in student learning, and examples of good practice. Influenced by contributors at a series of innovative conferences on creativity, I began to consider how creative learning spaces, as well as creative teaching, affected the student experience, and learned about many initiatives. At this time, I read about Di Williams' work at the University of Edinburgh, where she had introduced labyrinths as a quiet, contemplative environment for students and staff; I found this inspirational (Fox, 2007). Further research led me to consider how the labyrinth, already understood as a resource for spiritual and community development (Artress 2006a, 2006b), might also have applications in the support of teaching and learning through deepening reflection, quietening the mind, reducing stress and, as I later found, fostering creativity.

Back at Kent, a project steering group was formed comprising academic staff, development and guidance services and the Students' Union, a breadth of support that was to prove invaluable. We acquired our first canvas labyrinth in January 2008 and organised initial training for our group. A second canvas labyrinth was later purchased to support work on the Medway campus and further afield. Small enough to store in a suitcase, this provided a valuable resource for conferences and professional development. In May 2008, four of us went to Chartres, France, to train with Veriditas as labyrinth facilitators. In the summer of 2010, we were delighted to host the first Veriditas workshop and facilitator training to be held in the UK, in which a number of colleagues from Kent and other universities took part.

The year 2008 proved to be another major turning point when the opportunity arose to build a permanent labyrinth. The idea was inspired by the anticipated arrival of the Lambeth Conference, the international gathering of the worldwide Anglican community that meets every ten years. The building of the Canterbury Labyrinth was an extraordinary project. In the course of 13 weeks in total, the labyrinth was proposed, discussed and approved; expert designers and builders were chosen; funding was identified and the labyrinth was built on the grassy slopes to the south of the University, with wonderful views towards the ancient city and Canterbury Cathedral. Though still a building site, the labyrinth was available for the Lambeth Conference and was formally opened by the University's Vice Chancellor in October 2008. It was supported by, and was the first iconic project of, the University's 'Creative Campus' initiative, based within the Unit for the Enhancement of Learning and Teaching. As envisaged, the Canterbury Labyrinth plays multiple roles: open to all throughout the year, it is an art installation, a performance space and above all, a creative and peaceful space to support teaching and learning.

▷ Exploring teaching and learning with the labyrinth

Growing interest in the labyrinth led me to pilot its use in professional and academic development contexts as well as in the classroom, and I found others who were doing likewise. It gradually became clear that in the UK and internationally there was an exciting and growing body of practice and much to share, and this has led directly to the present book.

Until recently, the labyrinth has appeared in universities primarily as a landscape feature (including memorials in Canada and the USA) and as a chaplaincy initiative. We can now add another strand: this book is evidence of a surge of interest in teaching and learning with the labyrinth, and, as John Rhodes remarks in his chapter, a growing number of labyrinths have been specifically created with teaching and learning in mind. With good-will and flexibility, it seems very feasible that labyrinths in any one part of a university may be shared and used more widely. It remains the case that many universities have a labyrinth but do not make use of it in a learning and teaching context. In this respect, the present volume is a clarion call for exploration and collaboration. If you have a labyrinth on your doorstep, we encourage you to find out more and hope that this book will inspire the creative use of labyrinths throughout the sector, whether currently in existence or yet to be created.

It is of course common, in HE as elsewhere, to find the word 'labyrinth' as a synonym for 'maze', an indication of confusion and complexity. There is, however, a very different, and growing, strand of literature that reflects on teaching and learning with labyrinths, whether through labyrinth walking, working with the metaphor or both. As hospitals and health-related organisations were early adopters of the labyrinth as a resource for well-being (see, for example, Wright and Sayre-Adams, 2000; Griffith, 2002), it is not surprising that Nurse Education was one of the first aca-demic disciplines to explore use of the labyrinth to deepen reflection and reduce student stress (Sandor, 2005; White and Stafford, 2008). Michelle Bigard wrote about the labyrinth in 2009, discussing its introduction for Counselling Service outreach and its possibilities for wider university use. Ellen Goldberger found that her teaching of law students was enriched through using labyrinths and mazes *as tools for teaching the mediation process*' (2009). Shelton-Colangelo and Duvall (2007) describe two 'cir-cles of learning' with women's studies students, including the process of building and walking a labyrinth outdoors, and how these activities *are based on equality and communal exploration of ideas and meanings, which lead to more in-depth education of the whole person: mind, body, and soul* (2007, p. 43).

More recently, Murray includes labyrinth walking in self-knowledge development at graduate level (2012); Grace discusses her own experi-ences as a professor, reflecting on her changing approaches to teaching (2011a); Ruminski and Holba consider women's leadership development, with the labyrinth path as an image that empowers and give scope for complexity and change (2012). Knowles and Grant (2014) also work with the metaphor to explore the principles and approaches underpinning their writing retreats for doctoral students and academic staff.

In *Metaphors for, in and of Education Research* (Midgley, Trimmer and Davies, 2013), the idea of the labyrinth is woven throughout the introduction to support and illuminate the reader's journey. Janice Jones, in the same volume, explores the legend of Persephone, and *'re-presents [her own] doctoral experience as a metaphorical journey into the labyrinth'* (2013, p. 67). Bright and Pokorny (2012), in the context of contemplative education, report on a workshop that introduced a variety of HE staff to the labyrinth and explored possibilities for working with students and staff. Ideas included *'a group bonding process prior to peer working'* and *'raising awareness of pacing of self in context of e.g. time management, Personal Development Planning, study/revision, lesson planning, problem solving and creative thinking activities'* (2012, p. 24). Cook and Croft (2015) are experimenting with labyrinth patterns projected by light onto a library floor as an opportunity for students to alleviate stress and fatigue. My own work has focussed on the introduction of the labyrinth within a wide variety of university and college contexts, as a quiet, restorative and beautiful resource for teaching and learning, for well-being and for personal and professional development (Sellers, 2008, 2009, 2012, 2013; Labyrinth Society, 2011; James and Brookfield, 2014a, 2014b).

The present book draws together many examples of innovative and developing practice in teaching and learning with the labyrinth. In its diversity of approaches it is timely in offering a rich and creative contribution to the emerging literature in this field.

▶ Exploring this book

The book comprises a balance of substantial keynote chapters, shorter chapters (including research initiatives) and illustrative case studies of new and developing practice. Our contributors include academics, students, artists, photographers and poets, giving the book a rich breadth of illustration. Student feedback is evidenced throughout the book. Case studies provide snapshots of labyrinth work being undertaken, and are intentionally – perhaps tantalisingly – brief, even though all of them could well be expanded into longer chapters. In the spirit of good pedagogy, they are designed to get you thinking; to stir your imagination and encourage you to seek out further information yourself. To add to this, you will find (photocopiable) instructions on how to draw labyrinths, and templates of (internationally diverse) labyrinth patterns which can be reproduced to use as 'desk-top' or finger labyrinths (or, indeed, used for reflection in the course of reading this book).

Throughout, the underlying purpose is to deepen learning, foster creativity and enhance the development of the whole person. The book is structured in four strands: we invite you to explore.

Part I: First Steps offers a wealth of advice and shared reflections from contributors who have introduced labyrinths to their universities. They explore starting points, challenges, obstacles and successes in the context of art in the environment; Land Studies; Interior Design; Business and Education. To support first, experimental, steps in working with labyrinths we discover how to draw and create labyrinths with little or no budget, using what we have to hand. Two contributors discuss their own academic journeys in the light of the labyrinth metaphor, and in the final chapter of this section we follow a professor's journey from her discovery of the labyrinth to its introduction across the whole university as a resource for transformative learning.

In Part II: Teaching and Learning Perspectives, John Rhodes offers a comprehensive overview of labyrinth research, considers what the future of labyrinth research might be and offers guidance for both experienced and new researchers with a particular emphasis on quantitative methodology. We then embark on a fascinating exploration of academic innovation and creativity. We discover the impact of labyrinth walks at the beginning of the academic year, designed to deepen reflection amongst health studies students, and hear a student account of that experience. Our journey continues with initiatives in academic and staff development; Arts; Creative Writing; Midwifery and Social Work. We explore mindfulness in the context of Medicine and Theology; a conference labyrinth, and one in use for project evaluation. This section of the book explores successful ways in which students – and staff – are encouraged to 'think outside the box', fostering creativity and reducing stress and anxiety. There is something here for everyone to explore.

Part III: Campus and Community, takes a very different perspective. We hear first from colleagues in student development roles, in chaplaincy and in counselling, highlighting the pioneering work of chaplains in collaborative ventures in Canada, England, Ireland, Norway, Scotland and the USA, and the labyrinth as a pathway to foster student confidence and staying power. We move on to a powerful image of playfulness and freedom to learn without fear. Turning to the wider world, we hear how a labyrinth has found a place in both university and community and discover creative approaches to student, business and community engagement, from dance and museum education – enriching the learning of students and the life of local people – to enterprise, where people in the business world reflect on their careers and paths to come.

In Part IV: Moving Forward, we consider how to equip ourselves for the journey. Kimberly Saward's chapter offers a focus on sources and resources with an international perspective. This includes four finger labyrinth templates, supporting earlier chapters where authors have demonstrated the use of paper labyrinths within the classroom (and these beautiful patterns are equally appropriate for use at home). Our conclusion highlights ways forward and celebrates the path that we share, the gift that the labyrinth has to offer in these turbulent times.

Table 1.1 Labyrinths at HEIs and allied organisations in the UK. For the reasons stated above, the data can only be provisional

Higher Education Institution	Labyrinth
1 University of Aberdeen (Cruickshank Botanic Garden)	Turf, planted with crocuses
2 Anglia Ruskin University	Painted lines on lawn, with daffodils
3 University of the Arts, London	Portable calico
4 Ashridge Business School	Turf, with wildflower surround
5 University of Bedfordshire	1. Permanent: grass and cobblestones 2. Temporary creations as needed
6 University of Bristol	Portable canvas
7 Canterbury Christ Church University	Mown lawn
8 Coventry University	Portable canvas
9 University for the Creative Arts	Portable calico
10 University of Derby	Portable fabric
11 University of Dundee	Portable canvas
12 University of East Anglia	1. Portable canvas 2. Temporary creations as needed
13 University of Edinburgh	1. Permanent: fully paved, the Edinburgh Labyrinth 2. Several portable fabric labyrinths (canvas and calico)
14 Goldsmiths, University of London	Portable: finger labyrinths
15 Imperial College London	Portable fabric (jointly with Royal College of Art)
16 University of Kent	1. Permanent: stone path in grass, the Canterbury Labyrinth 2. Two portable canvases *continued overleaf*

Table 1.1 Labyrinths at HEIs and allied organisations in the UK. For the reasons stated above, the data can only be provisional *continued*

17 Kingston University	Portable canvas
18 Leeds Trinity University	Temporary creations as needed
19 University of Lincoln	Portable canvas
20 University of Liverpool (Ness Botanic Gardens)	Mown lawn
21 Liverpool Hope University	Hedge and pebbles
22 Liverpool John Moores University	1. Portable canvas 2. Occasional installations of luminary labyrinths
23 Northumbria University Newcastle	Portable canvas
24 University of Nottingham	Permanent: brick and grass (Millennium Garden)
25 Queen Mary, University of London	Portable canvas
26 University of Reading	1. Portable canvas 2. Portable fabric (PhD student project)
27 Royal College of Art	Portable fabric (jointly with Imperial College)
28 Staffordshire University	Portable canvas
29 University of Stirling	Permanent: grass and paving
30 University of Westminster	Portable calico
31 University of Winchester	Turf and gravel (Cosmic Garden)
32 University of Worcester	Mown lawn
33 Writtle College	Turf
Partner Colleges; Allied Organisations	**Labyrinth**
34 Goodenough College: The Burn, Angus, Scotland (study centre)	Permanent: river rocks
35 Schumacher College, Dartington, Devon	Trodden turf (path created by walking)
36 Westminster College, Cambridge	Permanent: paving and grass
37 Woodbrooke Quaker Study Centre, Birmingham	1. Mown lawn 2. Portable canvas

Notes

1 It is beyond the scope of this volume to explore the growing literature on walking, but the following may be useful starting points: Rebecca Solnit on the history of walking (2002); Francisco Careri on walking as aesthetic practice (2002); Tina Richardson on walking and psychogeography (2015); proceedings from the Walk21 Conference on Walking and Liveable Communities (2000–present). For a beautifully researched, personal account, see Robert MacFarlane's *The Old Ways: A journey on foot* (2012).

2 Sources of data (as at 1 July 2015): in attempting to count labyrinths in HE, my research has included the WWLL, online and literature searches, supplemented by exchanges of information with other enthusiasts including Jeff Saward and Di Williams. I have included universities, colleges and specialist institutions (offering degree programmes from BA/BSc level onwards) where there is a permanent or soft landscaped labyrinth, a fabric labyrinth or evidence of an ongoing initiative involving labyrinths. I have omitted HEIs with 'one-off' events but with no evidence of continued labyrinth use (for example, guest seminars and temporary arts installations). I have included one late addition, the new labyrinth at Canterbury Christ Church University, UK (created September 2015).

3 The lavender labyrinth at the University of Hohenheim, created in 2004, was preceded by a temporary maze built by artist Joseph Kosuth in 1993 to mark the University's 175th anniversary (Fellmeth, Quast and Wetzel, 2004). Kosuth's installation, though described as a labyrinth, was undoubtedly a maze, as a plan of the site within the book shows multiple paths and dead ends. This is just one of a number of so-called 'labyrinths' which turn out to be mazes on investigation, and therefore lie beyond the remit of this book.

Part I: First Steps

Poems from the Labyrinth

Boat

you float on the grass like a coracle
unstable, no tar to keep you watertight
all voyages are unpredictable
I embark once again, let you carry me

little boat, with your ribs of bent willow
weave of ash wood, made with no nails
I call you 'Labyrinth' and bless you
bless myself and all who sail in you

Victoria Field

Victoria Field is a writer and poetry therapist. She teaches in the UK at Canterbury Christ Church University; Metanoia Institute, London; and Tŷ Newydd, the National Writers Centre for Wales. These poems were inspired by coursework during a professional development programme, and influenced by labyrinth walking.

Introduction to Part I: First Steps

In Part I, we meet contributors who take us from the very beginning of their projects. In the first chapter, Jill Raggett and Steve Terry bring us moments of sheer beauty and considerable practicality as they explore what it means to seek, find and work with an artist in residence at their specialist college, discovering new approaches to teaching and learning. They offer examples of work with students in Finland as well as the UK, creating labyrinths of raked birch leaves, spirals of dew, temporary patterns with sand and candle-light. Jeff Saward continues the theme, teaching us to make labyrinths at very little cost with what we have to hand; his chapter includes practical diagrams on how to draw a labyrinth pattern. Part I takes us through the process of getting a project started, in many different contexts, forming a strong background to further exploration within and across disciplines in Parts II and III (those who want more diagrams will also want to explore Part IV, with labyrinth templates to copy).

How does a labyrinth project at a university begin? How to get started, who to talk to; what is needed? All of our contributors have introduced the labyrinth in a higher education context, on their own behalf or for others, and have tackled head-on the questions of how, what, why, where – and sometimes, what on earth for? 'You want to do *what?*' is one possible response. Read on for answers. Along the way, you will find (here as throughout the book) examples of teaching and learning with the labyrinth in different disciplines. Part I features Landscape Design and Horticulture; Business; Education, and Interior Design. We move from work within one discipline, to initiatives across disciplines; from the reflections of one doctoral student on her research journey in the UK, to the voyage of exploration that resulted in a permanent labyrinth and initiatives across campus at an American university. The possibilities are, to say the least, considerable: enjoy the journey.

2 Treading lightly: Learning, art and landscape

Jill Raggett and Steve Terry

Dr Jill Raggett is a Reader in Gardens and Designed Landscapes at Writtle College, Essex, working in the Writtle School of Design; an Adjunct Professor at the Dalhousie University, Canada; and recipient of a National Teaching Fellowship awarded by the Higher Education Academy for innovative methods of enriching student learning. Her doctoral and ongoing research focuses on the emergence and development of the Japanese-style garden in the British Isles and Ireland.

Steve Terry is a Garden Designer working in private practice with Studio Thadian Pillai and is the leader for the undergraduate Landscape Architecture programme at Writtle School of Design. His interests span the relationship between community and the wider environment and he has travelled the world working as lecturer, designer and horticulturist. This experience and understanding of art, community and environmental processes is integral to his teaching philosophy and his design work.

▶ Introduction

This is the story of how Writtle College, a specialist college in rural Essex, came to have a labyrinth and at the same time discovered new ways of viewing and understanding learning and teaching. Writtle College is a unique place and community, originally founded over a hundred years ago 'to educate the sons of farmers in the ways of the soil'. Men and women from around the world now come to study a wide range of subjects including Landscape and Garden Design, Horticulture, Floristry, Conservation, Equine and Animal Studies and Agriculture. Many of the disciplines are offered across a wide spectrum of educational levels, ranging from school leavers in Further Education at Level 1, through Higher Education degrees to doctoral studies. The College has a 250 hectare (618 acre) estate including a working farm, an ornamental plant collection and gardens, all managed for educational and biodiversity benefits. Much has changed in the curriculum over the years as agriculture and commercial horticulture have mechanised, needing fewer staff on the land. Other areas such as the management of parks and gardens have grown, along with landscape design. This chapter charts one of those areas of change, how it came about and how it has resulted in new areas of study and ways of studying.

▶ An artist in residence

By the late 1990s we had already spent a few years experimenting with ephemeral art, inspired by environmental artists such as Andy Goldsworthy and Richard Long, and artists working with willow such as Stephanie Bunn, Serena de la Hey and Claire Wilkes. The latter were relevant to the Writtle campus as we had large supplies of coloured stems of ornamental willows and dogwoods which were grown for their winter stem colour and then cut down in the early spring to encourage regrowth. As teachers we witnessed the reactions of the students, viewers and academic colleagues to these temporary art installations of stems, leaves and other natural materials collected from the immediate environment; we began to see the many benefits of creating the work. It helped students to appreciate how even a modest intervention by them in a shared landscape would be noticed and might – or might not – be appreciated. This is critical learning for students who will in their future careers make constant changes and amendments to shared spaces.

The positive reception of a new way of working and doing in the Writtle landscape led us to organise a conference in 1998 on 'Living Art in the Landscape'. This was warmly received by landscape professionals and those involved in the arts sector; as a result we forged supportive relationships with those who facilitated the arts in the Eastern region including Commissions East and the Arts Officers of Essex County Council. These were important allies, providing us with expertise and confidence as we took our next steps in developing our curriculum and experiential learning through the arts at Writtle College, which is primarily a science and land-based institution.

In 2000, to celebrate the millennium, Arts Council England set an ambitious target aiming to place 1000 artists in 1000 places across England. These to be at locations where it would be uncommon to find an artist in residence; we immediately felt that Writtle College was an ideal candidate. 'The Year of the Artist – Breaking the Barriers' took place from June 2000 to May 2001. To help us in our bid, we worked with Commissions East, first to secure the opportunity and then to appoint the most appropriate artist for our circumstances, a vital part of the process: we needed the 'right person', one who could inspire us and yet understood the responsibilities and constraints of working within an educational environment. We chose Jim Buchanan, an artist who had broken free of his employment in landscape architecture to establish a career as a land artist, with a reputation for building labyrinths and a desire to develop his techniques associated with land art (Buchanan, 2007). This was to be a symbiotic relationship with opportunities to learn and develop for the artist, the institution, the students and staff. It is important in these situations that the benefits are equally spread as it provides a much more valuable collaboration than simply employing an artist.

Jim Buchanan joined Writtle College as a resident artist, an 'Artist's Fellowship', from September 2000 to April 2001. For over 30 days he lived on the campus, mentored by a member of the management team who supported the project. Jim was charged with 'promoting the role of the visual arts in landscape development and management to create exciting and challenging public spaces'. Other aims included fostering the means for artists and landscape professionals to work together and to share and document the outcomes of the project.

The project prioritised use of on-campus materials, including recycling, from both a financial and sustainability perspective. The first workshops were classroom based, creating model landscapes with design students using previously unexplored materials. Next, a barn (normally in use for both teaching and storage) became a base within which to consider space and narrative as elements of landscape design, explored through the creation of labyrinths. Sand – held in stock for the construction of garden features – became arts material, as students worked in groups to outline and lay out four different labyrinths. The patterns emerged on the ground as the students followed Jim's direction with printed diagrams of the labyrinth designs.

Active participation in the creation of the four labyrinth types allowed students to compare and understand the relative simplicity of the designs. They realised that even apparently complex layouts could be easily achieved by engaging in teamwork. These students of Landscape and Garden Design made important discoveries, finding that each labyrinth provided a different experience and evoked different responses. This related to the size and scale of the labyrinth within a given space; the orientation of each labyrinth relative to its space and its surroundings; and perhaps, the students' involvement in the act of creation. Forethought itself became a point for discussion with regard to the permanent placement of such a feature within an existing environment. The use of sand as a drawing material allowed students to freely make mistakes without regret, being able to correct them easily, using the broom as an eraser and quickly redrawing elements of the design again. This freedom is something to be encouraged in all students but particularly those of Art and Design where experimentation and apparent failure can lead to discovery through the creative challenge (Dineen, 2006).

The simultaneous setting out and drawing of the labyrinths by the four groups created a vibrant atmosphere, with artist and teaching staff moving between each of the groups to help and support them. The labyrinths they created simultaneously raised the students' curiosity in their own work and that of the other groups, combining enjoyment and creative reflection in ways that stretched and deepened their learning (James, 2014). The speed by which the labyrinths came into being was a surprise to all taking part. On completion there was a sense of achievement, eagerness and anticipa-tion: the act of making led to a willingness to participate in walking the labyrinths. The excitement with which students can engage with labyrinths can often lead to running the path, and the pace at which the labyrinth is experienced certainly has an effect on the emotions of the user. With that in mind, groups were invited to participate with each of the labyrinths in different ways, walking in silence, holding hands as a group and walking rhythmically in pairs as if dancing. It is interesting that students willingly participated in all of these ways of interacting without reserve. This inti-macy of connection between individual participants and the walked expe-rience and between individuals as a shared experience is one of the most beneficial aspects of labyrinths and provides a rich seam for discovery and discussion with students.

Building on this experiment, Jim and the students decided to hold a 'Labyrinthine Experience – a labyrinth in a barn' to explain the purpose of the artist's residency and his work and to draw in the wider College com-munity, including families and friends. Students and artist analysed and selected the labyrinth they felt would be most appropriate and on the day of the event created a much larger sand installation that covered most of the concrete barn floor. At the time, core skills were very much part of the curriculum; as they worked in a row to lay out the paths of the labyrinth they amply demonstrated the collaboration required for 'working with others'. This labyrinth was designed to 'en-trance' the audience before they actually set their feet on the pathway: it was to be illuminated by candle-light and the audience were to observe the lighting of the candles as part of a performance. The design of the sand labyrinth incorporated semi-circular harbours to house tea lights. The sand cupped every light in a continuous sequence of serpentine semi-circles snaking back and forth along the larger curves of the labyrinth for its entire length (Figure 2.1). In the middle stood the 'Mother Candle' from which every light, over 600, was lit by students,

Figure 2.1 Labyrinth curves of sand and candlelight, Writtle College, UK.

Art installation by Jim Buchanan; photograph by Jerry Harpur, courtesy Writtle College.

one by one. Visitors watched the event from a balcony in the darkness. Each tiny flame added to the growing light until a soft glow filled the barn and the full extent of the labyrinth design was outlined. At that point Jim gave a brief talk about his fellowship, and his aspirations for his residency and collaboration with the College and wider community.

The audience were then encouraged to walk the labyrinth and go from an observed experience to becoming an active participant, a performer on the candlelit pathway. Finally, over 160 people interacted with the labyrinth and each other by walking, running and dancing around the candlelit sand labyrinth. At one point, most of the audience progressed through the labyrinth holding hands and, as they moved out of the labyrinth, spontaneously encircled it and applauded. This was a very special and memorable occasion. At the close of the evening the students and staff started to sweep away the labyrinth; it was then we discovered that the dampness of the sand left an after image in the concrete (Figure 2.2). We have subsequently found that most of the labyrinths we have made leave some form of after impression, as well as an individual and organisational legacy.

During his artist's fellowship, Jim played a full role in the life of the College and soon became known to the caretaking, gardening and catering staff. He won over 'hearts and minds' one chat at a time in order to

Figure 2.2 Labyrinth after-image, Writtle College, UK.

Art installation by Jim Buchanan; photograph by Jerry Harpur, courtesy Writtle College.

develop ideas and build community support and involvement. We discovered with subsequent artists in residence that this was an important skill,
demonstrating to students what it means to truly work with a community. Some important organisational lessons were discovered during this
first residency. These included how to achieve goals for both the artist's
development and the organisation, steering together through the bureau-
cracy of an educational institution. We were able to support the artist in
forming a complex web of alliances with both students and colleagues
in order to achieve the most powerful results. Every opportunity, expression of interest and offer of help was seized. In exploring labyrinth building materials, for example, the partner of a visiting professor spent long
hours in a polythene tunnel mixing Essex clay soils with various College
'waste' materials. This was very much part of Jim's practice and he worked
with a Writtle soil engineer to develop a suitable experimental process
to find the mixture with the most robust stability as a structure. This was
achieved through a soil slump test, which involves using a standard cone
form in which soil is moulded and then tipped out to measure stability. Soil
additives included College waste materials, our favourite being shredded
memos from College offices.

Drawing on this soil experimentation and experience of labyrinth building, in the final artwork Jim worked with the students in a field to create a
turf-cut labyrinth surrounded by turf-covered mounds, the latter the result

of soil spoil from the making of a car park. Soil as a sculptural medium, or as Jim put it in his workbook 'conversations with soil', resulted in rammed earth structures, which were developed into four standing monuments to College waste incorporating straw, wood chips, manure and horse hair and of course the shredded College memos, used as additives to the clay soil being dug up from the campus. These soil stacks, each two metres high (6 ft 6 in), marked pivotal points for laying out the labyrinth, while another stack created a fireplace and chimney on a nearby mound to act as a gathering point adjacent to the labyrinth.

The labyrinth was a major landscape intervention for the staff teaching Landscape Design. We spent many hours with the students discussing the most suitable location, sensitive to the Writtle landscape and the future use of the feature. The residency refined our ethical practice and policy of treading lightly on the landscape, so no hard landscape materials were involved. A turf cutter was used to make the labyrinth's soil pathway (418 metres or 1371 feet, about 500 'average' steps). With the help of the students the labyrinth emerged, sensitively placed within the existing rural landscape with the typical Essex view of a tree-lined horizon. This was a feature drawn on the land, a feature with a sense of place, to be entered by our landscape students as we encourage them to consider their work in 'place making'.

The culmination of the residency was a conference entitled 'Soil as Sculptural Medium' held in May 2001, which explored a range of issues concerning soil as an asset for growing, architecture and sculpture. The turf-cut labyrinth became the focus of a shared experience, a meeting point for delegates where professionals and students from a wide range of disciplines including Land Management, agricultural policy makers, horticulturists, landscape designers, artists and educationalists could discuss and share their views and ideas. All the delegates walked the labyrinth and were in contact with the soil and in the open air, away from the more normal confines of the lecture theatre. This created a very open atmosphere, and conversations across disciplines were much in evidence. There proved to be an additional benefit for Writtle College; a shift in the external perception of a college often seen as rather traditional in its approach. Through the labyrinth and the Artist's Fellowship we sent out a powerful message about the importance of landscape and our interactions with it through shared experiences and sensitivities to place. The capturing of some of those moments as a photographic record has provided striking images of the College as a forward-thinking organisation engaged with new ideas. These photographs provided powerful marketing materials, illustrating the College's educational aspirations. We were fortunate that the influential garden photographer Jerry Harpur was a friend and supporter of the College and gave his time and skills to record some of our event. We have discovered that a high-quality visual record is never wasted; it provides evidence of ability to succeed and supports progress on to the next project.

▶ The labyrinth at Writtle College

Jim's turf labyrinth was the physical legacy of his residency, and over 10 years later it is still much in use. Labyrinths take on a patina of wear that alters their appearance; at Writtle, its physical nature changes. With every step taken, the depth of the path increases; in addition, with climatic conditions and compaction, the grass area alters to favour different plant species. This gentle evolution due to use seems to imbue the labyrinth with vitality and validity. Every year the labyrinth has been used by over 3000 school children on a single day, as schools from around Essex visit the College. Conditions vary, but whether on sunny days, when the soil is dry, or wet days, when it is muddy, the children race around the path, often puffing and tired when they reach the end, getting fit without even realising! Every school should have a labyrinth for fitness and well-being, a tool to tackle obesity with fun. We discuss these issues and ideas with our own design and horticultural students.

Spatial design is a critical element in the design of landscape and gardens. Walking the labyrinth with our first-year undergraduates, they discover through experiential learning the importance of scale and proportion, spatial awareness, the appreciation of others engaging with and in the same space and the emotional experiences of walking alone or together. This is enriched by discussing the folklore, symbolism, historical significance and, in our case, the ecology of labyrinths, which becomes a very powerful tool for understanding culture, place and nature. We also used to have a maze at the College, an enjoyable temporary project that aimed to help our horticulture students understand the setting out of plants and plant establishment. It was always a good learning experience to take the students through both maze and labyrinth and let them experience the anxiety of the multi-route maze compared with the serenity experienced along the single line of the labyrinth. Both 'lines in the landscape' share a similar shape and form, yet yield such different experiences. This becomes an important lesson for young landscape and garden designers to learn, as their ideas will have a real consequence for people in the world.

From such a strong experience anyone might expect our students' designs will be full of labyrinths, but instead they learn the significance of when and where a labyrinth might be effective and useful in public or private space. They begin to learn how and why they can, and why they should, 'design out' frustrating, cramped and claustrophobic spaces in favour of appropriately scaled and engaging spaces where people want to be. The teaching of design with a labyrinth and the experience of using one, combine to offer a master class in siting a feature; creating an intervention; place making; and developing an awareness of the environmental impact of one's actions.

Students from all courses may happen upon our labyrinth while exploring the campus and we are reliably informed that students go there, they say, to 'chill out'. For students with stressful deadlines, for the wider College community dealing with the challenges of education and for visitors, the labyrinth provides a physical, emotional and intellectual experience, a thinking space and place for relaxation, and an opportunity to move with direction at one's own speed in fresh air as light, weather and seasons change. Nick Capaldi summarised the vision and hope for The Year of the Artist as *'Art conceived with integrity and imagination, well-crafted and produced, which has reached out and touched audiences, is distinctive, easily recognised and remembered'* (Capaldi, 2001, p. 3). This was and is true of Jim Buchanan's work at Writtle College.

There were other outcomes of the residency that were even more subtle but left resonances within the institution. These included a shift in perception concerning the less ornamentally planted areas of the campus and a realisation that outside space could be more than a grass field for impromptu football matches or from which views of the wider estate could be seen. The blending of art and science, considering the sensitivities of both and providing a meeting point for those discussions, caused us to grow in confidence. As part of a Higher Education Funding Council for England (HEFCE) initiative we proposed a Centre for the Arts and Design in the Environment (CADE), a bid that proved successful. Building on the achievements of work with Jim Buchanan and the artists preceding him, this Centre was to pave the way for other artists and designers to come and share their skills, talents and viewpoints to enhance learning across the College disciplines. Today the work of CADE, with students and artists at and beyond Writtle College, continues within Writtle School of Design.

▶ Teaching and learning with ephemeral labyrinths

In the following years a number of artists took up residency at the College, funded by external organisations. Each year we hosted an artist from France, supported by Essex County Council, and we were fortunate to secure what became a two-year residency funded by the Leverhulme Trust. By 2005 we decided it was time to challenge ourselves to a more daring venture and planned a conference that bought together two apparently disparate professional communities, namely farming and the arts. Our conference, entitled 'Agriculture and Art', explored possibilities where the two communities could interact and benefit from each other. The value of a labyrinth to bring people together in a joint endeavour was a technique we were keen to try again; we invited Jim Buchanan to return. Delegates were asked to arrive with a pair of waterproof boots for a post-lunchtime activity.

The Writtle campus is privileged to encompass a fine listed late-fifteenth-century timber-framed barn, complete with black weatherboarding, a tiled roof and much-respected resident bats. This is still a working barn, used to house working agricultural machinery and research equipment. In this setting Jim created a labyrinth projected onto a flooded floor. Machinery was cleared for the day and a low 'pool wall' was created by a thick irrigation pipe, attached to the concrete floor by silicon sealant; a thin layer of water then flooded the barn. Probably the hardest part of the installation was to black out the barn from any chinks of light, without disturbing the bats. The labyrinth was projected onto the water surface from a light source above, transforming the barn into a magical place where delegates of the conference would be invited to walk the path in their waterproof boots. There was no obvious connection between labyrinth and barn, but as reflections from the water played across the oak beams, the two were united in a poetic and dramatic interplay, linking the historic fabric of the building with immediate and ephemeral light and shadow. As delegates crossed the threshold from land to water and entered the labyrinth they made ripples which distorted the reflections and engaged participants with the whole installation. In the evening we shared the installation with the wider College community and with friends and family to celebrate Jim Buchanan's latest artwork.

Beyond the poetic gesture and new atmosphere given to the barn lay a more practical message, developed by the conference speakers. It is essential to Writtle's success as a specialist college that we share knowledge within and across our sector. With creative thinking, and the sharing of ideas between disciplines, the reimagining of workspaces can bring in new audiences at a time when farm businesses are looking hard at portfolio diversification that offers the potential for new customers. *(See also Alex Irving's chapter, offering another example of knowledge sharing with small and medium enterprises – eds.)*

As academics who wish to explore new ways to engender learning in our students, many of the frameworks for experiencing and seeing landscape discovered through our artist-in-residence programme are shared in the module 'Landscape Gardens and the Arts'. This provides a theo-retically based programme of study combined with experiential learning, allowing students to experiment with the College campus grounds and to apply concepts discussed in the classroom environment. The module aims to give students an opportunity to respond to place; to consider the beauty and value of the ephemeral. One year, to celebrate a Christmas exhibi-tion, the opportunity arose to apply the learning in the module by creating an illuminated snow labyrinth. This was set beneath the trees alongside our design studio, on the site of the medieval King John's Hunting lodge. Students have instigated their own works over the years, for example in outreach work in public parks, where they created spirals in fallen pink blossom beneath cherry trees. The labyrinth became a vehicle to see the landscape in its transient state, to respond to 'the place' and 'the time', however brief. *'The land connects us to a sense of time and space beyond the scale of our own lives'* (Tufnell and Crickmay, 2004, p. 242): walking lightly upon the land became our approach as a means of helping students to understand and see ephemerality, not just in landscape but all things.

In 2005 and again in 2006, as part of the Erasmus programme, we were invited to visit Leepa College, part of Häme Polytechnic, Finland, to deliver a condensed version of our 'Landscape Gardens and the Arts' module within their International Landscape Programme. Our brief – along with delivering the module – was 'to help students see the landscape anew'. Our first visit to 'the land of 1000 lakes' was inspirational, as autumn turned the birch trees to golden hues. Unexpectedly, the first year we delivered the course it was oversub-scribed with 57 students from across Europe, who had arrived just a few weeks before us. To help bond the group and for us to get to know them in a very short space of time we suggested a community activity. Having initially walked the campus grounds to gain a sense of logistical and practical issues and the aesthetic qualities of the landscape we intro-duced three possible sites for a 'landscape intervention'. Without reveal-ing too much of the surprise in store we offered cues to draw from the students their understanding of the campus and the country they were in, cues with a focus on considering the campus landscape as a material, an aesthetic and as a place. This led us to jointly select a grassy glade in the birch forest that formed a rounded peninsula projecting into a lake. The students were excited to discover that they were to come together to build a performance space in the form of a labyrinth from the materials found only from that site. We explored with them what these materials could be and set them in groups to rake the fallen birch leaves into semi-circles, forming the labyrinth. Once it was completed they stood back and marvelled at their joint achievement, reflecting on their use of materials and the impact they had made on the setting. The walking of the labyrinth in the fading light engaged them with the space, the place and the atmosphere. The last surprise was that we would return later in the dark when the labyrinth would be lit by paper lanterns.

The evening progressed with gentle music, eating and laughter as students walked the labyrinth together in groups or alone by moonlight and candlelight. As we cleared the lanterns with the students the next morning, we discussed environmental responsibility and the consequences of our activity on the land. A few tea lights had unintentionally captured some insects in the wax, drawn to the flame. These martyred invertebrates became a collective we called 'the unexpected guests' and were used with students to explore ideas of art and environmental responsibility. Our action of walking on the grass paths continually from the same entrance point had combed the grass into a striped pattern, alternate arcs of shiny or matt blades of grass angled towards or away from the rising sun. We returned to the labyrinth frequently that week as we worked in the campus grounds and watched the foliage outline gently turn from gold to brown and blow away, blurring the after-image of the labyrinth but not our memories of the event.

On home turf and more recently, the labyrinth continues to inspire students. 'Quick activities' are a collaborative, outdoor teaching exercise. In 2013, 'quick activities' inspired by the labyrinth included 'Walking a Spiral', a group activity where we, with design students, created a spiral on a dewy lawn by walking. A third-year undergraduate student reflected on this activity in his illustrated assignment for Writtle School of Design's module 'Landscape, Gardens and the Arts'. He showed the physical, emotional and intellectual journey he had been on:

> The materials used were the footprints of the community, highlighting the intimate links between the person and landscape with this type of mark making … The artwork was a very quick installation taking only ten minutes to create and promoted a lot of social interaction between the group … running around the spiral creating a joyous and fun atmosphere. This emphasises the value of environmental art and the community on emotions and well-being, linking its values and philosophies to environmental psychology … The creation of these artworks has made me realise the importance of connecting with the landscape and how some of the most successful community projects do not require regimented and heavily designed structures and programming but an event where people can unite and celebrate their local environment. (Chippendale, 2013)

CADE's aspirations were captured in this student's conclusion: the creation of these artworks offered *'a unique understanding of the local environment and a dynamic artistic palette that is constantly changing with the weather, seasons and life cycles in nature'* (Chippendale, 2013).

▶ Conclusion

Landscape architects are often heard to say that 'the success of a place is in its use'. With this in mind, the ephemeral labyrinth which appears periodically can continually re-engage a new student cohort or wider community, its joy being in the participation of siting, making, uniting and celebrating. In our teaching the temporary, site-specific labyrinth is more successful for us, our students and our landscape than the apparent permanence of stone or coloured paving labyrinth. These undeniably have their place and function. However, the ephemeral labyrinths that we work with, used both as a pedagogic tool and for sheer enjoyment, become powerful vehicles for synthesis. We have found that such teaching and learning enables our students and ourselves to synthesise not only our own understanding and reflections, alongside those of others, but also the complex and changing theories of Landscape Design and other environmental ideologies which are part of our academic and creative work.

3 Masking tape and magic: How to draw and make low-cost labyrinths

Jeff Saward

First captivated by the labyrinth in 1976, Jeff Saward is a world authority on the history and development of labyrinths and mazes, and the author of *Magical Paths,* a pictorial essay on the modern revival of labyrinths and mazes, and *Labyrinths & Mazes,* a comprehensive illustrated history. He is the editor of *Caerdroia – the Journal of Mazes and Labyrinths*, co-founder and director of Labyrinthos, the Labyrinth Resource Centre, Photo Library and Archive and administrator of the World-Wide Labyrinth Locator website. Travelling extensively to research the history of labyrinths and mazes, Jeff has an unrivalled collection of photographs from around the world.

▶ Introduction

This chapter provides practical advice and information on how to create an indoor or outdoor labyrinth at low cost, using materials readily to hand. Beginning with the process of drawing a classical labyrinth pattern on paper, I extend this principle to consider more complex patterns and a wide variety of materials and contexts. Some of these labyrinths are ephemeral, designed to last for just one event. Others – though equally low cost – may be created to last for a considerable time. These techniques can be used within and beyond the seminar and classroom, by students, staff and the community, offering a creative and artistic connection between the distant past and the present day.

▶ How to draw labyrinths

The knowledge of how to draw a 'classical' labyrinth, and how to transfer that skill to the construction of a full size labyrinth on the ground, has been passed from one generation to another, from one civilisation to another, for thousands of years. This pattern, known as the 'classical' labyrinth due to its great age, is first encountered as prehistoric rock carvings. The central core of the design (often called the 'seed pattern') can be further developed by adding or removing elements from the 'seed' to create similar classical labyrinths with differing designs.

The construction of simple labyrinth designs by this method is not difficult to learn, but does require some practice. Paper and pencil are the only materials required. You will surely make mistakes at first, but once committed to memory it is then a simple step to scale up the paper exercise to create classical labyrinths, indoors or out, with whatever materials are to hand. The technique is best explained by means of a diagram (beginning with Figure 3.1).

Exact dimensions for labyrinth making are discussed below, but the size of a labyrinth is often broadly described by the number of circuits that the path makes, circling the centre. This is practical knowledge; a seven-circuit labyrinth will often be smaller than an 11-circuit labyrinth, and the path to the centre will be a shorter one. In brief, the more circuits, the longer the path.

Forms other than the classical labyrinth, including complex medieval designs, such as the example from Chartres Cathedral, can also be created indoors, but bear in mind that additional circuits demand a much larger room for successful construction (as discussed below). For this reason, a series of 'compact' designs, with reduced numbers of circuits, have become popular for indoor use in recent years. Commonly formed from a series of concentric circles arranged around an enlarged central area (and therefore often better suited for use by larger groups of people), their layout will require the use of an instruction sheet, or at the very least a printed design to copy (Buchanan, 2007).

▶ Indoor labyrinths

One of the easiest options for a quick indoor labyrinth is to use masking tape to form the 'walls' of the design. This can usually be applied to carpet, wood or vinyl floors without problem, and the layout can be as precise or freehand as your confidence level allows. A tape measure or ruler is recommended to create the initial seed pattern for classical designs, to ensure a standard unit of path width, but equally a stick or your shoe length can be employed. Parcel tape dispensers can often be adapted to dispense masking tape; this is quicker and easier for those with bad backs.

Figure 3.1 The construction of a classical labyrinth from the so-called 'seed pattern' (three-circuit labyrinth).

Image by Jeff Saward, Labyrinthos.

Figure 3.2 The construction of a classical labyrinth from the so-called 'seed pattern' (seven-circuit labyrinth).

Image by Jeff Saward, Labyrinthos.

Figure 3.3 The seed pattern (left) used to construct the 11-circuit classical labyrinth (right).

Image by Jeff Saward, Labyrinthos.

Figure 3.4 The seed pattern (right) used to construct the eight-circuit chakra-vyuha labyrinth (Indian classical labyrinth pattern, left).

Image by Jeff Saward, Labyrinthos.

Start by creating the central seed pattern in the centre of the room (with the top edge of the seed on the centre line). Then create the concentric arcs accordingly, keeping the distance between subsequent arcs a consistent distance from the previous circuit, in just the same fashion as when drawn on paper. For more complicated concentric medieval designs, a series of simple circles is often the easiest starting point, with sections of tape then removed and reapplied to form the turns of the pathway. Angular designs will require the use of tapes and straight edges, but if your floor is covered with carpet or vinyl tiles the resulting grid can sometimes be co-opted to help with the layout process, whatever design you may have selected.

Creating a labyrinth that is practical to walk and will also fit the available space is an essential consideration. For an indoor labyrinth a path width of at least 30 cm (1 ft) is recommended for solitary walking, or a width of up to 60 cm (2 ft) for more comfortable walking, running or group activity. A standard seven-circuit classical labyrinth will have an overall diameter 15 times the unit width of a single path (plus a wall, if it has any significant additional width). For example:

▶ Making a 30 cm (1 ft) path gives a labyrinth 4.5 m across (15 ft).
▶ Making a 60 cm (2 ft) path gives a labyrinth 9 m across (30 ft).

As a starting point, think of a large seminar room or conference space. Dividing the available clear space by 15 (taking into account any pillars or other obstructions intruding into the floor space of the room) will provide the absolute maximum unit width to be employed, although a slightly smaller unit will certainly allow more room for error, as well as some space around the outside of the labyrinth for circulation of participants. If there is enough room, a masking tape labyrinth can be designed so that walkers simply move around awkward pillars, which become incorporated into the pattern, rather like a path winding past a tree.

While masking tape is ideal for indoor labyrinths, if delicate or unsuitable flooring is an issue there are many other materials to consider. Paper or plastic cups (see Figure 3.5) can produce a visually attractive labyrinth in minutes; tin cans, jars or fruit punnets can also be utilised (and could support a local food bank). Rope, string or yarn can also be laid out to form a small labyrinth, although the process is best if practised beforehand. With a large group of people, try using shoes laid end to end to form the walls, or pin down a long length of tissue.

Another option for temporary indoor installation (and outdoor with suitable equipment) is a labyrinth created by light projection *(illustrated in*

Figure 3.5 A chakra-vyuha (Indian) classical labyrinth created from paper cups in a university dining hall, University of Kent, UK.

Photograph courtesy Jeff Saward, Labyrinthos.

Chapter 8 – eds). Better suited to a room with a high ceiling or balcony, a digital projector or suitable spotlight fitted with an acetate or glass slide with a printed labyrinth design can project a labyrinth onto the floor space below. Some adjustment of the angle of the slide will be necessary to result in a design that is not too distorted, for which reason the highest possible projection point should be selected. The resulting ethereal labyrinth provides a fascinating playground of light and shadow for those on the path, but note that too many people walking a projected labyrinth at one time can result in chaos, as much of the design can be obscured by the walkers' own shadows.

▶ Outdoor labyrinths

Moving outside, the choice of materials for an impromptu labyrinth is limited only by the imagination, or more often by what is to hand. For a one-day or evening event, simple labyrinths can be laid out quickly using convenient or themed materials. Survey flags, plastic cutlery, lollipop sticks or feathers can be stuck into the soil; stones, pinecones or sticks can simply be laid on the ground. With a little forward planning, chopped corn or bird

Figure 3.6 Candlelit labyrinth at LightNight Liverpool 2011, created by Alex Irving, Liverpool John Moores University.

Photograph by Mark McNulty, courtesy of Open Culture.

seed can also be poured in lines to mark the walls, and will survive until the local wildlife arrives (Saward, 2009). Sand or lime powder could also be employed. A striking centrepiece for an evening garden party or facilitated walk is a labyrinth whose paths are outlined with glowing luminaries or lanterns made by placing tea-light candles in glass jars or on a bed of sand in small paper sacks. Local fire safety procedures will need to be taken into consideration; if necessary, electric tea lights can be used, as in Figure 3.6.

Creating a labyrinth on a paved courtyard or tarmac car park does not require expensive equipment or materials. Playground chalks or water soluble line-marking paint can easily fashion a pleasing labyrinth. On lawns or playing fields, the use of a traditional solution, such as lime-based tennis court or sports ground paint, is always a possibility, but can be awkward and messy to apply. Many Sports Departments or Estate teams will have line-painting machines, although the turning circle needs to be small enough to accommodate the design (one university groundskeeper found a small hand-propelled version ideal for the purpose). Surveyors' spray paint, while usually used for marking out a construction project, can be employed to produce a quick and easy labyrinth that will last until the first heavy rainstorm, or the lawnmower, comes along.

Figure 3.7 Using what is to hand: boulder labyrinth in the grounds of the Institute of Technology, Mumbai, India.

Photograph courtesy Jeff Saward, Labyrinthos.

One solution that will last for a summer season is to mark the walls of a labyrinth on a lawn with a suitable fertiliser. The first decent rain shower will soon be followed by lush new growth as the fertilised grass shoots longer and darker to this plan for the rest of the season, no matter how frequently the grass is cut.

Equally simple is the idea of mowing the pathway of a labyrinth into an open area of grass, although this often requires a sizeable lawn or meadow to be effective. A pathway cut closely into a lawn that is otherwise cut a shade longer is very effective, and in some climates can be successfully maintained year-round. A twisting pathway through a wildflower meadow allows the visitor to pass between banks of tall grass and admire the flowers without trampling them. Cutting the grass for the first time early in the season, to establish the pattern, requires some spatial planning and layout skills; a central stake and measured circuits defined by a line of spray paint or chalk dust to guide the lawnmower may prove helpful. It is easy to keep the path maintained throughout the summer season by simply mowing the path, ideally the same width as the cut of the lawnmower. Estates or Grounds teams may become creatively involved or enjoy a fresh landscape challenge.

As autumn approaches, labyrinths of raked fallen leaves can provide a touch of seasonal artistry, but are soon dispersed on windy days! During the winter months adventurous souls have been known to create labyrinths from banks of snow, or simply by stamping the design into deeper lying drifts. Looking ahead, a simple labyrinth planted with early flowering bulbs in a lawn area is an ideal way to celebrate the approach of spring and warmer days ahead. Crocuses are ideal (as at the Cruickshank Botanic Garden, University of Aberdeen, Scotland) and soon die back to leave the lawn open for the summer; a labyrinth formed of daffodils will require more space, but within a few years can become a striking feature.

Whatever your chosen materials, the width of the paths and the overall size of the labyrinth should be carefully considered at the planning stage. A labyrinth with narrow paths can prove difficult to walk – anything much less than 30 cm (12 in) is often considered too narrow, and a minimum path width of around 45 cm (18 in) is recommended. Obviously, if you have the space, a somewhat larger path width can be selected, especially if you are expecting a crowd to walk your labyrinth.

While it can be argued that too wide a path is a distraction from the focus required when walking a labyrinth, a broader path will be required for disabled or wheelchair access, which may dictate the construction of a labyrinth with fewer circuits. A small labyrinth with three or five circuits can be fitted into a confined space, but a full eleven-circuit replica of a cathedral labyrinth with generous path width will clearly require more room.

The question then must be asked: can a labyrinth be too large? Consider how long you think you might wish to spend walking your labyrinth, and whether potential visitors might have mobility problems. In general, labyrinths much larger than 30 m (100 ft) in diameter are not common, and with good reason: the pathway can soon become incredibly long!

Designing and building your own labyrinth, be it a temporary indoor labyrinth for a workshop, or something more permanent outside, is not as difficult as it might at first appear. With suitable materials, good preparation and a little imagination, there is no limit to what can be achieved.

4   # Setting up and sharing: Introducing labyrinth practice in two university settings

Debbie Holley

Debbie Holley is an Associate Professor at the Centre of Excellence in Learning at Bournemouth University; a Fellow of the Chartered Institute of Logistics and Transport; a Principal Fellow of the Higher Education Academy and a National Teaching Fellow. She is interested in supporting students by offering spaces for reflection, writing and creativity. Debbie has organised numerous student and staff writing retreats. As a trained labyrinth walk facilitator, her events often include a labyrinth walk, and have inspired writing across the disciplines.

In the end, why and how it works remains a great mystery.

(Helen Curry, 2000, p. 209)

▶ My journey begins

In this chapter, I aim to share the joys and barriers of an individual practitioner developing 'labyrinth' paths in two UK Higher Education Institutions.

My involvement with the labyrinth came very unexpectedly. At a Teaching and Learning Conference, exploring the poster displays before the conference started, I was attracted by some beautiful music. I found a woman in a nearby area laying out a large canvas 'carpet' on the floor and sorting a huge bundle of white socks into different coloured baskets. Intrigued, I asked what was happening, and my introduction to the labyrinth, through Jan Sellers and the 'Creative Campus' at the University of Kent, began (Sellers, 2014). That wet April morning, before anyone else came along, I walked a medieval canvas labyrinth and was entranced. I spent most of the next two days finding out more, and returned to my home institution with a request to be funded for a three-day labyrinth facilitators' training course, to be held at the University of Kent later in the year.

My line manager was bemused; as the leader of our Technology into Teaching strand in the Business School, my usual requests were for hardware or software packages to enhance the students' learning through different technical mediums. However, my request for funding was granted, and later in the year I packed my case for a one-day 'Journeys through the Labyrinth' workshop. This was led by Canon Lauren Artress, founder of the labyrinth training, non-profit organisation Veriditas and a pioneer of contemporary developments with the labyrinth (Artress, 2015). It was followed by a two-day labyrinth facilitator training weekend, hosted by the University of Kent and led by Di Williams, a senior Veriditas teacher and a University Chaplain (Williams, 2015). *(For more on the innovative work of university chaplains with labyrinths, see Di Williams' chapter in this book – eds.)* Our group was able to access the hardstanding, outdoor Canterbury Labyrinth, in its stunning location overlooking Canterbury Cathedral, as well as the painted indoor canvas labyrinth. The mix of students on the course amazed me – men and women of all ages, and from all walks of life, drawn to explore further the possibilities of the labyrinth.

▶ First steps

Returning home, I was keen to share my new experiences, and to develop a group of staff who might like to consider some aspects of the labyrinth in their working practice. Securing funding to run a one-day workshop for staff was not difficult, as I framed the request in terms of 'staff development in reflective practices', which *incorporated* the labyrinth. I then set about arranging the staff development day.

The early interest of colleagues and ease of funding were encouraging but, in stark contrast, one colleague objected strongly to the idea, stating that she felt the labyrinth to be a satanic device. Staff attitudes can be a barrier to the implementation of new ideas, and I was much perturbed to receive such negative feedback for an optional session. However, the staff development team was very supportive of well-being initiatives, and explained that it was not unusual for a member of staff to take exception to some of the courses on offer. On their advice, I left the email unanswered. At a later stage, I followed up on this issue, reading and reflecting on the theme of labyrinths and the Christian tradition, starting with Sally Welch's excellent chapter on this topic in *Walking the Labyrinth* (Welch, 2010, pp. 15–27). My colleague's email was, as I now appreciate, simply an issue of ignorance about labyrinths, and can be resolved by showing that labyrinths are ancient, in all cultures, and have a real place within the Christian tradition. Rather than being destructive, the labyrinth is a tool that enriches spirituality.

My first workshop comprised a morning session for support staff, with eight staff, who had various different roles, attending: careers advisers; study advisers; student services; counselling; plus one academic staff member unable to attend the afternoon slot. The afternoon slot was mainly for academic staff; 17 attended from Business, Computing, Psychology, Health and Education. The lunchtime session saw three 'walk in' staff members come and walk the canvas labyrinth that had been set out, with several others coming in to browse the books and take an information sheet.

The feedback from all the staff who attended was incredibly positive:

> *'I didn't know what to expect – glad I came.'*

> *'Loved it! Thanks for the opportunity. Look forward to using it more at Uni.'*

> *'Want to use in teaching – can we form a group?'*

The result was a University Labyrinth Users Group. Setting up a group mailing list offered a place to discuss ideas, to share practice and events, and it quickly grew as members of staff heard about the work. A great pleasure was the success of inviting mailing list members to attend events; for example, members of the group attended Jan Sellers' guest lecture with accompanying labyrinth walks at St. Giles Cripplegate, Barbican, London (Sellers, 2011).

Shared ideas led to the idea of a postgraduate students' creative writing day, featuring three different aspects of learning, comprising a library session, a creative writing session and a labyrinth session with a concluding plenary, aimed at supporting students about to undertake writing their master's thesis. Aspects of creativity, periods of silence and retreat have been a feature of my work with students ever since.

▶ Second steps

Moving from an inner city university to a university in a smaller town, I not only changed universities, but disciplines, from a Business School to an Education Faculty. I was keen to bring the labyrinth into my teaching practice, and to share the space offered with the wider body of staff and students. My first challenge was to find out where I could gain support for a labyrinth. My early hopes of new colleagues becoming involved were not realised, partly due to the pressures of preparing for an OFSTED inspection (the UK external school inspectorate regime) and partly the need to be supporting our trainees in schools and consequently not being on site for periods of time. Undeterred, I spoke to Student Services, where members of the Counselling Team were interested, and to the Chaplaincy Team.

The initial project was set up by the Department of Education, Chaplaincy and Student Services. The project brief was firmly based on students and their well-being and, after some discussion, funding for a classical labyrinth, painted on the grass outside the Access Centre, was given. The first painting and erection of the signs explaining the use and purpose of the labyrinth took place in early May, to be available for students to walk at a time of stress. The Chaplain persuaded a member of staff from the Surveying Department to lend us his surveying students to map out the pattern on the grass, and the Estates Director offered her grounds staff to paint the pattern. Labyrinth designer Jeff Saward talked me through how to plan the project, and my first labyrinth at my new location came to life. Having the labyrinth there generates a 'space', and it is noticeable how many groups visiting the campus stop and talk at this location.

To promote cross-university links for the future, the first Labyrinth Staff Development event was a combined 'Student Services, Chaplaincy and Department of Education' event. Developed as a labyrinth 'taster' workshop, it comprised a short presentation illustrated with photographs of labyrinths through the ages, sourced from Jeff Saward's extensive collection (Labyrinthos, 2015), and a facilitated walk. Around ten staff attended, once again from a wide range of roles and disciplines. Further publicity about the labyrinth and an invitation to join the mailing group was communicated through the in-house magazine (Cant and Holley, 2011). This led to a range of informal discussions, and an invitation to facilitate a labyrinth walk at the autumn student induction week, as a quieter space for reflection away from the busyness of other activities. I subsequently offered a facilitated walk for our annual Doctoral Students Research Conference, under the 'taster workshop' format. This comprised a short introduction to the labyrinth in a 30-minute scheduled slot, with a facilitated walk following immediately, accompanied by an open invitation to walk the labyrinth at any point during the day. Colleagues from Mental Health Nursing and Chaplaincy have since requested sessions for their students.

Offering the taster slots and physically painting the labyrinth two to three times a year has led to surprising events. Staff regularly report that students use the labyrinth when the campus is quiet, and talk about regular local community visitors. The grounds staff, who really enjoy painting the labyrinth, took it upon themselves last winter to plant out the grass pattern with daffodil bulbs; coming to work one wet and windy March morning it was stunning to see the whole labyrinth as a floral display.

Within my own department, I found an ally in Sara Knight, a pioneer of Forest School and champion of outdoor play for children, who uses the outdoor labyrinth as a resource for her accredited Master's summer school module (Comparing Outdoor Learning Experiences). The Chaplain, wearing his 'community' hat, put us in touch with the local park and woodland manager. This led to a collaboration where Sara's students, with community volunteers, planted a living 'Willow' labyrinth, and designed and erected an information sign. Funded by the Woodland Trust, this living labyrinth is available to the community (Knight, 2012). Once again, I started with a small labyrinth interest group. This is developing into an embryonic staff 'Well-being' Group, and our labyrinth is now formally embedded as part of the Health Visitors' curriculum, as one of a series of timetabled well-being activities.

▶ Walking with others

It is in terms of my own reflective practice and well-being that I most notice the effects of my labyrinth work. My fascination with the labyrinth has increased, not diminished, as I seek out different spaces to develop my own practice outside the workplace.

Recently I was privileged to be invited to work with the community organisers at the Saffron Walden 'Amazing Maze' weekend. Saffron Walden's labyrinth was built in 1699 on the town common and is Europe's largest historic turf labyrinth. Despite the event title, this was actually a community labyrinth weekend, with activities including a knitted labyrinth, and indoor and outdoor labyrinths. Seeing the whole community, old and young, enjoy the time and space offered by different labyrinth walks in both inside and outside locations was inspiring (Saffron Walden, 2013).

The educational impact of the labyrinth continues. The small initial mailing group has now grown significantly. The Staff and Educational Development Association (SEDA) funded a labyrinth-making workshop, developed and run by practitioners from the first small group meeting, which was attended by fifteen interested parties from across the university sector. As reported in Bright and Pokorny's (2012) article, the delegates went away to share and develop their own labyrinth practices.

And for me? I have continued to read, walk and guide others; working with health practitioners has raised questions about the evidence base for well-being and labyrinth walking. A report on 'Commonly Reported Effects of Labyrinth Walking' (Rhodes, 2008) summarises research findings from a number of studies, and benefits such as 'peace; calming; centredness and clarity and a decrease of agitation' are described by participants, along with physical benefits such as the equalisation of blood pressure, stress reduction and a feeling of relaxation. These studies are consistent across culture, gender, ethnicity, employment status, age and those of faith or no faith. Helen Curry (2000) summarises the appeal of the labyrinth across such a wide audience, and notes that ultimately, while valuing research, we need also to value that which is mysterious. '*Words fall short. We limit things when we try to explain them through words*' (pp. 214–215) and as her quotation at the beginning of this chapter states, '*in the end … it is a great mystery*' (p. 209).

It is encouraging to know that in an increasingly technical and pressurised world, we are able to reach back to earlier times and learn again how to access the simplicity of an ancient practice. Thus, relatively few paces can gently take us on an unconscious voyage towards enhancing our own well-being. I would encourage the reader to take those first steps; develop friendships and find encouragement; make contacts in surprising places; enrich your life and the lives of others – all through sharing a simple walk – a walk of exploration and discovery around a labyrinth.

5 Adding a new dimension to design

Katja Marquart

Katja Marquart is a design educator certified by the National Council in Interior Design Qualification. She currently serves as Associate Dean and Division Head with the Division of Interior Architecture, University of Wisconsin – Stevens Point, USA. Through her research and creative work, she explores the transformative character of built and natural environments where labyrinths play a significant role, serving as tool, object, and symbol. Katja has been engaged in labyrinth-related activities for over fifteen years, is a Veriditas-trained labyrinth facilitator, and is trained at the Reiki Master level.

▶ Learning about space

This is an account of how I have shared the labyrinth with university students in various stages of their own academic pursuits. It is also a personal story of how the labyrinth has influenced my academic studies and professional research.

The story begins in 1998 when I was an undergraduate interior design student. On a beautiful fall weekend, I attended a women's retreat and walked a labyrinth for the first time. As my feet started following the path I was struck by the powerful symbolism of the labyrinth as space. Moving along the labyrinth's winding path affected me on a deeply spiritual and intellectual level: I connected with the pattern visually as a two-dimensional design, and physically, as a three-dimensional immersion into space. The labyrinth helped me realise that space is more than what is visible to the eye. While walking, I was struck by the understanding that the experience of moving through space, and the sequences of its varied components along the way, has a significant effect on a person physically and spiritually.

Following this experience, I questioned why my design studies did not include learning about space in this context. These inquiries led to further research on labyrinths and sacred spaces, and laid the foundation of my future professional work. In the years following this experience, the labyrinth has continued to be a significant element of my personal life, academic research and classroom instruction.

▷ Learning and teaching with the labyrinth

While in graduate school, the labyrinth became a tool that I used to facilitate my thinking process. Its physical design greatly influenced the final creative products of my design studies work. The metaphor of journey associated with walking a labyrinth also served to guide my mental and spiritual processes as a whole throughout this intense period of academic and personal growth and exploration.

My Master of Science thesis, 'Choice, Experience, and Transformation: Space as Metaphor', examined the topic of sacred space through written word (a thesis) and visual imagery (a creative project). Following an extensive literature analysis, I chose to define sacred space in this study as:

> a place or environment that facilitates transformation on both physical and spiritual levels and serves as metaphor or symbol, of our life and spiritual cycles through its varied components of sound, light, texture, color, structure, and movement patterns. (Marquart, 2004, p. 5)

This definition informed a decision to base my research process on the labyrinth as a visual symbol and experiential space. The process I followed in conducting my research was much like walking the path of a labyrinth. It was a journey that constantly brought me close to a goal and then away from it as I gathered and refined information.

For my visual project, I sought to give physical shape to common sequences found in existing sacred spaces, based on my literature review findings. Influenced by the physical design of the labyrinth pattern, this resulted in the creation of abstract spaces that diversely communicated the forms, architectural elements and dichotomies in sacred places. These were initially created on 3D computer modelling programmes, then physical architectural models and finally an exhibition installation.

For my Master of Fine Arts thesis and exhibition I examined the labyrinth pattern more closely in terms of its shape and structural qualities. In general, I was exploring various ways to visually interpret the winding and spiralling path characteristics of a labyrinth pattern while maintaining the experiential qualities of a physical labyrinth walk. The final installation of this creative process resulted in a complete transformation of the gallery space into a labyrinthine journey. Though not representative of a 'typical' labyrinth pattern in any way, this installation focused on a contrast between zigzag pathways and spiralling pathways. Guests walked through the installation and were asked to reflect upon their experience in an informal survey. A main component of the survey was to determine whether guests found the zigzag path or the spiralling path to be more engaging. Of those who responded, the spiralling pathway was by far the more engaging of the two options.

During this time I also introduced the labyrinth to other graduate students through workshops for the Graduate Student Collaborative, a professional development and graduate student support organisation at the University of Wisconsin, Madison (USA). These workshops were designed to help graduate students explore their research topics more deeply through cross-disciplinary connections, creative activities for idea generation and a facilitated labyrinth walk. The labyrinth was introduced as a tool that can help facilitate creative thinking and personal reflection. Prior to walking, students were given a basic introduction to the labyrinth, including a historical overview, contemporary uses of the labyrinth and general guidelines for how to approach and walk the path. Students were also encouraged to reflect upon a specific problem or question they were facing in their studies prior to starting the labyrinth walk. After the walk, students were asked to spend time in quiet reflection making note of any significant thoughts or feelings that arose during their walk. The group then reassembled to reflect and share their experiences.

More often than not, students expressed surprise at how easily their thoughts began to flow once they were following the labyrinth path. Many noted that although their thoughts began along one line of inquiry, they often found themselves thinking about something completely different by the end of the walk: sometimes this shift in thinking provided new ideas or new ways for them to explore their original line of inquiry. Almost all reported a sense of deeper relaxation and overall stress reduction.

For those familiar with labyrinth walking, these results are not unexpected. The process of walking in, through and out of a labyrinth is a metaphor for divergent and convergent thinking processes. They provide a place for focused attention. A technique known as 'walking with intention' allows a problem to be held in mind whilst walking the labyrinth with an openness, an accepting awareness. Drawing on this technique, a steady flow of thoughts can emerge, which often result in solutions or new insights on the problem.

I have also used the labyrinth as a tool to facilitate creative thinking in the design studio classroom throughout a semester, with third-year undergraduate students (at the University of Wisconsin, Stevens Point). The project began with a basic introduction of the labyrinth, demystifying the pattern and distinguishing it from mazes. Relevant historical applications were shared and I discussed contemporary uses of the labyrinth that would be of particular interest to these design students, such as the rise in popularity of labyrinths used in hospital settings and in hospitality design (spas and retreat centres).

Following this introduction, I discussed how a labyrinth can be used as a problem-solving tool and emphasised this as our main purpose in the activity. For this project, students were asked to always approach its use 'with intention' and to establish specific questions or goals before using the labyrinth. I emphasised the importance of being 'present' for the activity and encouraged students to slow down while tracing the labyrinth pattern. Given my prior experience working with students in the design studio who are often sleep-deprived, stressed and anxious to check activities off their to-do list, this instruction was critical in helping to create a meaningful experience for the students.

At the time of this project, there were no labyrinths on campus or in the local community for students to use. I therefore provided paper copies of several different patterns to explore through finger tracing, including the seven-circuit classical labyrinth and the Chartres labyrinth. Students were encouraged to keep these copies with them at all times and to trace them at different times of the day, both inside and outside of the studio classroom. Following each use, students were asked to record their experience. *(See chapters by Fran Grace, Nina Johnson and Kimberly Saward for further examples of paper labyrinth use and for templates – eds.)*

I also designed a classroom activity utilising the labyrinth patterns. Students were divided into small groups and asked to generate ideas relevant to their studio project. Following this activity, students were asked to spend some time in personal reflection and idea generation, during which they were invited to trace the labyrinth pattern as they reflected upon the session.

Student reflections on both of these activities at the end of the semester were varied and positive:

> *Tonight when I was at the studio, I was beginning to get frustrated with my project. I took out one of the labyrinths that was given to us. It helped me refocus on what I needed to do.*

> *Afterwards I felt more relaxed and could think more clearly. It was a nice quick way to take a mental breather.*

> *It was interesting doing this technique. At first it felt kind of silly, but I did it twice in the morning and before I went to bed and it really helped me to relax and focus.*

> *Doing this exercise in the morning helps get my mind going. I never really thought I would enjoy this one because it seems like such an easy and quick task, but it really works.*

My design students have also made use of the labyrinth by incorporating the pattern as part of their design project solution in their studio work. One third-year student learned about labyrinths during one of our course lectures in Interior Architecture, and subsequently decided to utilise the pattern for the design of a commercial office space. The fictitious client for this project was a company providing a full-service office environment for telecommuters, small groups and individual workers seeking a professional atmosphere in which to meet and conduct business. The design programme called for a space that stimulated creativity, innovation and networking, including an indoor park-like area. The student included a labyrinth in the design of the park as one way to meet these project requirements.

Labyrinths have remained influential in my teaching; I continue to seek opportunities to engage my students with labyrinths, whether through encouraging personal use or through integration within studio project requirements. The labyrinth has also remained influential in my professional growth and development since leaving graduate school and entering the professional academic community.

▶ Shaping a career

This focus on labyrinths has created interesting professional challenges in my career development. As a new faculty member I was constantly faced with the need to explain what labyrinths were and why they were a relevant topic of study in my field. A body of work for 'labyrinth research' related to the design fields was (and remains) virtually non-existent. This challenge has forced me to research labyrinths from a variety of angles. Initially, I focused on the scholarship of teaching and learning, resulting in a series of conference presentations on the use of labyrinths in the classroom (Marquart, 2006, 2008). My institution supports and encourages this type of faculty research, enabling me to build a body of research while pursing tenure.

I also began to focus more on the use of labyrinths in the built environment (Marquart, 2007) and in the development of creative works. 'Creative scholarship' is a fairly new form of accepted research practice in my field and it was natural for my work to evolve in this direction, given my previous labyrinth work in graduate school. Through these projects I used the labyrinth both as subject and tool, combining digital and hand-woven practices as I explored new ways to express different labyrinth patterns (Marquart, 2009, 2011).

My research focus continues to evolve. At present, I am researching the environments in which labyrinths are installed with the eventual intention of creating design guidelines for indoor and outdoor environments that will contain labyrinths (Marquart, 2013, 2014). The guidelines will be available to professional designers, labyrinth builders and the general public when creating a new permanent labyrinth.

Much like a labyrinth walk, the journey of navigating through this process of teaching, research and creative exploration has brought times of confusion and clarity; frustration and reward. I have come to know the labyrinth in ways never imagined during that first labyrinth walk so long ago. As space and object, the labyrinth's physical design has significantly influenced my research. As tool, the labyrinth has become a useful classroom resource. As symbol, it has served as metaphor to guide my thinking through all of these activities. Finally, as gift, the labyrinth brings depth and meaning to my life. It has provided opportunities to build relationships and connect with others around the world through professional organisations, research and travel.

6 Case study: Labyrinths and learning – reflections from a research engineer

Faye Thomsit-Ireland

Faye Thomsit-Ireland is a doctoral Research Engineer at the School of Agriculture, Policy and Development, University of Reading, UK. Following a BSc in Ecology and an MSc in Ecological Applications, Faye's EngD research is on overcoming the barriers to retro-fitting green walls in an urban setting. Previous roles include research on Alzheimer's disease; working for Adult Social Services in Scotland; and work at the wildlife garden at the Natural History Museum, London.

▶ Starting out

I am a research engineer half-way through my doctorate, studying green walls and ivy in conjunction with buildings. My research explores whether ivy and other directly clinging plants can work in harmony with domestic and commercial buildings.

My first experience with a labyrinth was at university in Norwich, where I walked the labyrinth in Wensum Park. It felt strange but was a pleasant way to calm my mind for a moment. Fifteen years later in Scotland, my curiosity was piqued again, this time with respect to mindfulness and as a form of walking meditation when I walked the Edinburgh Labyrinth.

My love of labyrinths continued to blossom when I returned to London and the Religious Society of Friends (Quakers), where I was able to walk a canvas labyrinth, which took up the entirety of the hall at Wanstead Meeting House. It was a moving experience, especially when I considered my path in relation to those around me and how we wove in and out, with the children racing around. I felt that the labyrinth experience was good for me, and I wanted a labyrinth close to me.

When I began to study for my Master's degree, I printed a labyrinth that I hung above my workstation, so I could trace it – as a finger labyrinth, following the path by hand – when I needed a sense of perspective. I got a labyrinth brooch that I wore whenever I needed self-assurance, such as during interviews, exams and my wedding. Tracing the labyrinth would always remind me that things seem darkest just before the dawn: in the labyrinth you are typically furthest from the centre when you are on the final part of the journey. Once I was 'tuned' into labyrinths, I started spotting them everywhere. There was a finger labyrinth in a little community garden in Vauxhall (south London), that I traced while I sat in the sun, after an interview. Then 'Art on the Underground' commissioned labyrinths as part of the 150th Anniversary of the London Underground and a labyrinth wall plaque was installed at every Underground station in London (Wallinger, 2013).

▶ Life and research: One step at a time

Suddenly I realised the similarity between walking or tracing a labyrinth and following a journey, be it searching for a new job, pursuing studies or any other endeavour. I suspect however that inklings had been forming for some time. On entering a new venture, everything seems possible. In the same way, on entering the labyrinth, the first steps are straight towards the middle; you can see the centre, but just when it seems immediately at hand, you turn away from it to continue the journey.

This rang true. I remembered experiencing this series of emotions many times before. I would be excited about starting a project, then something would happen and my energy would evaporate. What I found so pleasing about the labyrinth was that the centre, the apparent 'goal', does not matter. It is not a trick or a puzzle; simple persistence enables arrival. That too was concordant; so far, anything I had put my mind to, I had achieved. This rarely occurred in the way I had anticipated (the straight route into the centre), but by a highly convoluted route, where the experience of the journey was enlightening.

Dealing with depression

I have depression and I find the movement in the labyrinth balancing, like the tide. I enjoy the ebb and flow towards the centre and from one side to the next and back again, constantly looping back; it grounds me in the present moment.

Walking and looking at labyrinths is very reassuring. The path can be followed quickly or slowly, in a day-dream or not. Even if 'nothing happens', no unexpected or powerful insight, something may still start to crystallise; and it is a calming, mindful walk.

I now like to have a labyrinth at hand. It is easy to draw one on something frequently carried – a purse, or small piece of laminated card *(see Jeff Saward's chapter for drawing techniques – eds)*.

Goal centred, process centred

I see walking and tracing labyrinths as a way of valuing the journey. Yet this was something that until the last year or so I saw as pointless. Physically, I don't travel well, so from childhood I developed the habit of sleeping through journeys, a practice I called 'TARDIS' travel.[1] I would fall asleep in one place and wake up in another, psychologically eliminating the journey. My mind was driven by achievements and the next goal, almost ignoring the process of how I got there. Yet I am learning that the 'process' is where joy, peace and contentment lie. Miss the journey, and you miss the point.

During my doctoral research, the labyrinth reminds me to have faith that despite the complexity of the journey, continually moving forward with a sense of my overall aim will eventually bring me to the centre – no matter how intimidating the journey appears or how concerned I feel at times.

Travelling with others

Walking a labyrinth with other people is quite a different experience to that of walking alone, or moving through a finger labyrinth. It is now a dance, passing people, moving to one side to let them pass, and my speed naturally alters to match others around me. The dynamics constantly change like friendships in flux; someone who was close at one point may appear far away at other moments, constantly moving around. Unconsciously, each of us would become the leader, then led, sometimes walking in parallel, and even walking in opposite directions. Best of all, with labyrinths there are no rules. To leave, you can walk back along the track, hop from one track to the next or walk straight down along the edge; it is just a question of doing what feels right.

This flow has been reflected in my team of supervisors and sponsors for my project, especially as regards leading, being led and going in opposite directions. Some parts of the project that seemed so close from my supervisor's perspective, just on the next track, were the equivalent of an endless path to me, and those areas that appeared challenging to them, were for me just a hop and a skip across.

▷ **Next steps: Bringing the labyrinth to more people**

During my time as a doctoral student I have joined a Peer Support team, a trained group which provides students with a fellow student to talk to, whether as a listening ear or for help and advice. As part of our stress management and well-being events we follow the TREAT yourself principle: Try something new, Relate to others, Exercise, Appreciate and Think of others. To accompany this, I am providing two portable labyrinths that I have hand-painted on tarpaulin, using the classical labyrinth design. My aim is to introduce labyrinth walking as a way of stress management and relaxation, sharing what I myself have learned through the opportunity that the Peer Support scheme offers.

Note

1 'TARDIS' travel (Time and Relative Dimension in Space) is a reference to time and space travel in the television drama series, *Doctor Who:* see www.bbc.co.uk/programmes/b006q2x0

7 Transformative learning: Introducing the labyrinth across academic disciplines

Diane Rudebock

Dr C. Diane Rudebock is a Registered Nurse and Professor Emerita in the Department of Kinesiology and Health Studies at the University of Central Oklahoma. She coordinated the UCO Campus Labyrinth Project as well as the Graduate Wellness Management, Health Studies Program. As a Veriditas-certified labyrinth facilitator, Vice President of the international Labyrinth Society and Chair of the Society's Research Committee, she is passionate about utilising labyrinths in her research and teaching. She has presented at local, state, national and international conferences on ways to incorporate the labyrinth personally and in university settings.

▶ Introduction

Through the centuries, colleges and universities, both public and private, have created rich environments that foster learning and transformation to better prepare students to become engaged and productive citizens. At the University of Central Oklahoma (UCO) in Edmond, USA, transformative learning experiences are at the heart of the campus learning environment, supported by the University's Center for Excellence in Transformative Teaching and Learning (UCO, 2014a). One unique characteristic of the campus is a dedicated space for transformative learning: a permanent campus labyrinth. Artress (2006a) describes a labyrinth as a moving meditation. In *Walking a Sacred Path: Rediscovering the Labyrinth,* she refers to the labyrinth as a *'blueprint for transformation'* (p. 147) and shares the transformative experience of her first labyrinth walk.

Whether using the labyrinth as a part of a class activity or as an individual walking the labyrinth path in solitude, the labyrinth provides a unique space for students to experience transformative learning. Nohl (2015, p. 45) states that ' ... *transformative learning may begin unnoticed, incidentally, and sometimes even casually, when a new practice is added to old habits'*. Walking a labyrinth can become a new practice, and labyrinths in university settings invite students to nurture their inner being through a contemplative walk: for example, using the labyrinth prior to creating a required course project; walking before taking an exam; planning activities at the beginning of the day; reflecting on experiences at the end of the day; or simply taking a break from the constant demands of their campus and work schedules. Sellers' work in the UK also provides readers with creative ways that labyrinths can be used in university settings (Sewell, Sellers and Williams, 2012). The 2014 XI International Transformative Learning Conference, 'Spaces of Transformation and Transformation of Space' (Nicolaides and Holt, 2014), emphasised the significant role that space plays in creating transformative experiences. Universities seek ways to enrich all aspects of students' lives, including the campus environment; the creation of an inclusive space such as the labyrinth brings another dimension to learning available not only to students, but also to faculty, staff and community members.

Students arrive at the University of Central Oklahoma from varied backgrounds and cultures and often feel overwhelmed with the demands of school, family and work; it is vital to recognise these issues. As Beer et al. (2015, p. 163) stated, *'the importance of reflection, trust and individualized attention is paramount in transformative learning'*. In this chapter I will explore the introduction of the labyrinth to the UCO community and its integration across academic disciplines, in the context of UCO's Six Central Tenets of Transformative Learning (discussed below).

▶ The University of Central Oklahoma campus environment

The University of Central Oklahoma in Edmond, USA, is a metropolitan university founded in 1890 and is home to over 17,000 students. As the first public university in the state, the spacious 210 acre campus welcomes students, faculty and staff from around the world and is noted for its attractive teaching, learning and living environment and commitment to 'green' environmental practices (UCO 2015). Collaboration among divisions and academic disciplines is valued, and many opportunities exist to foster collaborative efforts, an essential component of creating transformative environments.

The provision of spaces such as the labyrinth strengthens wellness beyond physical health, fosters the intellectual pursuit of knowledge and becomes a foundation for transformative learning to occur. This approach to learning, an 'expanded wellness model' discussed by Kolander, Ballard and Chandler (2005, p. 15), is at the centre of transformative learning and incorporates all components of health, including physical, intellectual, emotional, social, occupational and spiritual. Based on the commitment to provide an environment which fosters transformative learning, administrators, faculty, students and staff embraced the vision of creating a permanent outdoor labyrinth on campus (Rudebock and Worden, 2012). Dedicated 6 September 2013, adjacent to the Y Chapel of Song in Heartland Plaza, and surrounded by Oklahoma native trees, the 11-circuit red and grey paver labyrinth offers by its presence an invitation to step on the path, to engage in a walking meditation (UCO, 2013a). The labyrinth is 42 feet and nine inches (13.03 metres) in diameter, a replica of the ancient labyrinth in Chartres Cathedral, France. The full walk, from the entrance to the centre and back out to the beginning, is one-third of a mile (0.5 km).

▷ Finding life's meaning through the labyrinth journey

In his book *Man's Search for Meaning,* originally written in 1946, Viktor Frankl told of his experience and survival in Nazi death camps. As a result, Frankl believed that our greatest quest on our life journey is to find purpose and meaning, with experience itself offering one path towards the discovery of meaning (Frankl, 2006, p. 145). The labyrinth has provided such meaning and purpose to my day, to my life and in my career; it has also become a space for me to enjoy quiet time for contemplation on a regular basis as well as a model for problem solving as suggested by Curry (2000).

I welcomed in the New Year of 2001 by walking my first indoor labyrinth at a local community centre. As my husband drove for an hour along the snow-packed roads to reach the event two miles away, he inquired repeatedly, 'What exactly are we doing?' and 'What is this labyrinth?' My response was always the same: I did not know, other than that one walks along a path painted on canvas, and I felt strongly I was to attend (Rudebock, 2014).

This was a time in my life when there were not enough hours in the day to meet the deadlines of my full-time position as a Public Health Nurse Program Manager at our county health department, combined with my struggle to finish my doctoral dissertation. Taking a break to engage in a walking meditation seemed like the ideal way to begin a new year, and I had secretly hoped that I would receive insights that would keep me motivated to complete my doctoral work.

My husband and I received a warm welcome once we arrived to walk the labyrinth. We were greeted by two women, who suggested that we approach our labyrinth walk by focusing on our life journey. They invited us to write a reflection upon completing our walk to acknowledge the significance of the experience. I loved the ambience of the candlelit room with soft sounds of flute music; for the first time in months, I felt myself slowing down both physically and mentally. Even though I could not determine exactly where the meandering path would lead, I did not seem to mind. Metaphors began to emerge as I neared the centre of the design, and I realised that while finishing my dissertation was certainly part of my life journey, there was more. I sensed that I was on the verge of entering a new era in my life, something which had a deep meaning, although I did not have words to describe it.

In the days to come, the labyrinth frequently occupied my thoughts. I had crossed a threshold on that first labyrinth journey that would become the foundation for my life's work. I returned each month to walk the indoor community labyrinth, and in spring 2001, my husband and I created a labyrinth in our back yard. In the coming months, I was invited by the two women who were present for my first labyrinth walk to join a local Labyrinth Guild, which offered monthly walks for the community; soon after, the Guild funded my training with Veriditas to become a certified labyrinth facilitator. In return, I committed to volunteer with the Guild to offer monthly labyrinth walks and, after 14 years, still continue to do so.

▶ Introducing the labyrinth in a university setting: Labyrinth 101

Because of the calming benefits I gained from my personal interactions with the labyrinth, it became natural to share my labyrinth experiences with others. I joined the UCO faculty in 2003 and in the next few years easily found ways to incorporate the labyrinth, both in the health-related classes I taught and in campus events. The following examples illustrate my own journey to bring the labyrinth to the campus environment; dates are included to demonstrate the progression of the labyrinth story on the UCO campus.

In 2004, having completed my training with Veriditas, I began to use the canvas labyrinth from the Labyrinth Guild to offer a variety of workshops on campus. This included a regular component of the Student Affairs Division's leadership training (for student leaders) and the Center for Counseling's stress management series. As interest grew, more and more faculty and students engaged in labyrinth walks, and in 2005, the Kinesiology and Health Studies Department (KHS) purchased an 11-circuit medieval canvas labyrinth. It was offered at the first 'Work of Women' campus event, 'Embracing and Honoring Women'. The following year, a seven-circuit medieval canvas labyrinth was added to meet the growing number of requests from student groups. Labyrinth activities became a regular part of a variety of campus events, including Earth Day in 2006 when a seven-circuit classical labyrinth was painted on the grass by KHS faculty; students created signage around the labyrinth focusing on conservation and sustaining a healthy environment. Interest in using the labyrinth continued to evolve in 2006, and a campus grant funded a student research assistant as a part of the newly formed interdisciplinary labyrinth research team.

The labyrinth landscape was expanding on the UCO campus. Undergraduate students were awarded campus grants that utilised the labyrinth for their research projects, and grant funds were used to purchase labyrinth resources including books, hand-held wooden labyrinths and items to create a labyrinth display. The labyrinth became a part of the curriculum for my students in the undergraduate Community Health and graduate Wellness Management classes, and soon faculty in other departments and disciplines requested 'labyrinth time' in their classes based on their specific discipline or topic, such as leadership.

While walking the Chartres Cathedral labyrinth in France in July 2009, I knew that building a labyrinth on our university campus was more than a dream. Walking the stone path in Chartres, step by step, and journeying with others on the path, was inspirational: to bring a permanent labyrinth to our campus, we embraced the metaphor of the labyrinth as journey. We would travel with others who shared and supported this vision, staying on the meandering path, trusting that we would arrive at our goal – just as, when we physically follow the path of the labyrinth design, we arrive at the centre. It was through self-reflection that I discovered that the labyrinth itself became the blueprint for moving forward with the creation of a permanent labyrinth on campus.

In January 2011, an 11-circuit medieval labyrinth was painted on the campus grounds, part of a research study by the campus labyrinth research team which I led. Permission was received from the UCO Facilities Management team to maintain the painted grass labyrinth after the research study was completed due to requests from students, staff and faculty, who walked the labyrinth over several months. For the next two years, in the heat of the Oklahoma summers, and the cold days of winter, every two weeks, with the help of my husband and students, I repainted the lines of the labyrinth on the grass.

▷ Connecting the labyrinth with transformative learning in a university setting

Higher education, according to Mullen, Hatton and Frankland (2011), by its very nature is a transformative experience. Many opportunities exist in university settings for students and faculty to explore their own understanding of themselves and the world as they expand their knowledge base in given areas. As a result of these experiences, a change in perspective occurs which is referred to in the literature as transformative learning; Mezirow's work in transformative learning in the late 1970s was originally introduced in Europe as 'the theory of reflectivity' (Wang and King, 2006, para. 8).

The repetitive painting process in 2010 was also a time for my own reflection: my experience on the Chartres Labyrinth lingered in my mind, as well as the question from those who had walked the temporary and canvas labyrinths on campus over the past seven years: *'When can we have a permanent labyrinth on campus to walk?'* I recalled all the stories from students from various disciplines who had experienced the labyrinth and realised that the labyrinth was 'transformative learning in action'. Ongoing self-reflection is an integral part of the transformative learning journey as educators and students (Cunliff, Franz and Romano, 2014). As Mezirow stated (1997, p. 5): *'When circumstances permit, transformative learners move toward a frame of reference that is more inclusive, discriminating, self-reflective, and integrative of experience'.* As a result of engaging with the labyrinth, students were changing and learning – they learned how to become present in the moment, spend time in contemplation and reflection and be open to their creative processes. It became apparent that the labyrinth could be utilised in any academic discipline to help students learn.

It became my mission to find ways to connect the labyrinth experience with the 'Central Six Tenets of Transformative Learning' (UCO, 2014b). These had been developed in 2006 in a collaborative environment of campus divisions with the focus on 'high impact' student-centred learning, predicted to have far-reaching benefits for students' lives (Barthell, Cunliff, Gage, Radke and Steele, 2010, p. 56). Fortunately, in February 2010, I was invited to be the luncheon speaker at the Transformative Learning Conference on the UCO campus. The title of the conference was 'Reflections: Where We're Going and Where We've Been'. Even though many labyrinth activities had been offered on campus since 2004, it was important to take this opportunity to present the labyrinth in a more formal setting; the 200 participants included university administrators, faculty, staff and students. My presentation, 'The Path of Transformation: Using the labyrinth as a metaphor for learning' (Rudebock and Adair, 2010), included collaboration with a graduate student who had received a grant to assist with labyrinth projects. I began with a brief introduction about labyrinths and included images of the labyrinth in Chartres Cathedral, our Kinesiology and Health Studies Department canvas labyrinths, students using wooden finger labyrinths and the 11-circuit medieval pattern – with one of the six tenets in each of the petals in the centre. Following this came an experiential session: participants were given an individual pack containing an 11-circuit medieval paper labyrinth, guidance notes, a pen and paper for reflections. The instructions for the experience were verbally given and included:

▶ Pausing at the opening and focusing on the word, 'transformative'.
▶ As they traced the labyrinth path, they were invited to remember the times they had experienced transformation.
▶ When they arrived at the centre, it was suggested that they think of times when they observed their students experiencing transformation.
▶ As they moved out of the centre and back to the beginning, they were asked to be open to ways they could create transformative experiences for their students in their respective disciplines, using the paper available to take time to write a reflection.

A hush fell across the room while quiet flute music played in the background; it was deeply moving to observe the process. Participants traced the labyrinth design on paper and moved easily into writing a reflection. This was followed by small group discussions in which participants shared their experiences. Such was their enthusiasm that several people volunteered to share their insights with the entire conference; participants embraced the idea of a labyrinth and could readily see how they could use a labyrinth in their academic discipline.

As educators, we assist learners to discover their quest for life-long learning, and our role is to provide experiences which foster reflection and critical thinking. In this process, students have the opportunity to restructure or confirm the beliefs they hold. Cranton (2000, p. 195) believes the role of educators is to bring *'taken for granted assumptions into critical awareness so that appropriate action can be taken'*. She also suggests that *'activities and discussions that encourage learners to become aware of their habits of mind, engage in discourse and reflection and critically question their perspectives have the potential for fostering transformative learning'* (p. 199). The labyrinth is a powerful example of such activity: offering the labyrinth in this conference, and the discussion and reflection that followed, illustrated how the labyrinth could be used as a metaphor to demonstrate the Central Six Tenets of Transformative Learning at UCO. These comprise:

1. Discipline Knowledge.
2. Leadership.
3. Problem Solving (Research, Scholarly and Creative Activities).
4. Service Learning and Civic Engagement.
5. Global and Cultural Competencies.
6. Health and Wellness.

Transformative learning was described as *'a holistic process that places students at the center of their own active and reflective learning experiences'* (UCO, 2014a, para 3). The centre of the labyrinth design was used as a symbol for student learning, with the path to the centre being symbolic of the student's journey as they pursued their education. The campus leaders who created the Central Six tenets attended the Transformative Learning conference and participated in the labyrinth experience as a part of my presentation. I believe that this was a turning point. Many key campus leaders as well as students had the opportunity to have a personal experience with the labyrinth; administrators, faculty, students and staff embraced the vision of creating a permanent outdoor labyrinth on campus, based on Transformative Learning and using the Central Six tenets as the foundation. A formal proposal to move this forward was presented to the university administration in 2012 (Rudebock and Worden, 2012; Rudebock, 2014).

Integrating the 'Central Six' with the labyrinth seemed to be organic, and the campus community came together to support and develop the labyrinth experience across disciplines and in a broad spectrum of university and community contexts, as illustrated in Table 7.1.

Table 7.1 Activities with the labyrinth in relation to each of the six tenets of transformative learning at the University of Central Oklahoma

1st Tenet: Discipline knowledge
Students use the labyrinth prior to taking exams; students use the time to focus on what they have learned as they journey along the path.
In the Department of History and Geography, students use the labyrinth during their coursework in medieval history.
Students in the Community Public Health course are invited to focus on community as they navigate the winding paths of the labyrinth.
Speech pathology students were introduced to the labyrinth with a focus on inclusion.
Students in the Nursing Department learned about the labyrinth and participated in a labyrinth experience as a part of their class on the importance of reflection.

continued overleaf

Table 7.1 Activities with the labyrinth in relation to each of the six tenets of transformative learning at the University of Central Oklahoma *continued*

2nd Tenet: Leadership
Student Leaders participate in a retreat prior to the fall semester, and the labyrinth was offered in a retreat setting which focused on important attributes of leadership.
Students in the Leadership and Ethics in Health Education course walked the labyrinth, focusing on leaders who have made an impact in their lives.
Students in the graduate Organizational Behavior and Leadership Course use the labyrinth as a metaphor for learning about the various aspects of organizational culture.
3rd Tenet: Problem solving (research, scholarly and creative activities)
Research
A Labyrinth Research Team was created which included students, staff and faculty.
An introduction to the campus labyrinth was presented at UCO's Fall Faculty Collegium. Four faculty from three disciplines (Dance, History, and Kinesiology and Health Studies) provided examples explaining how they used the labyrinth with students in their classes (Rudebock, Webster, Kambor and Gregory, 2013).
Nine students received funding for research grants in relation to the labyrinth. They subsequently presented their findings at a Regional Research Day.
Several students went on to present their research at an international conference.
Creativity
Theatre students (College of Fine Arts and Design) were introduced to the labyrinth by their professor when they studied rituals.
Kaleidoscope Dance Company students (College of Fine Arts and Design) participated in a collaborative project and created a dance performance based on the journey of the labyrinth.
Fashion marketing students used the labyrinth as inspiration as a part of their Creative Problem Solving Class when they began a new class project.
4th Tenet: Service learning and civic engagement
A labyrinth walk was part of activities held during the inauguration of the new campus president in 2012. Students from the Leadership and Ethics in Health Education class were hosts for this event, making signs that included the six tenets of transformative learning.
A labyrinth workshop was created for students attending a local 'Sober High School', using the 12 steps of recovery.
Students in the Introduction to Community and Public Health class and the Leadership and Ethics in Health Education classes completed Community Service activities by assisting with community and campus labyrinth events, including presentations about the labyrinth for community groups.
The campus was the host for the first Institute of Coordinated School Health in the state of Oklahoma: 60 teachers and nurses from elementary, middle and high schools in Oklahoma were introduced to the campus labyrinth, focusing on the components of the new school health approach, which is an integrated model involving teachers, students, school staff and the community.
Girl Scouts experienced the labyrinth as part of requirements to obtain their Labyrinth badge.

continued overleaf

Table 7.1 Activities with the labyrinth in relation to each of the six tenets of transformative learning at the University of Central Oklahoma *continued*

5th Tenet: Global and cultural competencies
The labyrinth was available to walk as a part of World Peace Day, 2013.
The labyrinth is gaining in popularity as a moving meditation and is unique, since the labyrinth can be experienced by incorporating other forms of meditation while one walks along the path. This is particularly appealing to our international students.
Through the Labyrinth Society's annual conferences, students have not only presented their findings but have had the opportunity to learn about labyrinths in many cultures, faith and community traditions, and to meet international experts in this field.
6th Tenet: Health and wellness
As a part of the Healthy Life Skills course through the Department of Kinesiology and Health Studies a labyrinth section and an assignment using the labyrinth were created in the 'Healthy Life Skills' textbook. This course is a requirement for all students attending UCO and provides practical knowledge for personal health and wellness.
Students in a Yoga course used the labyrinth space for their yoga, placing their mats on the permanent labyrinth.
The University Center for Counseling and Wellbeing offers stress reduction events which use the labyrinth.
The peer health leaders of UCO held a Gratitude Walk for campus during November.
Officers and members of the Community Public Health Club offered a labyrinth event for students during the week prior to finals.

When evaluating the opportunity to create a labyrinth on a university campus it is important to consider the campus community as a whole and incorporate the university mission as a foundation in the process. By focusing on creativity and global and cultural diversity, labyrinths can be a wonderful addition to any campus, since labyrinth designs are found around the globe. University settings are ideal places for labyrinths, since most university campuses have faculty, staff and students from other parts of the world; the labyrinth is a place of inclusion where all are welcome to journey the path together. It is open to all beliefs and traditions. Using the labyrinth in a university setting as a part of the Central Six Tenets of Transformative Learning supports the University's goals towards providing the optimum environment for students to thrive, and allies with new approaches in the current literature on transformative learning (Taylor and Laros 2014; Illeris, 2014).

Reflection is an integral part of the labyrinth experience and is also at the centre of Mezirow's expanded model of transformative learning (Kitchenham, 2008). The labyrinth offers a space to engage in an experience and, as Mezirow (1997) suggests, reflect on the inner meaning of that experience. Numerous students have shared with me their insights after walking the campus labyrinth. One of my senior students emailed me after walking the new campus labyrinth: he was excited by the experience, saying that it gave him an opportunity to stop what he was doing and ask himself what would motivate him to accomplish his life goals. A common experience reported by students who walked the labyrinth was that it gave them time to de-stress and clear their minds. Dr Don Betz, President of the University of Central Oklahoma and a firm supporter of the labyrinth initiative, stated at the dedicatory event that the campus labyrinth provides an *'oasis of serenity amid an otherwise bustling campus'*. He noted that:

> The process of reflection is essential to lifelong learning. It is through reflection that we find new opportunities and fresh perspectives. The labyrinth certainly enhances our mission to create a culture of learning, leading, and serving at Central. (UCO, 2013b)

Other strong supporters of the campus labyrinth were Dr Pat LaGrow, Assistant Vice President of Academic Affairs, and Dr Jeff King, the Executive Director of the Center for Excellence in Transformative Teaching and Learning. Dr King believes that the labyrinth is:

> perfectly suited to our [UCO] campus for a number of reasons, one of which is that contemplative instruction practice can be a key strategy which prompts for Transformative Learning experience. Another is that labyrinth walking as a form of active meditation benefits students' cognition and attention. (Personal communication, 31 March 2014)

Creating and researching the effects of labyrinths is like *'mapping the unknown'*, to use a phrase by Holford, Jaris, Milana, Waller and Webb (2013, p. 685). Since labyrinth experiences are diverse, and our understanding of what occurs when one walks the labyrinth has not been fully explored, we are positioned to move labyrinth research forward due to the availability of labyrinths that dot the landscape. Labyrinth research is in its infancy, offering the opportunity for future collaboration and adventure with a multitude of professional and academic disciplines as the journey continues.

Many people in university settings may not be well acquainted with labyrinths, their history or ways in which they can be incorporated in an academic setting. Reflecting on my own experience of working with the labyrinth over the past 15 years, I have identified ten key ideas to keep in mind when planning to introduce the labyrinth to enhance learning in a university or other academic setting.

1. First, it is vital to consider the mission of the university and to frame labyrinth events and proposals for a temporary or permanent labyrinth within the context of the mission and core values of the institution.
2. Allow your personal enthusiasm for the labyrinth to motivate you in your ongoing journey to integrate the labyrinth in a university setting.
3. Be alert to campus opportunities which could incorporate a labyrinth activity.
4. Maintain positive relationships with staff and faculty in all disciplines and departments on campus.
5. Identify faculty, staff and students who share your enthusiasm of the labyrinth and enlist their assistance with labyrinth events, offering the labyrinth opportunity in their courses and student events.
6. Collaborate with members of the community who provide labyrinth events.
7. Create a formal presentation and handouts which can be used with the labyrinth activity.
8. Develop a Research Team including faculty, staff and students, who can begin to use the labyrinth as a part of their research projects and can present their findings at local, state, regional and international professional conferences.
9. Identify faculty in administrative roles who are available to assist in moving the labyrinth project forward.
10. Continue to walk the labyrinth as a part of your own routine, remembering that insights emerge along the path.

▶ Conclusion

The labyrinth on the UCO campus has been fully embraced by community members, as well as students, faculty and staff, since it was dedicated in September 2013. Connection with the surrounding community is vital as a part of civic engagement and transformative learning. These interactions strengthen and deepen relationships; community is where we live, work and play, and having a permanent labyrinth on campus has added a new and welcome dimension. The labyrinth is used by individuals who seek moments of quiet reflection and those who wish to walk the path in community, and its use over these past two years has been truly diverse. In addition to teaching, this has included research projects; creative art activities; courses which focus on leadership; staff development conferences; gratitude walks; peace walks; World Labyrinth Day Celebrations; school health workshops; sorority and sorority alumni groups; and teachers from area high schools. Frequently those who are introduced to the labyrinth are anxious to share their experiences and insights after walking. Whether it is a faculty, student or staff, first-time walkers or those who walk regularly, a common theme is that insights were gained and the feeling of calmness and peace motivates them to return again to the path.

It has been an honour to be the campus labyrinth champion and to bring the vision of a permanent labyrinth to reality. It has also been gratifying to see the enthusiasm within so many aspects of university life for developing the creative uses for the labyrinth. The permanent labyrinth is an interactive work of art that invites all to journey on a path of transformation. This work nurtures a wide vision for learning, teaching and well-being, and emerging from this transformative space is an invitation for all to step on the path.

Part II: Teaching and Learning Perspectives

Poems from the Labyrinth

Choice

Canterbury

this way, there's an oak tree
that way, a eucalyptus

uphill, a vast sixties university
its Templeman Library
below, Lanfranc's medieval cathedral

over there, my house across the valley
over here, a cycle-path climbing the hill

how can I choose between a library and a cathedral
a heavy-branched native oak
and silver ribbons of imported eucalyptus

decide whether to head home
or take a bike ride to the coast

listen, says the labyrinth,
there's no here nor there
just the path
one way, an oak tree
the other, a eucalyptus

Victoria Field

Introduction to Part II: Teaching and Learning Perspectives

In Part I we have set the scene and sketched in some of the important background material that will help you appreciate the complexity and beauty of this artefact. We have also given examples of creative ways in which the labyrinth has been introduced and developed both in the UK and in America.

Part II brings us to what in many ways is the heart of this book. As Sally Brown reminds us in her series editor's Preface, creative and imaginative approaches to teaching and learning are the heartbeat of our academic endeavours. One of the joys of editing this book has been our engagement with such a wide range of thoughtful, imaginative colleagues who have grasped the opportunity which the labyrinth offers, and have run with it in various directions, all to benefit the learning experiences of their students.

We are acutely conscious that research and teaching are at best mutually interdependent. Although the labyrinth is relatively new as a learning and teaching tool (if we may call it thus) we are keen to emphasise that a research basis to our work with the labyrinth must feature strongly in this section. Admittedly, it is still early days: we are still able to call ourselves pioneers, working at the cutting edge of this aspect of teaching and learning. But research is crucial. John Rhodes therefore makes a seminal contribution to the book with his perceptive overview of the current state of labyrinth research, and suggests ways forward for future research projects.

Part II offers you as a reader a combination of in-depth discussions about how the labyrinth is being used across a fascinating range of academic and professional disciplines, and some punchy snapshots and case studies aimed to stimulate your own thinking and reflection about how you might adapt these approaches to your own disciplines. We encourage you therefore to explore subject areas that may at first glance seem a long way from your own, to see how they are making the labyrinth experience come alive in teaching and learning settings. There is something for everyone in each of these contributions.

8 Research and the labyrinth in Higher Education

John W. Rhodes

John W. Rhodes, PhD has more than 40 years' experience in public and private secondary and higher education. He has held a variety of positions, including the position of Vice President for Academic Affairs at Shenandoah University, Winchester, Virginia, USA. Dr Rhodes has been associated with research in the field of education for more than 30 years. Additionally, he has taught 'Tests and Measurement' courses at graduate level. He became involved with labyrinths in 1998, and has served as chair of the research committee as well as president of the Labyrinth Society.

▶ Introduction

The World-Wide Labyrinth Locator (WWLL) lists more than 4700 labyrinths in at least 75 countries (the Labyrinth Society and Veriditas, 2015).[1] While not exhaustive, it certainly is the most comprehensive labyrinth database available. At the time of writing, the World-Wide Labyrinth Locator lists 129 labyrinths on college and university campuses. Why? One has grown to expect labyrinths at churches and other faith-based institutions and retreat centres (the WWLL lists 1687) and at hospitals and other healthcare facilities (the WWLL lists 175), but why the growing number of labyrinths on the campuses of colleges and universities? One possible explanation is that the labyrinths are being used by the various faith-based groups on campus. Another possible explanation is that the labyrinths are being used by the various healthcare programmes and professions on campus. However, another very important use is emerging: the use of the labyrinth to support teaching and learning. According to Dr Jan Sellers, who introduced the labyrinth at the University of Kent, in Canterbury, UK:

> We think that this may be the first university in the world to build a labyrinth specifically to support teaching and learning across the disciplines.

We see it primarily as a teaching and learning resource, so people will come and walk the labyrinth individually, as opportunity for quiet reflection – a breathing space in their studies – and this, I think, is going to foster reflection, and that fosters creativity. (DVD interview, The Labyrinth Society, 2011)

Is there evidence to support the use of the labyrinth in this context, to support teaching and learning? More broadly, is there evidence to support the use of the labyrinth in any context, for any purpose? Is there, in fact, any identifiable labyrinth effect?

To be sure, the field of labyrinth research is a fledgling, emerging field of inquiry. Some may even question whether labyrinth research is a legitimate field of inquiry, given the often-ephemeral, very personal nature of individuals' reported labyrinth experiences. However, over the past ten years a picture is beginning to emerge regarding possible labyrinth effects.

Figure 8.1 Time for reflection. A 'light projection' labyrinth created by artist Jim Buchanan at the Labyrinth Society's Annual Gathering, Delray Beach, Florida, 2014.

Photograph courtesy Jan Sellers.

▶ A context for labyrinth research

The history of labyrinths continues to evolve as new discoveries are made. The age of the earliest examples, such as the petroglyphs of Spain, cannot be determined with any precision but they are considered by experts to date back to c. 2000 BCE. There is a substantial body of research, developed over many years, that addresses historical and archaeological questions about the designs, locations and uses of labyrinths. Classics in the field include work by Doob, Kern, Saward and Wright, to name but a few; the journal *Caerdroia* (edited by Jeff Saward) reports much current research. However, early in the twenty-first century, perhaps for the first time, people began asking different sets of questions about the labyrinth. These related to the reported effects of walking labyrinths or of interacting with labyrinths in a variety of ways. Questions also began to be raised about the psychological, physiological and emotional aspects of perceived and often-reported 'labyrinth effects', and whether or not these 'effects' could be isolated and measured. In her book, *Pondering the Labyrinth* (Geoffrion, 2003, p. 8), Jill Geoffrion raises the following question: *'How does the labyrinth "work" in creating the shifts that people describe?'* Lauren Artress (Artress, 2006a, p. 189) adds, *'A ... challenge to the Labyrinth Movement is the need for empirical research. Thus far we have relied on anecdotal information to illuminate the effects of well-being that occur in the labyrinth.'* Anecdotal reports regarding the effects people have experienced as a result of interacting with labyrinths in a variety of ways are numerous (for example: Artress, 1995, 2006a; Curry, 2000; Schaper and Camp, 2000). Efforts are underway to document empirically the effects that have been only reported anecdotally until now.

▶ Basic assumptions of labyrinth research

When a new field of research begins to emerge, it is important that a set of basic assumptions be presented to provide a base for and to guide the development of the new area of inquiry. The basic assumptions outlined here were developed and first presented in 2006 (Rhodes, 2006a, 2006b, 2007). They serve as a focus as well as a springboard for thought and discussion.

A first assumption relates to **authenticity**. Labyrinth research must be authentic to the labyrinth and to labyrinth experiences. For example, individuals who have been trained to facilitate labyrinth events are taught as guiding principles that each person's labyrinth experience is different, that the same person experiences the labyrinth differently at different times and that a person's expectations regarding a labyrinth experience might interfere with the labyrinth experience itself. In terms of labyrinth research, this tells us that, simply because of the nature of labyrinths and the experiences of those who walk them, labyrinth research studies often will provide results that are event specific. The results might not be predictive of other labyrinth events or experiences and they might not be broadly generalisable to other situations and/or populations. This is an artefact of the nature of labyrinth experiences, and not necessarily the result of research design flaws. For this reason, much useful and valuable labyrinth research might not meet the 'gold standards' regarding controllability, predictability and generalisability applied to much empirical research.

A second basic assumption relates to **intrusiveness**. Except in clearly defined and controlled research situations, labyrinth research should not interfere with (or at least be minimally intrusive of) people's labyrinth experiences. This is a vital consideration for action research that is conducted during 'real' labyrinth events. From quantum physics we learn that any time one observes or studies something, no matter how unobtrusive one attempts to be, the observer interferes to some degree with what is being observed or studied. The classic description of this effect from quantum physics is that light can behave as a particle or as a wave. When researchers attempt to study the wave actions of light, the particle characteristics are suspended. Likewise, when researchers attempt to study the particle actions of light, the wave characteristics are suspended. In labyrinth research it is important that researchers know and acknowledge that whenever an attempt is made to measure something related to the labyrinth, especially an effect, the attempt often interferes with the very effect that is being measured. Even when the research is as simple as asking a walker to complete a questionnaire following walking a labyrinth walk, the inquiry could have an impact on the effect of the person's walk. To some degree their attention is being directed to what it is being measured.

A third assumption relates to care in **interpreting** the results of labyrinth research studies. The interpretation issues of **predictability** and **generalisability** have been mentioned previously. Another interpretation issue relates to the direction of the effects observed and interpretations of their '**desirability**' as effects. If, for example, research studies indicate that individuals are more relaxed after walking a labyrinth than they were prior to walking a labyrinth, and if other research indicates that individuals' blood pressure, as a whole, is lower following labyrinth walks, caution needs to be exercised in identifying these effects as 'good' or 'desirable' effects, or that walkers who exhibited these effects had 'good' labyrinth experiences or 'better' labyrinth experiences than those who did not exhibit these changes.

These effects could be 'desirable' if the labyrinth were used as a tool for meditation or reflection. However, it is quite possible that, as a result of a labyrinth walk, an individual who was dealing with heavy personal or emotional issues could feel more agitated and have higher blood pressure upon completion of a labyrinth walk. For this individual, a state of increased agitation and higher blood pressure could well be indicative of a meaningful labyrinth experience.

Research studies that measure and quantify under controlled situations physiological, psychological and/or emotional changes resulting from various ways of interacting with labyrinths are highly desirable. Unfortunately, the current labyrinth research literature includes very few studies that meet this desirable level of rigour (although there are exceptions, including, for example, Zucker, 2012; Zucker, Villemaire, Rigali and Callahan, 2013). However, it is anticipated that potential topics and designs for research of this level of rigour will arise from the other categories of useful labyrinth research that have been and are being conducted.

Following her question, *'How does the labyrinth "work" in creating the shifts that people describe?'* Jill Geoffrion (2003, p. 8) continues, *'While we wait for scientists and others to investigate more fully, we must admit we don't know. Fortunately, mysteries do not have to wait for full comprehension before bestowing their gifts!'* Also relevant is a quote attributed to Albert Einstein: *'If we knew what it was we were doing, it would not be called research, would it?'*

▷ Commonly reported effects of labyrinth walking

The most frequently researched labyrinth effect is the effect of labyrinth walking on stress. Of the 107 citations in the current *Bibliography of Articles and Studies Related to Labyrinth Research* (Rhodes and Rudebock, 2015), fully 15 per cent address in some manner the relationship between labyrinth walking and stress reduction. Also reported are studies of the relationship between labyrinth walking and variables such as blood pressure, calmness and peacefulness. While these studies have evident relevance for university counselling and health teams, they will also be of interest in the wider field of student well-being. In referring to such qualities as mental calm and clarity, they may also be valuable for lecturers and educational developers interested in creative approaches to deepening reflection.

▷ Fairbloom (2003) reported that study participants found walking the labyrinth offered 'time out' in a hectic workplace environment and created opportunities to 're-energise', 're-focus', 'reduce stress', 'seek clarity', 'facilitate calm' and 'nurture the soul'. Participants thought the labyrinth would be helpful in teaching healthcare providers to care for themselves better at work and to improve their coping mechanisms in demanding and stressful workplace environments.

▷ Mariscotti and Texter (2004) related that study participants who walked an eleven-circuit labyrinth reported higher levels of disengagement, physical relaxation, mental quiet and peace, as well as lower levels of somatic stress, worry and negative emotions than a control group.

▷ In a study titled, 'The Labyrinth as a Stress Reduction Tool for Nurse Interns during the Journey of Their First Year in Practice' (2007), Weigel, Fanning, Parker and Round considered the impact of labyrinth walking for incoming nurse graduates at Mercy Hospital (Oklahoma City, Oklahoma). The experimental group, who were taught labyrinth walking in addition to their other training, showed a 14.2 scale point lower score on the 'Index of Clinical Stress' after 90 days compared to the control group, whose training did not include labyrinth walking. Additionally, the Index of Clinical Stress score for the control group increased while that of the experimental group decreased.

▷ Wood (2006) reported on Jeanne Miller-Clark's study, conducted with 75 patients at South Seminole Hospital in Longwood, Florida: *'She found that walking the curved paths increased patient's hope, decreased stress, and equalized their blood pressure. Patients with bipolar disorder showed the most improvement'* (p. 6).

▷ Wirth (2005) carried out a small-scale project to measure the effect of tracing a finger labyrinth on the stress levels of those who used it. A 46 cm (18 in) wooden finger labyrinth was placed in the meditation room of the hospital where the researcher was health education director. Instructions and a short survey were displayed near the labyrinth. Of 30 respondents, 28 (93 per cent) reported 'some' stress or 'lots' of stress prior to tracing a finger labyrinth. After tracing a finger labyrinth, 28 (93 per cent) reported that they were 'more relaxed' or 'very relaxed'. (Wirth describes this as a 'casual' research project but these are nevertheless interesting results.)

▷ Sandor and Froman (2006) found that systolic and diastolic blood pressures showed essentially no changes when pre-labyrinth walk and post-labyrinth walk measures, using four-group, repeated measures design, were compared. (The repeated measures design is one in which multiple, or repeated, measurements are made on a particular group of subjects, for example, weekly systolic blood pressures measured under different experimental conditions. An advantage of a repeated measures design is that it allows statistical inferences to be made with fewer subjects.)

In contrast, Wood (2006) reported that walking the labyrinth equalised patients' blood pressure (i.e. the blood pressures of the group of participants became more similar to each other, following a labyrinth walk).

▷ In a study by Mariscotti and Texter (2003), 11 respondents reported feeling 'calm' following the labyrinth walk, compared to only three participants reporting feeling 'calm' prior to the labyrinth walk. In the same study, 27 respondents reported feeling 'peaceful' following the labyrinth walk compared to no participants reporting feeling 'peaceful' prior to the labyrinth walk.

▷ In a 2004 study by Rice, walking the labyrinth was used as a treatment method to induce relaxation. Several independent sample t-tests demonstrated that gender, ethnicity and employment did not significantly impact relaxation, contentedness, health and friendliness.

A small number of studies refer specifically to creativity and creative processes. This clearly has direct relevance to Higher Education and would be fascinating territory for further research.

▷ Danielson (2004) reported that walking the labyrinth creates a calming, meditative state that opens one up to one's intuitive, creative nature and allows for a shift in consciousness.

▷ DeVito and Dunlap (2012) conducted a replication study to determine if mindful labyrinth walking has relaxing effects on the labyrinth walker. Their replication suggests that labyrinth walking may produce a higher sense of consciousness that might heighten a sense of creativity. (A replication study involves repeating a research study, using the same research design and methods, but using different subjects and by different researchers, to determine if similar results can be obtained.)

▷ In *Into the Labyrinth: Excursions and Applications for Creative Process*, Francisco (2006) surveyed, analysed and organised implicit references to creativity in labyrinth literature to assess the validity and context within which the labyrinth could be used as a creativity tool to facilitate creative change. In her work she discovered explicit links to the creativity concepts, processes/tools, models and outcomes required to facilitate creative, transformational change. She suggests that research is needed concerning the placement of the labyrinth within the repertoire of tools useful in the Creative Problem Solving Thinking Skills Model, particularly the ability of the labyrinth to generate 'in-the-moment' benefits of incubation.

▶ The labyrinth as a walking meditation

Perhaps the most commonly used descriptor of the labyrinth experience is that of a 'walking meditation'. For example, Artress (2006b, p. 38) states, *'I teach the use of the labyrinth as a walking meditation since there is a pressing need to quiet our minds and to find an effective way to meditate. In this area the labyrinth is truly a gift.'* She states further:

> People on the labyrinth seem to gravitate toward what I have come to call a process meditation. This meditation moves between silence and image, so the focus does not remain solely on quieting the mind as in a contemplative practice. This meditation also uses what is very close to a guided imagery process. (Artress, 2006a, p. 77)

Does walking a labyrinth produce results similar to those of other forms of meditation?

The Labyrinth Walk Questionnaire (Rhodes, 2006a) is a non-intrusive instrument that allows respondents to report the effects of their labyrinth-walking experience on ten variables: relaxation; anxiety; clarity; peacefulness; centredness; stress; openness; quiet; agitation; and reflectiveness. Participants are invited to complete the short questionnaire after concluding a labyrinth walk by responding to the stem statement, 'Comparing how I felt before I walked the labyrinth with how I feel now, I feel …' Participants respond to the stem statement by circling a number on a Likert Scale related to each of the ten variables. Other questionnaire items allow respondents to list and rate additional variables that are relevant to their labyrinth experiences, list and rate environmental factors affecting their walk, and provide pertinent demographic information. This questionnaire adequately addresses the basic assumptions of labyrinth research previously described that relate to authenticity and non-intrusiveness.

According to the most recent summary of Labyrinth Walk Questionnaire results (Rhodes, 2011), for a majority of walkers, labyrinth walking increased levels of relaxation; clarity; peace; centredness; openness; quiet and reflectiveness; and reduced levels of anxiety, stress and agitation. 'Majority' here is between 64 and 82 per cent of walkers who completed the questionnaire, as discussed below. These action research results – data collected following many, real-life labyrinth walks, rather than controlled situations – are consistent with the expected outcomes of various forms of meditation, while adding the additional aspect of movement. For example, describing a particular type of meditation, Newberg and Waldman (2009, p. 35) state:

> Numerous studies have shown that the mere repetition of a sound, phrase, or finger movement over a period of time significantly reduces symptoms of stress, anxiety, depression, and anger, while improving the practitioner's perception of quality of life and spiritual well-being. *In fact, the addition of movement to any meditation should significantly enhance the cognitive performance of the brain.* (italics added for emphasis)

Results obtained using the Labyrinth Walk Questionnaire are summarised in the following two tables. They represent data collected from September 2005, through March 2011. The study compiles Labyrinth Walk Questionnaire results from 524 respondents and includes data collected from 34 labyrinth events and 44 labyrinths on three continents (Rhodes, 2011).

Table 8.1 Labyrinth Walk Questionnaire results. Before and after walk: 'I feel more ...'

'Comparing how I felt before I walked the labyrinth with how I feel now, after walking the labyrinth, I feel:'

'Much More/More' (Number/Per cent)		
n = 524	Number	Per cent
Relaxed	428	81.68%
Clear	346	66.03%
Peaceful	420	80.15%
Centred	398	75.95%
Open	347	66.22%
Quiet	354	67.56%
Reflective	408	77.86%

Table 8.2 Labyrinth Walk Questionnaire results. Before and after walk: 'I feel less ...'

'Comparing how I felt before I walked the labyrinth with how I feel now, after walking the labyrinth, I feel:'

'Much Less/Less' (Number/Per cent)		
n = 524	Number	Per cent
Anxious	350	66.79%
Stressed	367	70.04%
Agitated	333	63.55%

A factor analysis of data from an earlier compilation based on 160 respondents to the Labyrinth Walk Questionnaire identified two different components (factors) that contribute to the differences in the scores (Rhodes, 2006b). The primary factor appears to relate to a physical dimension while the second factor appears to relate more to a 'state of mind' dimension. One possible interpretation of these results, based on the two factors identified and the order of the factors, is that walking a labyrinth can enable a set of physical responses (relaxed, unstressed and so forth) that allows for the emergence of a set of 'state of mind' responses (reflective, centred, clear and so on) that contribute to the so-called and frequently-reported 'labyrinth effect'.

▷ The emerging use of the labyrinth in Higher Education settings

In the 1980s and 1990s, the focus of labyrinth usage was in churches and other religious and spiritual contexts. Therefore, the focus of labyrinth research at that time was on the labyrinth as a spiritual tool, primarily a tool to enhance prayer, meditation, transformation and other spiritual practices. Approximately 25 per cent of the citations in the current *Bibliography of Articles and Studies Related to Labyrinth Research* (Rhodes and Rudebock, 2015) relate to the use of the labyrinth in religious, spiritual and/or meditative settings. In the late 1990s and the early part of the twenty-first century, focus shifted somewhat towards using the labyrinth in hospitals and other healthcare environments. At this point the focus of labyrinth research shifted to studying the physical, psychological and emotional effects of the labyrinth. Both of these foci (religious/spiritual and healthcare) continue to dominate the still-emerging field of labyrinth research. Currently a new focus appears to be the use of the labyrinth in educational settings. This occurred first in elementary and secondary schools and now in higher education. Therefore, labyrinth research is only just beginning to reflect this trend. A new focus of research is how the labyrinth can be used effectively in educational institutions to enhance teaching and learning as well as other aspects of the educational environment, e.g. in conflict resolution.

However, whether being used as a tool to deepen prayer and contemplation, reduce stress and anxiety related to illness, release feelings of grief, provide a container for quiet reflection during a hectic school day, or as a tool to enhance teaching and learning, *the common denominator appears to be the documented meditative effect of the labyrinth.*

The current *Bibliography of Articles and Studies Related to Labyrinth Research* (Rhodes and Rudebock, 2015) lists only seven citations that relate directly to the use of the labyrinth in educational settings. Mariscotti and Texter (2014) report their findings from a study of school-age children, where the researchers explored similarities and difference in reported responses and levels of relaxation. Otto-Diniz (2008) reports a qualitative case study where she uses the idea of the labyrinth in analysing the aesthetic experiences of a group of elementary school age children who participated in an art museum discovery club (the children themselves were not involved in labyrinth walking).

The remaining five citations report the use of the labyrinth in various manners in institutions of higher education.

▷ Bigard (2009) reports on the use of the labyrinth as one systemic approach that counselling centres may use to conduct outreach that targets the college community. Her article describes the labyrinth's introduction on one university campus. Additionally, she outlines practical considerations when incorporating the labyrinth in college counselling centre outreach efforts. (In the present volume, Bigard takes this work further in an initiative related to student retention.)

▷ The intent of a study presented by Norton (2008) is to serve as a catalyst for additional research related to the use of labyrinths as design elements by landscape architects. Her qualitative study interviewed twelve individuals at five sites in the Dallas/Fort Worth, Texas, metropolitan area. The sites comprised two hospitals, two churches and one college campus. The findings indicate that those who commission labyrinth projects have a very specific knowledge of the subject and are seeking to enhance their organisation by providing an interfaith space for walking meditation, contemplation and relaxation.

▷ In their study, 'Promoting Reflection through the Labyrinth Walk', White and Stafford (2008) report the results of a reflection study assigned to 25 registered nurse (RN) students returning to college to pursue the Bachelor of Science in Nursing degree (BSN). The authors report anecdotal comments of the students and conclude that, *'The labyrinth walk and/or other forms of reflective practice experiences should be an essential part of nursing education'* (White and Stafford, 2008, p. 100).

▷ Bright and Pokorny (2012) provide an overview of some benefits of contemplative practices and write about using the labyrinth as one alternative for introducing the benefits of contemplative practices into higher education experiences. They report on a workshop they conducted that centred on using the labyrinth as one tool for providing contemplative time. After learning basic information about labyrinths and assisting in construction of a temporary labyrinth, workshop participants, all of whom who were working or had previously worked in higher education, were invited to walk the newly-constructed labyrinth. Following the session, the participants generated a variety of ideas for the use of the labyrinth in higher education settings. The writers conclude that the *'labyrinth is but one approach to bringing mindful practices to students and staff in higher education'* (p. 25). Further, they conclude that, *'It would be instructive to engage in research to discover how the implementation of such practices affect staff and students – whether in terms of wellbeing or in terms of enhanced learning'* (p. 25).

▷ Sellers (2009) reports on her use of a labyrinth as a means to foster reflection and creativity. The article describes her journey of discovery and identifies possibilities for using labyrinths as creative resources in university teaching and learning. (See also Sellers, 2013 and James and Brookfield, 2014.)

This dearth of research should not be surprising or unexpected, as the use of the labyrinth in college and university settings is only beginning to be explored. Examples of new research are included in this book; see, for example, Nina Johnson, Jayne Dalley-Hewer and Joanne Opie's accounts of their contrasting projects. Other chapters describe current and emerging practices of using the labyrinth in the context of higher education: each of these chapters and approaches provides a potential context for research and inquiry. What shapes and forms might this inquiry take?

Initially, it is vital to *gather, compile, analyse* and *report* existing and emerging anecdotal information regarding the various ways of using and interacting with labyrinths in a higher education context, as identified in the immediately preceding paragraph. A large amount of anecdotal evidence attesting to the various purported effects of interacting with labyrinths in other arenas has been reported in books, magazines, by word of mouth and through other sources. Other potential sources of anecdotal information include journals kept at university-sponsored labyrinth events, as well as detailed journals kept by students, faculty and/or university staff. Additionally, anecdotal reports regarding the efficacy of using the labyrinth in various teaching and learning contexts will be informative. What is needed is a compilation and analysis of these anecdotal reports. This compilation and analysis likely will point the way for other researchers as they look for fruitful areas of inquiry. Detailed journals kept by individuals also could provide rich sources of information for qualitative and case study research.

Another step would be to *verify* and *quantify* the effects reported as occurring as a result of the various ways of incorporating the labyrinth into higher education settings. Studies conducted in this category often will be action research type studies. Many studies of this type will take place during active use of the labyrinth in teaching and learning and other applications, rather than under controlled circumstances, so the basic assumption related to intrusiveness is very applicable here. It is also possible for controlled studies with some degree of randomised assignment of participants to be conducted within action research. Many of the studies will be perceptual in nature. Such 'soft data' can be very compelling; however, to make a strong case, researchers need to quantify as much as possible, within the conditions of the Basic Assumptions cited earlier in this chapter. A growing number of action research studies, conducted under a variety of conditions, with different populations and involving different applications of the labyrinth in the university setting, will provide valuable data to verify and quantify the effects/shifts that are initially reported anecdotally.

It would be fruitful to *relate* and *correlate* the effects reported as the labyrinth is used in higher education settings with existing validated instruments that purport to measure the reported effects. These types of studies likely would be studies conducted under structured conditions, using experimental and control groups and experimental or quasi-experimental research designs. For example, if an anecdotally reported effect of using the labyrinth in an instructional setting is increased relaxation and decreased anxiety, the levels of reported participant relaxation and anxiety before and after using the labyrinth could be correlated with scores on instruments that have already been developed and validated to measure relaxation and anxiety responses.

Another useful method of inquiry would be to *conduct, analyse* and *report* short term as well as longitudinal case studies regarding the effects reported as occurring as a result of various ways suggested for using the labyrinth in higher education settings. In addition to the 'backwards analysis' of existing journals kept by labyrinth walkers suggested previously, this would enable longitudinal, case study research to be conducted using a 'front loaded' design. In these studies, participants (students, faculty, staff and others) would agree in advance to keep journals of their labyrinth experiences in congruence with the study design. Also, the participants would agree to the terms and conditions of the longitudinal study, as well as to being interviewed by the researchers at predetermined intervals.

Although the 'gold standard' of the double-blind research design likely will not be met in labyrinth research, it is important to *measure* and *quantify* under controlled situations effects resulting from the various ways of using the labyrinth in educational settings. These studies likely will be studies that meet the strict requirements of rigorous empirical scientific research. Many of these studies will feature experimental/control group designs, as well as randomised assignment of study participants and identification and control of intervening variables. The basic assumption related to intrusiveness is less applicable here than to the other types of research suggested above. It is expected that potential topics for this level of research will be identified from among the action research studies, case studies, anecdotal reports and other studies conducted using the other types of research methodology.

It is hoped that individuals with research expertise, interested in incorporating the labyrinth into higher education settings, will see the great potential in the ideas and developments outlined above. Equally, it is hoped that those who might not be trained as researchers will see within the broad suggestions provided above an area of research inquiry that interests them, prompting them to seek the specific research assistance from knowledgeable researchers that they might need to make research contributions. It needs to be remembered that multiple measures of effects are 'better' and more robust than single measures. Also, it must be remembered that several people replicating the same study, in different locations, under similar or different conditions, with similar or different samples of participants, is stronger than one person doing one study in a single location. If effects prove to be similar across a variety of studies, this helps address the generalisability issue mentioned earlier in this chapter.

At first, the various labyrinth practices suggested in this book, as well as others, must necessarily inform the research. Then, as the research base becomes more extensive, reliable and robust, the roles reverse and research will begin to inform the practices for using the labyrinth effectively as another powerful tool to enhance teaching, learning and creativity at the various levels of higher education.

Note

1 The number of entries in the World-Wide Labyrinth Locator is constantly subject to change as the Locator is updated. In consultation with the editors and with Jeff Saward, who maintains the WWLL, a date of 1 July 2015 was chosen as a 'cut-off date' for the purposes of this book.

9 Introducing reflection to health care students: Curriculum development and the labyrinth

Jayne Dalley-Hewer and Joanne Opie

Jayne Dalley-Hewer and Joanne Opie are Senior Lecturers in Physiotherapy in the Faculty of Health and Life Sciences at Coventry University, UK.

Jayne has a special interest in reflective practice. For some years this interest has focused on the teaching and facilitation of reflection in undergraduate students. She has developed this further by studying how physiotherapists use reflection in real world practice and the implications that this has for fostering reflection in students.

Joanne is the module leader for a cross-faculty module teaching the foundations of communication and professionalism to all the first year health profession students. Within this module, students are introduced to the concept of formalised reflection and are encouraged to become more self-aware as practitioners. Her research interest is in professional identity with specific regard to the integration of people with disabilities into the profession of physiotherapy.

▶ Introduction

A desire to promote meaningful reflection in first-year students on health profession programmes led to staff exploring a variety of teaching strategies and class experiences. At the same time, the university teaching strategy was moving from more didactic approaches to alternative forms of pedagogy, such as the flipped classroom (Bristol, 2014) and inquiry-based learning (Cleverly, 2003). These factors facilitated experimentation into new approaches in the teaching of reflection, including the introduction of labyrinth walking.

▶ Background and context

Reflection in education has been written about since the 1930s (Dewey, 1933) and the theoretical consideration of reflection gathered pace as it became applied to the health professions – first in nursing, and then in the allied health and social care professions. The importance of being reflective practitioners has been emphasised for the last 20 years and the practice of reflection is now a required skill in each of these fields (Health and Care Professions Council, 2014; Nursing and Midwifery Council, 2015). There are many definitions of reflection, for example:

A generic term for those intellectual and effective activities in which individuals engage to explore their experiences in order to lead to a new understanding and appreciation. (Boud, Keogh and Walker, 1985, p. 19)

Thinking or attentive consideration in order to make sense of thoughts and memories, and to make appropriate changes if required. (Taylor, 2010, p. 6)

The range of definitions share common elements, suggesting some consensus. The two most consistent elements are 'thinking' and 'change' (Taylor, 2010). This change can take various forms. Moon (2004, p. 84) includes the following as outcomes of reflection: learning, knowledge and understanding; the building of theory from practice observations; the making of decisions and the resolution of uncertainty. There is also some consensus on the attributes required for reflection. Hargreaves and Page (2013) describe a reflective practitioner as engaged, open to learning and self-aware so that each professional encounter can enable learning and performance improvements. Burton (2000) reports that the skills of critical analysis and self-awareness are considered crucial to the ability to reflect. Bassot (2013) suggests that critical evaluation and self-awareness are required in order to examine our knowledge, skills or attitudes. It was this critical awareness of their own thinking that the module staff wished to promote in the students.

It had been observed by academic staff that the focus of past teaching had been on writing reflection and the use of reflective models, rather than developing deeper and more effective reflective processes and strategies. During a research study into the practice of reflection by physiotherapists (Dalley-Hewer, 2012) it was noted that practitioners equated reflection with writing rather than a thinking process. This is the case even though both written and dialogical modes of reflection are recommended in teaching. For example, Fook and Gardener (2007) use discussion for group reflection; Driscoll (2000) facilitates reflection in clinical supervision conversations. Recent work has explored additional tools for developing reflection including the use of storyboards in the classroom (Lillyman, Gutteridge and Berridge, 2011), and the pictorial River Kawa model to promote reflection on life events (Iwama, 2006; Opie et al., 2014). Nevertheless, advice on facilitating reflection often focuses on written reflection, typically in the form of diaries, assessments or portfolios (as in, for example, Bassot, 2013).

A newly developed cross-faculty module sought to facilitate communication skills and professional attributes as a basis for professional practice. The module was the first part of a collaborative curriculum running through all years of professional education, with the educational approach of inquiry-based learning. Students of Nursing (adult, child, mental health and learning disability nursing), Midwifery, Occupational Therapy, Dietetics, Physiotherapy, Paramedics and Operating Department practitioners began this module in week one of their training. The module included a strand on reflection, which commenced by introducing the students to labyrinth walking as a tool for increasing self-awareness and reflection. The strand continued with reflection using visual modes, through viewing pictures or drawing Kawa models, and culminated with an introduction to documenting reflection using formal models which are used by health professionals to meet professional requirements. However, documentation of reflection was not introduced until week seven of the module. The decision to introduce labyrinth walking in the first two weeks of the programme was in order to promote self-awareness and reflection right from the beginning of their programmes.

▶ **The practicalities: Challenges and resolutions**

The main challenges were the construction and location of the labyrinth, introducing it to staff and students, and managing the student numbers through this experience.

Location

To house the labyrinth a room was needed with sufficient size and which was available for sustained periods of time across a calendar week. The project was undertaken in partnership with the Spirituality and Faith Centre. In addition to providing a suitable room, Centre staff were able to informally monitor students' use of the labyrinth and talk with students about their experiences should they wish. Some Centre staff were experienced in using labyrinths from their work elsewhere and some had walked labyrinths previously; their enthusiasm and support were very valuable in setting up the project. The Centre also offered a choice of quiet spaces or specific faith rooms which the students could use following their walk should they wish.

Materials

Finding the space for the labyrinth was linked with how the labyrinth would be created – what materials it should be made from and how temporary it would be. The decision was made to begin with a portable labyrinth as a pilot. Outdoor labyrinths were excluded due to the unpredictability of the weather, given the need for activities to take place in a specific academic week. Fortuitously, a one-off source of funding became available and a canvas labyrinth was chosen to fit the size of the room, a 4.5 metre (15 ft) canvas painted with a five-circuit labyrinth. A canvas labyrinth enables the labyrinth to be taken up when the room is used for other purposes; it is quick to lay out and remove and allows for the labyrinth to be used in other situations and places. Having chosen a fabric labyrinth, hygiene and general maintenance were managed by requesting everyone to bring a clean pair of socks to wear while on the canvas. In case of forgetfulness, a supply of spare socks was also provided in the room, together with a laundry bag.

Student numbers

There were approximately 600 students on the module, divided into 23 timetabled seminar groups with up to seven seminars running simultaneously. The organisation of such a large cross-faculty module meant that up to 23 different staff drawn from various professions would be facilitating the seminars. Multi-professional classes drew students with different individual timetables into each class. Because the labyrinth walk was to be offered as module content there was a need to give each student the same opportunity to experience the labyrinth. Students were therefore introduced to the concept of labyrinths in class and offered the opportunity to walk the labyrinth outside of class time. This enabled the logistics of high numbers of students and available walk time to be reconciled. It also permitted students who did not wish to take part in a walk to 'vote with their feet' by not taking up the opportunity. An electronic scheduling tool embedded into the university virtual learning environment was used for students to book their walk time.

Introducing the labyrinth to staff

It was expected that most staff would have little or no previous experience of labyrinth walking. This was such a new concept that staff receptivity was uncertain and there was concern that staff unfamiliar with this approach would be limited in their ability to encourage students to attempt it. Various sessions introducing labyrinths and their use for reflection were given to the staff team, for example as part of an away day preparing for the new curriculum. During the away day, the topic of labyrinth walking was approached through the subject of reflection, beginning with the idea that real-life reflection is not usually conducted in 'I am reflecting now' time, but whilst undertaking other daily activities such as walking. The link between walking, creativity and problem solving (and thus, implicitly to reflection) has already been made (Baird et al., 2012; Manning, 2012). Following this, an illustrated talk introduced labyrinths and their use, leading to the concept of a walking activity to promote introspection. Staff were invited to experience a labyrinth walk for themselves on a separate day, prior to the module. Teaching materials (a PowerPoint presentation and lesson notes) were provided for each class tutor. Staff were mostly open-minded and curious, whilst concerned about communicating to students something with which they were unfamiliar. Invitations were also extended to staff who were not on the module who might be interested in the labyrinth as an educational tool or student support adjunct. This included staff with special interests in education and student support staff from the university health centre. Staff who chose to experience the labyrinth for themselves reported responses such as calming the mind, seeing things in perspective and feeling less anxious about work issues.

Introducing the labyrinth to students

Students were introduced to the idea of a labyrinth walk in class, where it was linked to their development of self-awareness. Further instructions and information were available online, and in the labyrinth room. These included practical instructions and suggested approaches to labyrinth walking, such as the release, receive, return approach (Artress, 1995) or 'just walk'. It was suggested that students might consider their personal journey towards being a health or social care practitioner while walking the labyrinth. This aligned the experience with the module focus of developing personal awareness and insight. It was recognised that equitable access to the experience was required for all students whatever their physical ability, so table-top brass finger labyrinths in two designs were available in the room as an alternative to walking the canvas. These are popular amongst experienced labyrinth users although there is little exploration of the way in which these might differ from the experience of walking.

▶ Evaluation

Approximately 125 students experienced a labyrinth walk. Feedback was acquired formally through an online audit, and informally through anecdotal accounts from the students, including the content of assessed reflections which addressed their development over the module.

The successes

Many of the students who walked the labyrinth had a positive experience which demonstrated development of reflective ability. Some students made plans to incorporate some form of 'space' in their routine lives, for example, by going for a walk; several expressed the desire to walk the labyrinth at a later point. From the questionnaire results, of the 58 students who had walked the labyrinth and completed a questionnaire, 40 students found the experience calming, 21 reported experiencing insights or inspiration and 33 reported that it helped them to reflect or to be more aware of themselves:

> It made me realise how calm it was possible for me to feel; it also inspired me to make a real effort to find a quiet five minutes at home to help me reflect on the day.

> I had a good reflective opportunity and afterwards felt I was able to easily express/articulate my feelings and thoughts with others.

Some accounts were profound and moving (as in Mustafa Jaafir's reflections following this chapter). Several students tried the finger labyrinths as well as walking the canvas. This idea of experimenting with different methods for reflection was consistent with the module philosophy.

Concerns from the teaching team that using the Spirituality and Faith Centre might deter some students from trying this experience appeared in practice to be unfounded and the support provided by the Centre staff was instrumental in the success. Staff in the Centre perceived the development of deepening reflection and self to be consonant with the Centre's aims and goals and welcomed the introduction of many students so early in their programmes to the Centre facility and services.

The obstacles

Not all students considered the labyrinth walk to be helpful. One student said *'I was shocked to see that it looked like a rug'* and another that *'walking round shapes made me feel as though I had wasted my time'*. However, some of the obstacles concerned problems with logistics or expectations. The campus, timetables and IT systems were all new to most students, and they struggled initially to book their walk in the allocated week. Subsequently, the labyrinth was made available over two weeks in recognition of this. There was also a mismatch between students' expectations and their experience, the most significant factor being that they expected to be the only person in the room while the booking schedule anticipated an over-lap. Having booked 'their slot' some students objected to the presence of others, feeling that it interfered with their concentration and made them aware of others rather than of themselves. It is possible that the absence of a labyrinth facilitator in the room heightened their awareness of the strange-ness of this novel activity and thus hindered their introspective awareness. Some students felt that a larger labyrinth would have helped them 'get into it' more.

Impact on teaching and learning

This was a positive experience for many of the students and several chose to share their experience with staff, either in their cross-faculty seminar group or with staff from their own profession. This enabled discussion about the uses and availability of labyrinths, about the use of walking for reflection and about each student finding their own methods for introspection that suited them best. These discussions enabled the tutor to give recognition and value to the importance of developing self in the professional context. It was sometimes an opportunity to hear the students' personal accounts of their individual reasons for entering their profession, and the place of that decision in their lives.

Some students were able to take the idea of creating reflective space and find a sustainable means of doing so in their routine life – through walk-ing or swimming, for example. The labyrinth, therefore, created a platform to continue to develop reflective thinking through the later years of their professional programme. At this stage, it is not possible to judge the long-term impact of this attention to introspection on future health and social care professionals.

▶ Conclusion

The introduction of labyrinth walking was considered a useful component of several strategies in the module for facilitating reflection. This experimentation with labyrinth walking has suggested that creating space for students to consider their own personal development can be a valuable addition to their professional education. Good planning and the preparation of staff and students aid the success of the venture. Future plans include making the labyrinth available at different points in the academic year, and considering whether student evaluation of the experience might change after walking the labyrinth several times or at different points in their programmes.

10 Reflection: On walking the labyrinth, a first-year student's response

Mustafa Jaafir

Mustafa Jaafir is a student in Operating Department Practice at the University of Coventry. This reflective account was written as part of Mustafa's participation in the Orientation events discussed in Jayne Dalley-Hewer and Joanne Opie's chapter.

Today I walked the labyrinth and I have decided to reflect on what I experienced. I have never walked a labyrinth before, so as a first timer I was really eager to know what it is like and how I would go about it for the very first time. I did some research beforehand to have an understanding of what a labyrinth consisted of.

As I went into the room, I was alone and it was silent. I could only hear a few people in the background from surrounding rooms, which I used to my advantage as I wanted to use this surrounding sound to be able to block off. I read the instructions after sitting down and putting on a new pair of socks.

I saw that there were stones of pale and dark colours, which varied in size, on the table. I sat down and thought how I was going to walk the labyrinth. I felt the need to pick five stones which represented five different aspects on my life that are most important to me. A feeling of awe and respect permeated me as I walked the labyrinth. I entered with respect and left feeling like I have overcome so much fear, hatred, negative emotion. The labyrinth walk caused me to reflect on my journey of this past year. The walk represented what I have overcome recently. The finality of the walk represented a new beginning for me and represents hope and peace. The labyrinth is a reflection of your devotion and love for life. Each turn offers a new perspective. Walking with a consistent slow pace makes every step have a meaning. As I got to the middle I used placement of my stones as indications to me, telling me the order of importance of these five different aspects of my life. I determined this from the order I placed the stones in the circle.

Walking out of the labyrinth I felt cleansed and spiritually awakened as I took my last step off the mat back to reality.

I would definitely recommend this to everyone.

11 Twists and turns in staff and educational development

Bernard Moss and Jan Sellers

▶ Introduction

It is a sad indictment of contemporary Higher Education that we can talk about rhetoric and reality when it comes to the important issue of staff development. HEIs speak proudly of their staff as being their prized asset. There are international schemes dedicated to celebrating excellence in teaching and learning such as the UK Higher Education Academy (HEA) National Teaching Fellowship Scheme and its Canadian counterpart, the 3M National Teaching Fellows. The UK Staff and Educational Development Association (SEDA) has its own fellowship scheme as does the HEA, and internationally equivalent schemes also seek to foster a deep sense of professional pride, a striving for excellence, a greater commitment to staff development and the importance of clear-sighted effective management with the well-being of education as a core value.

And yet, at the sharp end of everyday practice, academic colleagues are under increasing pressure. Workloads increase; the uncertainty of student recruitment in some HEIs raises the spectre of redundancy and job losses. Part-time contracts undermine commitment to consistent best practice and high levels of student satisfaction as the 'last in first out' culture bites deep. The professional delight of scholarship, research and publication is enjoyed mainly by a favoured – even privileged – minority. Add to the mix the varied personal styles of Vice Chancellors or Presidents, their relationship to their (sometimes dysfunctional) senior management teams, and how genuine leadership is exercised in times of uncertainty alongside the necessary business management skills, and the picture can look bleak.

This is not to deny that we live in challenging times, where the impact of economic downturn will continue to have a massive impact upon the sector. Wooldridge (2013, in Outram, 2013, pp. 7–9) captures this well in his farewell message as the first Chief Executive of the Leadership Foundation for Higher Education:

The critical skill is about managing uncertainty, coping with emergent change, as opposed to planned strategy development. There is a need for more agile approaches to scenario planning ... Above all, the challenge is to be able to create a more entrepreneurial and enterprising culture in the institution without losing the concept and values of the university.

No pressure then! And yet without clear leadership and a sense of vision and purpose the risk of various HEIs descending into a rudderless anonymity and eventual disappearance is higher than ever before. To be wholly reactive is to run the risk of being driven by the next brewing storm.

As one senior colleague remarked:

It's like being in a maze – you can't see the wood for the trees – you can't see where you are going and the risks of running into an expensive, financially draining cul-de-sac give you sleepless nights. It's a treadmill, it really is! (personal communication)

That is what a maze feels like. And it poses the question in staff development terms about how to get off that treadmill and to begin to see things more clearly.

What a labyrinth offers of course is no easy fix – nor even a difficult fix! In fact it does not provide answers at all. But it is not a confusing maze: the labyrinth offers us that indefinable moment of quiet reflection that enables us to de-clutter – to stand back – to seek a fresh perspective. These are essential ingredients for effective leadership, both at an individual and at team level. The following discussion draws on staff-centred examples; these approaches are equally applicable to leadership development involving students (and see also Alex Irving's chapter relating to business leadership).

▶ Considering appreciative inquiry

Academic leaders at all levels are supposed to be good at clear thinking; seeing the deeper issues; championing – and modelling – the values that underpin higher education. At their best they are also the encouragers of best practice and positive career development, with an awareness that real education is not about 'quick fixes' or knee jerk reactions to the latest crisis. Rather, it is about laying long-term foundations for both students and staff to develop their knowledge-making skills that will stand them in good stead throughout their lives.

Within the current challenging, even turbulent, context, staff development assumes much greater importance, not just to help colleagues develop survival skills, but for cherishing, developing and maintaining the core values of the organisation, and indeed of the sector. In her discussion of Appreciative Inquiry (AI), Taylor (2013, pp. 23–26) suggests that, unlike traditional problem-solving approaches, which promulgate a 'deficit model' by focussing on what to fix through action plans and interventions, *'Appreciative Inquiry assumes that an organisation is a source of limitless capacity and imagination, creating an appreciative culture'* (p. 23). Taylor draws attention to the four inter-related themes of AI – Discover, Dream, Design and Destiny, and suggests that for educational development – and this means senior managers as well as staff delivering modules – this can be a powerful and effective model or cycle.

The starting point – or the moment of discovery – is not a crestfallen lament about all that is going wrong and threatening to overwhelm us. On the contrary the focus needs to be both investigative and affirming: *What gives life to this organisation or team? What are we best at? When are we at our most alive and vibrant?*

Taylor then explores the Dream phase in the cycle: *'How can we imagine and creatively envisage ways in which our excellence can be expanded? What would we look like and be like if this Dream came true?'*

The next stages involve practical collaborative work around Design, shaping or re-shaping to facilitate the achievement of the Dream, and looking forward (Destiny) to how this will be sustained.

Even this all too brief description of AI opens up immense possibilities for creative imaginative approaches in staff development that have the potential for quickening the spirit and raising morale as colleagues realise that this is *what we are really good at!* and also, *we have the capacity and resourcefulness to make it work.*

The challenge is to find the space and the creative moment to enable the potential of an AI approach to take hold. This is where labyrinth walks come into their own. There is something powerful in the indefinable creative chemistry generated by the disciplined, reflective engagement with this unicursal pathway that makes few demands but opens up limitless possibilities. In this regard AI and labyrinth walks are comfortable and respectful fellow travellers. If a senior management team, for example, were to take the core 'Discover' questions with them on a reflective labyrinth walk, it could open up the possibilities of new ways of thinking, working, imagining and developing their management style and the ethos of their organisation. If a group of staff, or a mixed group of staff and students, were to adopt a similar approach to issues of mutual educational concern, it could open up

the possibilities of new ways of thinking, working, imagining and developing their curriculum and module design. In other words a labyrinth walk
can provide a creative context in which the AI approach could really begin
to flourish.

▷ Exploration: An Appreciative Inquiry seminar

An example of this was at a staff seminar convened in an HEI in the Midlands,
UK, to explore dissatisfaction with various modules being delivered. Staff
themselves felt that they were not giving of their best; student feedback
confirmed it. The labyrinth facilitator encouraged the participants not to
focus on the 'doom and gloom' but rather to identify (in the Discover phase)
what they were really good at; what experiences they had had when working with these students, when energy, motivation and enjoyment ran high;
when did their teaching and learning come to life? These questions were
taken by the participants on their labyrinth walk, and to their surprise when
they came to jot down their thoughts and reactions after the walk they all
had some powerful stories to tell. It was fascinating to find that they all
reported one thing in common: there was something about the structured
reflective walk on the labyrinth that had released creative energy in ways
they had not expected.

One major theme – objective even – for contemporary staff development, therefore, is the recognition, releasing and nurturing of the creative energies and potential in colleagues at all levels in an organisation. AI
provides a valuable approach: labyrinth walks offer a creative moment and
space in which such creativity can emerge and thrive.

▷ Wider perspectives

Within or outside an AI context, the inclusion of a labyrinth walk in staff
and educational development can bring unexpected gifts. To call these outcomes 'gifts' is to use the language of participants: something received,
something given, something that can be taken away to use in future.

The following discussion draws on the experience of leading labyrinth
workshops (including the opportunity for a labyrinth walk) in a number of
HE contexts in the UK since 2008 (Sellers, 2013). Inevitably, the purpose of
these events has been two-fold. Because the labyrinth (for educational purposes) is a new concept for many, one self-evident purpose of these workshops has been to introduce the idea of the labyrinth: what exactly is it?
How does it differ from a maze? This aspect of the workshop introduces the

Figure 11.1 The mown grass labyrinth at Woodbrooke Quaker Study Centre, Birmingham, UK (home of the Centre for Postgraduate Quaker Studies), is often walked by conference, retreat and course participants.

Photograph courtesy Woodbrooke Quaker Study Centre.

labyrinth, across centuries, countries and cultures, as a truly international concept and artefact. Coming to the present, we consider the contemporary resurgence of interest, with specific examples of educational use of the labyrinth (and wider uses where professionally appropriate to the group; for example, health-related use for Health Studies). We then move to the main theme of the workshop, specifically tailored to the group and context.

Engaging with the labyrinth is a highly participative activity. We explore here, briefly, some practical strategies to support student and staff involvement. Note that there are a wide range of accessible resources available and that participants will be their own best judge of what assistance, if any, is needed.

Quietness and silence

A labyrinth walk can offer a time of deep quietness. This can be profoundly refreshing but may be unsettling for some. For groups unaccustomed to silence, peaceful music may help.

No 'wrong way' to do this

There is no wrong way to walk a labyrinth. The only ground rule is respect for other walkers. It can be very liberating, especially for students, to take part in something where it is not possible to get it wrong; on the other hand, people do not always believe this.

Shorter walks

Because there is no wrong way to walk the labyrinth, it is perfectly accept-able to just undertake half of the journey, say to the centre, quietly leaving afterwards. It is helpful for the whole group to know this and it may benefit people with invisible disabilities and health problems such as arthritis or high fatigue levels.

Freedom of choice

No one has to walk a labyrinth: the experience will not be valued unless it is freely chosen. It is useful to provide supplementary materials (relevant literature; finger labyrinths; drawing materials) and people may build con-fidence through watching.

Ground rules

The primary ground rule is respect for, and between, participants: those who are fully engaged should not be disturbed by those (few or none in our experience) who choose not to take part. This includes respect for the quietness, without use of mobile phones. Most groups readily accept this and it is rarely a problem in practice.

Finger labyrinths

These small, table-top or plinth-mounted labyrinths (where the pattern is traced by hand) can be beautiful artefacts and have universal appeal. They are helpful in introducing labyrinth patterns to a group, make a valuable alternative to walking for people with mobility problems and are also wel-comed by people who are blind or partially sighted (see Kimberly Saward's chapter for resources).

▶ Drawing on experience

The authors have worked with their own portable canvas labyrinths and other temporary installations, as well as permanent labyrinths such as the Canterbury Labyrinth, but for the purposes of this chapter our focus is on temporary indoor installations using a canvas labyrinth where practical. There is always the question of finding sufficient space, but with goodwill and a network of labyrinth facilitators to draw on, it has proved to be the case that almost without exception a room has been found and a labyrinth found to fit it. On one memorable occasion, the room measured by Estates staff as amply sufficient had mysteriously 'shrunk' in size by the time the facilitator arrived, as it was certainly too small for the purpose! Sheets of plastic were hastily gathered so that the labyrinth could be laid on the outside lawn. It is also possible to 'draw' a labyrinth on the floor with masking tape, as at the National Association of Writers in Education, 2009, or to create one outdoors as at the HEA Conference, 2010 (see the case study by Jan Sellers, and chapters by Jeff Saward, Jill Raggett and Steve Terry for more ideas). Time to set up is important in creating a calm atmosphere; for example, furniture removed or screened is an improvement on towering stacks of chairs in full sight. There is no doubt, however, that a labyrinth can transform the most mundane of teaching spaces, as we have personally experienced in venues ranging from state-of-the-art conference centres to an underground, 1960s concrete gymnasium. These canvas labyrinths are hand-painted works of art, designed to be walked on: they are beautiful (and valuable) artefacts. To hold a labyrinth walk is to offer people the opportunity to engage in a very immediate way with something beautiful, and this itself is a gift: people do feel valued and recognised when someone within their HEI has organised something beautiful for them to take part in.

The following illustrative quotations are drawn from participant feedback at several HE events.

▷ Workshop, Marian University School of Nursing, Summer School, Harlaxton College, Lincolnshire, 2014:
- *[The labyrinth event] came at a time when our students and faculty could use quiet reflection, a slowing down and time of relaxation. Simply perfect.*
- *[This] labyrinth present has given us a universal (global) tool to use with our patients and self for relaxing reflection.*

▷ Project evaluation workshop, University of Staffordshire, 2014:
- *A wonderful vehicle for reflection, past, present and (possible) future pathways. Relaxing and yet dynamic.*

▷ SEDA Day School, University of Westminster, 2013:
- *Labyrinth is a metaphor but walking it becomes an active experience – connecting with the inner self – emotional and profound.*
- *A lovely metaphor for my journey – an educational, or life journey – being present; it really is about the journey, not the destination, and it is about*

how you decide to tread your path, who meet along the way, and how you choose to interact with them.

▷ Cave of the Heart Conference, 2012, St. Mary's University, Twickenham:
  • *Amazingly peaceful and powerful. Problems surfaced and began to untangle. Inspirational.*

▷ Specifically tailored labyrinth workshops

The examples below are as applicable to student contexts as to staff. In addition to academic development, the first two of the following workshops have been successfully held in student learning development contexts; the third draws extensively on research and practice in learning development. Suggested applications are included below.

1: Deepening reflection

This workshop may include a specific theme (for example, exploring personal and professional values – SEDA 2008) with time for discussion, followed by a labyrinth walk, in turn followed by time for shared reflection. The labyrinth walk may then be influenced by a set of issues or questions developed within the earlier discussion. The suggestion then for walkers is not to think through these questions actively, but to choose a question or theme, and to hold an awareness of it (as if one is carrying the question in one's heart, or in one's hands) as one walks. The response from walkers, frequently, is that fresh insights are gained. The labyrinth serves as a meditative path, with no need for prior experience of meditation; in stilling and quietening the mind, fresh insights may arise. This applies equally for colleagues who may have experience of meditation: such colleagues tend to remark on the sense of recognition of this quiet inner space. (For examples of similar workshops with students, see chapters by Katja Marquart and Michelle Bigard).

2: Preparing for the next steps

This workshop focuses on moving to a different stage, moving on in some way, perhaps a career change or a major step on one's life journey. Here, one possibility is to use the image of a suitcase. What are the strengths we already have that will support us in this transition? What are the challenges we face, for which we will need to find support and guidance? What may we need to leave behind? The use of positive language is deliberate and affirming: by the end of the workshop, participants have a clear sense of what will support them (including their own strengths and values) in moving ahead. This workshop is of value at turning points in the academic year, at conferences where personal and professional development is explored and also for students at times of major transition such as graduation or the beginning of postgraduate studies.

3: Releasing our inner writers

This half-hour workshop was held at the Labyrinth Society's Annual Gathering in Florida, 2014; it is included here as it was solidly rooted in the experience of teaching, learning and guidance in HE in the UK. The structure was a talk, paired work and a question and answer session; no labyrinth walk was included (Labyrinth Society Gatherings are already wonderfully full of labyrinths and walking opportunities). Participants were introduced to several academic concepts and practical approaches that (though not ostensibly related to writing) have proved valuable to the author in supporting university students' academic development. These include threshold concepts (Land, Meyer and Smith, 2008); impostor syndrome (Gravois, 2007); gendered differences in help-seeking behaviour (McCarthy and Holliday, 2004) and finally, stress management, through the use of a one-minute relaxation exercise. The labyrinth, in this workshop, represented liminal space: the unknown, the hazardous, the space full of uncertainty which we must enter as writers to fulfil our potential. Though brief, this workshop alleviated the sense of isolation frequently experienced by writers, offering fresh insights to counter problems that are common to writers and also the academic community. This workshop, first presented in 2014, could be readily expanded and adapted to explore and support issues of academic writing and indeed, student confidence, across a wide range of disciplines at undergraduate or postgraduate levels. (For more on academic writing, see Knowles and Grant's (2014) detailed discussion of writing retreats for doctoral students and for academic staff, seen through the lens of the labyrinth metaphor).

▶ Conclusion

These examples illustrate practical yet creative ways in which the labyrinth is currently being used for staff and educational development, and is making a profoundly positive impact upon very real contemporary challenges for higher education. Inevitably an element of risk is involved: putting one's faith in what might emerge from a labyrinth walk can feel counter-intuitive to many managers, leaders and practitioners in Higher Education. But as our examples show, it is a risk well worth taking.

Figure 11.2 A labyrinth walk during a teaching and learning symposium at the University of Westminster, UK.

Photograph courtesy of the labyrinth project team: Jennifer Bright, Jenni Nowlan (copyright holder), Helen Pokorny, Sobia Razzaq and Beryl Young.

We report with delight, therefore, that a growing number of universities are acquiring their own labyrinths and initiating their own labyrinth projects. For example, recent additions in the UK include the University of Bedfordshire's permanent outdoor labyrinth (2014); the mown lawn labyrinths at the University of Worcester (2014) and Canterbury Christ Church University (2015) and the University of Westminster's portable fabric labyrinth (2015), illustrated in Figure 11.2. To offer a labyrinth walk or labyrinth workshop is to offer a precious breathing space. Such events bring the gifts of quiet time; slowness, and permission to slow down; a sense of stillness and of peace in a rushing world; beauty, and harmonious time for reflection so that major decisions can be tackled creatively, and the values and ideals of higher education can be cherished and deepened. These are rich gifts to share.

12 Case study: A conference installation – volunteers, goodwill and chicken-feed

Jan Sellers

The Higher Education Academy Conference 2010 celebrated 10 years of the National Teaching Fellowship Scheme. As a National Teaching Fellow, I offered a labyrinth installation for the Conference: this was to be a peaceful space for reflection for all, and an opportunity for a group to experience making a labyrinth from scratch, at minimal cost.

We needed volunteers, a lawn, temporary storage and permission from Conference organisers and host university – all readily secured after initial discussion and a 'scoping' visit. On the day, we had eight volunteers. We used rope; measuring tape; tent-pegs; plastic scoops (made from soft drinks bottles) and three sacks of chicken-feed (chopped corn), which created golden lines on the grass. We moved in circles, guided by rope, pouring the lines of the pattern as we went. The seven-circuit, classical labyrinth measured approximately 9.1m x 11m (30 ft x 36 ft).

This imaginative approach was initially created by Jeff Saward (and is demonstrated online: Saward, 2009). It proved to be a highly enjoyable team activity. It was rewarding to see the lines falling – literally – into place as the shape of the labyrinth emerged. Following installation, the labyrinth offered a distinctive outdoor space for quietness, with basic guidelines available nearby for walkers. The labyrinth also attracted children from a conference for young mathematicians. We have used this technique at the University of Kent for a Schools Liaison team-building day and a combined event for (adult) primary school volunteers and drama students (Figure 12.1).

The biggest challenge was the (unusual) stipulation that the chicken-feed on the grass should be swept up afterwards: this is not something to try more than once. (See Jeff Saward's chapter for alternative materials.) Often it is a pleasure to see wildlife cleaning up, but I have had one proposal rejected due to a rodent problem. This method should not be used in spring, when there is a risk of young birds choking.

Figure 12.1 Students, staff and volunteers create a chicken-feed labyrinth.
Photograph courtesy Jeff Saward, Labyrinthos.

In video feedback, one delegate commented:

This Conference, I've enjoyed seeing the labyrinth here … It's good to see people being a little bit hesitant and then taking the plunge and walking it. I used it myself this morning, before my presentation, and it just gave me that few minutes out – to just be reflective and calm my mind. (Higher Education Academy, 2010, cited with permission of delegate)

13 Case study: A creative 'Away Day' for mid-term project evaluation

Emma Dawson Varughese

A Global Cultural Studies scholar, Dr Emma Dawson Varughese is the author of four books including the forthcoming *Genre Fiction of New India: Post–millennial receptions of "weird" narratives* (2016, Routledge). As a creative practitioner and academic, Emma also runs 'Karvan' (see worldlits.com), working with a travelling caravan to create participatory arts and world literature events.

I commissioned this Away Day as a rare opportunity for our team of community arts developers. We were completing the first year of a three-year Arts Council-funded project in a city in the Midlands, UK. This city has a proud craft history but exceptionally low levels of contemporary engagement with the arts. The 'Away Day' saw five of us come together to experience the labyrinth, as a means to reflection and through metaphors of 'journey' and 'finding your way'. Much 'journeying' had taken place over the first 12 months of the programme. The 'Away Day' was designed to explore this experience in some detail. In the midst of copious written evaluations, the event was a breathing space, time for our own creative and arts-based responses to the story so far. As project researcher, based at a local university, I joined the team for the day with their permission.

We used one venue, but two spaces: a gymnasium (for the canvas labyrinth) and a graceful room with spacious views over the city centre, where the team had been working with various communities over the year. It was valuable to move from one space to another, finding stillness and quiet with the labyrinth whilst associating planning and documenting with the high-level space.

The morning was a time of individual reflection. Through the labyrinth walk, we explored our own journeys, our paths into our new roles. The afternoon focussed on team and project. Quiet time downstairs was balanced by creativity upstairs: we created a spectacular table-top model of the project journey, sketched freely on window panes, laughed a lot, shared experiences and, not least, recognised the challenges we had faced and overcome. At the end of the day, we gathered our craftwork and photographs, planning to continue work on this as an arts-based evaluation of the project's first year.

Several of us felt inspired to take the labyrinth into our communities: ideas included a labyrinth in a park and a community estate labyrinth. Walking the labyrinth allowed both space and time for reflection, and we recognised that this had been in short supply over the year. Our wishes for the future included more creative time together, and more opportunities for this depth of honest, shared reflection.

14 Towards medical practice – a mindful journey

Helen Malcolm

Revd Dr Helen Malcolm is the Deputy Director of Medical Student Education at the Shepparton campus of the Rural Clinical School, University of Melbourne, Australia. She is also a practising General Practitioner and an Anglican priest. She was instrumental in having a labyrinth installed at the RCS in Shepparton and uses it both educationally and as a stress management, mindfulness, self-development tool with students, patients, staff at the RCS, health professionals and community groups.

When you practise walking meditation in the morning, your movements will become smooth and your mind will become alert. You will be more aware of what you are doing all day long. In making decisions, you will find that you are more calm and clear, with more insight and compassion. With each peaceful step you take, all beings, near and far, will benefit.

Thich Nhat Hanh (Anh–Huong and Nhat Hanh, 2006, p. 54)

▶ Introduction

The above quotation provides the perfect description of a good doctor – someone who is calm but alert, who does not appear rushed and is mindfully present with their patients all day; a doctor who is clear in their decision-making and shows insight and compassion so that others benefit.

How do we prepare medical students to become doctors like this? Thich Nhat Hanh provides part of the answer – to practise walking meditation daily. The labyrinth, as one form of walking meditation, provides this space, but offers much more in the education of our future doctors and other health professionals. To take Thich Nhat Hanh seriously, we would have a labyrinth in every medical school, hospital and health centre.

The labyrinth is also a metaphor for the hero's journey as summarised by Campbell (1968, p. 30): *'A hero ventures forth ... fabulous forces are there encountered and a decisive victory is won: the hero comes back ... with the power to bestow boons on his fellow man'.* McDougall and Davis (2011), in their paper on reflective practice for educators, use the idea of the hero's journey as a reflective tool. They quote Dirkx, who sees transformative learning as *'a heroic struggle to wrest consciousness and knowledge from the forces of unconsciousness and ignorance'* (Dirkx, [1997], in McDougall and Davis, 2011, p. 436).

The word 'education' derives from the Latin term to draw out, which, in turn, suggests time and space for reflection and thoughtful consideration. The labyrinth provides the opportunity for this reflection, this drawing out, this mediating of transformative learning. This contrasts with the common medical student desire for educators to 'put in' – to impart facts, lists and conclusions that they are to learn. While this may enable students to pass exams, it is not the transformative learning that is needed in higher education, enabling graduate students to be ready for their role in the world, whether that be as engineers, nurses or accountants. This is particularly true of medical education, where patient-centredness, listening skills and ethical judgments are equally important in diagnosis and management as anatomy, pharmacology and procedural skills.

▶ The challenge

The world of higher education demands a lot of students, educators and supporting staff. Clinicians teaching prospective doctors carry a responsibility to ensure they prepare safe, competent interns who will help, rather than harm, patients. They must do this while maintaining their own clinical practice and often with minimal or no training in teaching. Similarly, students have large amounts of knowledge and skills to acquire and apply. Thus for educators, learners and the staff who support them, medical school can be a stressful place. Maintaining their own emotional well-being is vital for everyone involved in this endeavour.

The potential challenge that this presents was starkly illustrated in a 2013 study in Australia by *beyondblue* (2013), the national depression and anxiety initiative. The research showed that:

▶ One in five medical students and one in ten doctors had suicidal thoughts in the past year, compared with one in 45 people in the wider community.
▶ More than four in ten students and a quarter of doctors are highly likely to have a minor psychiatric disorder, like mild depression or anxiety.

In the first year of medical school, students' mental well-being, from being similar to that of the general population, deteriorates, with a significant increase in the prevalence of stress, depression and burnout (Hillis et al., 2010). Simultaneously, empathy decreases, especially during the clinical years (Chen et al., 2012). Sadly, *'graduates who were more emotionally sensitive were more likely to become burnt out and exhausted during the difficult transition from university to workplace'* (Sweet, 2003, p. 355).

From these sobering figures it becomes evident that measures are needed to decrease the stress caused by medical studies as far as is possible and to arrest the parallel decline in empathy. Some of the causative factors cannot be obviated – the personality of people who want to become doctors; the responsibility for other people's lives and health; and that medical students are at the bottom of the hierarchy in a busy, stressful environment. Because their teachers are often involved in their assessment, it is difficult for students to voice their uncertainties. The issue of 'cognitive dissonance', where what students are taught does not match what they see happening in hospitals and consulting rooms, is a further source of stress (Meyer and Xu, 2005), causing students to question which is correct – theory or practice. Financial concerns, the need to pass exams and the pressure to get an intern place on graduation add to the stress of being a medical student. Underlying all of this is that students may confront their own mortality for the very first time, as they learn from patients who suffer from, or do not respond to, medical treatment and as they watch doctors convey heart-breaking news to patients and their families.

The Rural Clinical Schools (RCS) of Australian Universities, set up by the Commonwealth Government to encourage students to return to work rurally as doctors, take medical students for at least one year of their training. Students may opt to study at the RCS or may simply be allocated there. Students who undertake a long placement at a rural University campus, especially those who did not choose to be placed there, may be exposed to additional stressors. They are dislocated from the support of family and friends and live together with other medical students with whom they might not get along. Additionally, there is the perception that it will be harder to get the intern position of their choice.

Staff placed in rural areas may also face added stress. Factors include the 'fishbowl' effect of a small community – constantly being visible to patients and students; and the lack of the required range and number of clinicians to deliver the curriculum, requiring staff to teach outside their area of expertise. The *beyondblue* study (2013) confirmed that doctors working in more remote areas have higher levels of psychological distress and disorders.

▷ The requirements

The Australian Medical Council (AMC), which accredits Australian medical schools, has a set of requirements that students must demonstrate at graduation (AMC, 2012). These inform the Graduate Attributes of the University of Melbourne's Doctor of Medicine (MD) degree (Melbourne Medical School, 2013), which include the following goals:

▷ *An understanding of the principles of reflective practice, the ability to apply them, and a recognition of their importance in health care;*
▷ *An understanding of the principles of empathy, compassion, honesty, integrity, altruism, resilience and lifelong curiosity, the ability to demonstrate them and a recognition of their importance in health care;*
▷ *The ability to maintain their own physical, emotional, social and spiritual health.*

In the USA, the Accreditation Council for Graduate Medical Education (2013, pp. 9–10) similarly requires residents to demonstrate qualities including *'compassion, integrity and respect for others … sensitivity and responsiveness to a diverse patient population'*. This makes clear that medical professionalism *'depends heavily on the quality of a physician's inner life'* (Palmer, 1998, p. 197), reflecting the need for this to be nurtured during medical training.

Another skill which medical students need to acquire is that of teamwork. Working effectively with doctors, nurses and other health professionals is vital for complete patient care, but also for learning. A further Graduate Attribute of the University of Melbourne MD is *'an understanding of the principles of teamwork and the ability to work effectively in a team, including as a leader'* (Melbourne Medical School, 2013).

Parker Palmer (1998, p. 211) uses several terms to describe team learning where students not only learn more but also act more compassionately. He refers to such teams as communities of truth, of discernment, of congruence, or *'circle[s] of trust, my name for the kinds of relationships that facilitate deep and difficult learning'*. The labyrinth lends itself to supporting such learning amongst students. It can be used as a team-building tool and assist in problem-solving by providing a reflective space for the creative, intuitive mind to assert itself.

▷ Solutions

Mindfulness and reflective practices

The University of Melbourne has introduced several new measures into its postgraduate MD course, while continuing the Empathic and Ethical

Practice (EP) sessions from the previous undergraduate course. EP sessions allow issues that are unavoidable in the medical training context to be openly addressed. Students discuss, in confidential groups facilitated by an experienced practitioner, their own reaction to illness, constraints on treatment choices, side-effects of medical treatment, ageing, death and other issues, often coloured by their own family experiences as well as what they see on the wards.

EP also provides the *'reflective ... small group discussions'* advocated by Meyer and Xu (2005, p. 79) to ameliorate nursing students' stress from cognitive dissonance, another unavoidable facet of medical training.

The labyrinth can provide a useful metaphor for confronting 'demons' in these areas that may derail learning or medical practice. The Greek myth of the Minotaur is valuable here: we confront, and overcome, our deepest fears. Being mindful of these 'demons' and reflecting on them in a safe, supported environment allows them to be put in perspective and a way negotiated through the stressful path of medical training and on to insightful and compassionate medical practice, to reiterate Thich Nhat Hanh.

Initially introduced into the students' first clinical year, EP sessions are being expanded into subsequent years.

The MD includes a session in the third year Mental Health curriculum, 'Health practitioners' wellbeing: a mindful approach', which discusses the need for and usefulness of self-reflection and mindfulness practices and allows students to experience one or more such practices, including walking the labyrinth. In the fourth and final year of the MD, a module on Emotional Skills and Self-care is undertaken by all students. This includes reflection on stressors, risk factors and protective factors for mental health problems and consolidates advice on having a mindfulness discipline, as well as taking students through a mindfulness practice. These sessions are taught by educators who already have a mindfulness practice of their own.

In Victoria, Australia, Monash Medical School in Melbourne incorporates a stress management course into its medical degree. The students learn stress management techniques and practise mindfulness meditation. Hassed and Chambers (2014), in 'Mindful Learning', outline the process of introducing mindfulness teaching. Hassed et al. (2008) report the outcomes, showing an overall improvement in student wellbeing during the pre-exam period, when well-being is traditionally at its lowest.

Similar measures have been introduced into the City University of New York (CUNY) School of Law to help students *'find inner peace as they navigate the intensive, demanding rigors of law school and social justice careers'*, paralleling those confronting medical students and doctors (CUNY, 2010, p. 8). The Law School delivers a one-semester class, 'Contemplative Practice for Social Justice Lawyers', where students can learn a number of different approaches to mindfulness and stress reduction (including walking the labyrinth). One student (echoing Thich Nhat Hanh) said, *'It's practising compassion for yourself that makes it possible to be even more compassionate toward others'* (p. 8).

The labyrinth in learning environments: the university campus

At the Shepparton campus of the Department of Rural Health (DeptRH), University of Melbourne, medical students and other health professionals are educated in a rural setting. In 2011, an 11 metre (36 ft) diameter outdoor tiled labyrinth of the 11-circuit Chartres-style design was laid out – the first such labyrinth at an Australian University campus. Students and staff, along with other local health professionals, were introduced to the labyrinth through a presentation at 'grand rounds' and additional workshops have been held specifically for students and staff.

Students use the labyrinth prior to exams, to clear their minds when faced with a challenging personal or academic problem, or simply for exercise. Both professional and academic staff walk it when pressure of work seems overwhelming, or when a particular problem needs a calm mind for a solution to surface. Workshops introducing the labyrinth for stress management, as a tool to use with patients and carers or as a team-building exercise have been held for specific groups involved in both clinical work and teaching future health professionals.

Medical students are focussed on obtaining all that is necessary to not only pass, but also to excel at, their exams; anything that they perceive does not directly contribute to that goal can be seen as a waste of their time. It is a challenge for educators to assist them to understand the need to learn the 'art' of medicine and self-care. Parker Palmer (1998, p. 205), in *The Courage to Teach*, proposes that, in educating new professionals, *'we must teach – and model for – our students what it means to be on the journey toward an "undivided life"'*. To achieve this, Palmer suggests, we must *'validate the importance of our students' emotions as well as their intellect'* (p. 205). This also means attending to and supporting the teachers' inner lives. By placing the labyrinth adjacent to student accommodation and staff offices, the DeptRH makes it easily accessible for everyone concerned with the complete education of our future doctors.

By modelling mindfulness, educators in medical schools will hopefully influence their students to see the benefit of this skill and seek to acquire it. Rechtschaffen (2014, p. 43) emphasises this as he encourages teachers to lead by example: *'Information is imperative in education, but transformation is where maturity, morality and wisdom come from. When you are on a path of personal growth, you are modelling to your students the true meaning of mindfulness.'*

The labyrinth in learning environments: hospitals

While hospitals, hospices and palliative care centres are increasingly installing labyrinths for patient care, they are also using them in the education of their staff. A study with incoming graduate nurses at Mercy Hospital in Oklahoma City showed a decrease in the Index of Clinical Stress scale for those who walked the labyrinth (at least twice a month) compared to those who did not (Weigel et al., 2007). The Dean of the Christine E. Lynn College of Nursing (Florida Atlantic University) commented that the campus labyrinth provides students with the opportunity to learn to centre themselves and reflect on practice (Wood, 2006).

In Australia, The Children's Hospital at Westmead, Sydney, installed a labyrinth in 2012 for the use of patients, families and staff (Children's Hospital, 2013). Robert Ferré, writing in an American context, believes that we are reaching a stage where no progressive architect will design a health-care facility without including a meditation labyrinth, and patients, staff members and doctors will insist that their existing facility install a labyrinth (Ferré, 2012).

▶ Conclusion

In a world of increasing technology we risk forgetting that our students (and patients) are people with their own stories. To subscribe to a narrow view of educational excellence is to risk neglecting the importance of reflective practice for both educators and students; the opportunity to engage with our own story and discover those of others, the stories that make us human. The labyrinth, as a place for reflection, allows us to acknowledge our own hero's journey and to use what we have learned (perhaps through confrontations with our own minotaur) in service to our students and to encourage them to do the same in the service of their patients.

Victor Sierpina, Professor in Family Medicine at the University of Texas Medical Branch (cited in Kermeen and Kermeen, 2012, p. 42) reminds us of the wider responsibility we all hold and the role of the labyrinth in fulfilling that responsibility:

> If you intend to be doctors of tomorrow, you will need to know how to heal yourselves. It is no longer simply about curing cancer or stitching wounds, it is about healing souls. To do this well, you must be on your own path of personal healing. The labyrinth is a powerful tool for centering, focus and personal transformation for healers and their patients.

15 Case study: Loss and grief in social work practice

Bernard Moss

All human life is here. This sums up a social worker's case load as they grapple with the challenges and complexities that occur 'from lust to dust' in many people's lives. The experience of loss occurs in many such situations, and social workers need to feel prepared to deal with the emotional and spiritual turmoil that can so often 'knock people for six'.

To be prepared for such encounters requires more than head knowledge and a working grasp of relevant theoretical perspectives. Perhaps more than any other aspect of social work, dealing with loss is 'heart and gut' territory, where one's personal experience can significantly impact upon professional performance.

At Staffordshire University, UK, social work students were introduced to the labyrinth as part of their professional studies around grief and loss. They were encouraged to reflect upon their own experiences of loss, its impact upon their lives and their chosen worldview, whether secular or religious. The twists and turns of the walk suddenly brought to life for them some of the conflicting emotions they had experienced, and the importance of finding ways to deal with their own 'baggage' so that it did not get in the way when dealing with other people experiencing similar feelings.

Using pebbles or large stones to symbolise their own experience of loss, the students were encouraged to use the central point of reflection in the labyrinth as an opportunity to let go, and to gain confidence in their social work role. In this area of work particularly, the social worker is not the expert, but rather is a fellow traveller (Holloway and Moss, 2010, p. 111) with people in pain, an insight highlighted by meeting each other on the labyrinth walk.

Significantly, several students reported afterwards that the labyrinth walk had been a powerful and emotional learning point that no lectures or seminars could have achieved. It emphasised their basic shared humanity and reminded them of what a privilege it is to be in the social work profession.

16 Case study: Writing and walking the labyrinth

Sonia Overall

Sonia Overall writes fiction and poetry. She has a strong interest in form, intertextuality and performance-based approaches to text. Her current practice explores constraints, randomness and game-playing in writing, including a 'labyrinth' novel. Her chapbook *The Art of Walking* (Shearsman, 2015) reflects her interest in psychogeography.

Sonia has written and abridged work for street theatre and has published two novels, *A Likeness* and *The Realm of Shells* (HarperPerennial). She teaches at Canterbury Christ Church University and the University of Kent. www.soniaoverall.net

Much undergraduate creative writing teaching involves seminar-based, desk-bound writing and discussion. I try to incorporate interactive exercises and outdoor activities wherever possible, and frequently use the campus labyrinth for notebook work and inspiration. Labyrinth sessions are particularly effective when the students near the end of an intensive period of study or in the run-up to deadlines. They are a welcome break after a difficult or challenging subject. They also provide powerful opportunities for creative writing.

Using an outdoor labyrinth entails embracing the elements. Below are two instances of working with different student groups in sun and rain, and some suggested writing exercises.

▶ Walk in the rain

This session was with second year creative writing undergraduates during a fiction workshop, just before Reading Week.[1]

9.30am: Rain check. The slopes of Eliot footpath muddy but passable. The labyrinth lightly littered with sticks. Walking and kicking them aside attracts the attention of a muddy-footed terrier, two excitable children and two women in wellies and macs. One is, I realise, a local poet. We talk about the labyrinth as a place to escape, think, write. The children jump, hop, skip to the centre. The sky is clear. The dog dances with twigs.

10.00am: The rain starts.

11.00am: Seminar on postmodernity and the novel. We negotiate a path through the texts of Lyotard, Jameson and Baudrillard. We talk about smashing through the Spectacle, consider conspiracy theories, the reflective surfaces of *White Noise* and the fragmented maze of meaning in Pynchon's prose.

12 noon: Workshop. Students present their ideas for writing manifestos. What should writing do? There are rants, metaphors and playful typography. The drizzle continues. I propose the labyrinth. Several students whinny nervously.

1.30pm: The labyrinth. (Light) rain. I offer encouragement: this is a place for emptying the head, focusing ideas. It's not a race, I say. Think Sebald, I tell them. Think Borges. The students jump, hop, skip and slide to the centre. Some mime a minotaur. They clutch damp notebooks. One of them actually writes things down.

2.00pm: Rain stops. The students squelch away, some smiling, some grumbling.

▷ Using the labyrinth for creative writing: three ways in

The nugget. Before you walk, focus on one nugget to write about. Maybe you want to brainstorm a setting or character, or you are into

Figure 16.1 The walk in the rain.
Photograph courtesy Sonia Overall.

a text and a question needs answering. Walk to the centre, thinking about your nugget. When you arrive at the centre, stop, get out your notebook, write your ideas down. Walk back out the way you came: your notes will echo in your head. Sit down when you return to the beginning: keep writing. It's miraculous, but it works.

The hiatus. Take a piece of text – a short passage of prose or poetry – and read the text to yourself as you walk. Whenever the path changes direction, stop and mark that point in the text. When you have finished the walk, use those marks to rework your text. Turn them into line breaks, or end points for cut-ups. Make them peaks and troughs. Let the labyrinth reshape predictable sentence constructions.

The stream. Freewrite as you walk. Avoid all punctuation. Stop when you get to the centre. Walk back again, reading the text to yourself. Use twists and coils in the path as moments to pause, punctuate and edit.

▶ A summer school workshop

This workshop was an introductory session at a creative writing summer school. The participants were adult learners from community settings.

The labyrinth lends itself to generating ideas and giving writers the space to focus, as well as involving them in an unusual shared experience. This is very useful when working with a group who do not know each other well. At the beginning of this session, we used the labyrinth for a warm-up group 'relay' walk, with participants reading aloud extracts of text, using the space between them to direct the speed of their reading – a valuable icebreaker. I then offered participants a selection of self-led writing exercises to choose from. Initial exercises used the labyrinth to generate creative text, drawing on the immediate environment, found text, freewriting and seed words. The shape of the labyrinth was incorporated to direct line lengths, patterning or repetition.

Further exercises used points in the labyrinth as prompts for editing, punctuating or cutting up the generated text. Some participants used the walk to focus on a specific creative idea for development.

By the end of the workshop all participants had created fragments or completed passages of prose or poetry. The participants then chose to continue writing and editing or to use their text in a group exercise.

Individuals used the labyrinth as directed by their chosen writing exercises. Some participants walked first, and then wrote in the centre or outside; others wrote while walking.

Participants commented: *'It made me realise what my mind is capable of.'* *'It really helped me get in touch with my emotions.'* *'Great for generating new ideas.'* *'A good writing tool.'* *'It was interactive.'* *'A different environment which was conducive to writing.'*

Creating poetry

This is an exercise that uses the shape of the labyrinth to direct the creation of a poem. It is suitable for individual use and for group writing workshops. Participants generate a poem during the walk itself, making notes as they go. The nature of the exercise is free enough to generate a variety of responses, although it lends itself particularly well to creating 'shape' poems and mirror sequences.

If using this for a group workshop, facilitators may wish to provide a theme or seed words to get ideas flowing. Encouraging participants to draw words randomly from a hat is effective.

Pattern and repetition

Before starting the labyrinth walk, write out a list of four to six words or short phrases that you wish to work with. These can be suggested by a theme or associated with an image.

As you walk, construct a poem incorporating your chosen words.

▷ Use the shape of the labyrinth to suggest where to include the words in your piece – at a turn in the walk, perhaps, at compass points, when you change direction or near the centre.
▷ Each time you reach this 'trigger' on the walk, use one of your words.

Stop to rework your piece at the centre, or continue working back out again, creating a mirror sequence.

The following short poem was generated using this exercise, walking part way into the labyrinth and back out again. I wrote the poem as an example while facilitating a labyrinth workshop for creative writing students at the University of Kent, 31 May 2012.

Chosen words / phrases to work with: lifted; around me; small journeys; raised; levelled

Hulk

I didn't move from this spot
lifted by the swell of water, waiting
as everything around me worked its way upwards,
flotsam in small journeys climbing my sides, raised to my waist, levelled.

I didn't move as the tilting circles slapped, levelled, the raised whorls
draining surely, their small journeys ebbing,
sucked away to leave a pitted bed
around me, my lifted ribs.

Note

1 An earlier version of 'Walk in the Rain' was published as a Centre for Creative Writing blog, University of Kent, 25 February 2014.

17 Case study: The power of the labyrinth – an 'AcrossRCA' inter-disciplinary project

Qona Rankin

Qona Rankin is Dyslexia Coordinator at the Royal College of Art. Initially trained and subsequently employed as a designer, she continues to design and make jewellery. In 1997 she re-trained in Dyslexia Support. Her research, in collaboration with an inter-university group formed by her in 2004, explores dyslexic/dyspraxic student perceptions and challenges in 'drawing well' and has been published widely. This inspired Qona to set up the Creative Mentors Foundation, which she now runs (www.creativementors.org).

Every year in the autumn term the Royal College of Art holds 'AcrossRCA'. This week of projects brings students from diverse programmes of study together, to work and develop their skills by trying something different. AcrossRCA also offers staff the opportunity of working within a different context; this can contribute to staff/student relationships in very positive ways and can often lead to exceptional and unexpected cross-disciplinary projects.

This year, two colleagues and myself had been discussing a way of combining our fields of expertise. Our aim, quite simply, was to offer students the opportunity to consider personal journeys of understanding and idiosyncratic ways of being creative, away from their own programmes. As chaplain (Andrew Wilson), counsellor (Jane Andain) and dyslexia coordinator (myself), the three of us have quite different and specific responsibilities. However, we do have a shared interest in how students meet spiritual, psychological and educational challenges. It seemed to us that the labyrinth would be an ideal springboard for our project; and that our various areas of expertise would enable us to encourage students to think about how the brain makes creative links, what happens when it stops doing so, and the effect that balancing the left and right hemispheres of the brain has on learning and spiritual and emotional health. We anticipated that the outcomes might have a practical application but not necessarily be object-centred; they may equally be system or process focused.

We called our project 'The Power of the Labyrinth'; it involved 11 students from nine separate disciplines. The project began on a Monday with a briefing and time to learn about, and explore, labyrinths including two labyrinth walks (using our own fabric labyrinth and that of a guest speaker). Once students had decided whether to work alone or in groups for the duration of the project, they began to develop their ideas, initially with each other and with staff. They then chose a single focus to take through to prototype stage, including costings and practical issues of making. A project meeting midweek offered time to discuss progress and highlight areas of difficulty. By Friday, students were completing prototypes and preparing a presentation, in readiness for an extremely lively and interesting crit, which included advice on further development and promotion of their prototypes.

Shared themes emerged to do with journeys, experiencing the present and being acutely aware of one's surroundings, but the six outcomes from the projects were as varied as the 11 individuals who took part, both in project development and in presentation.

1. A group of students, studying diverse practices (Information Experience Design, Printmaking and Global Innovation Design) were inspired by what they had felt when they walked the labyrinth: in particular how we access the subconscious mind through conscious language and how the conscious and subconscious mind work together. The group created a (downloadable) podcast to lead the listener through a sensory journey. Walking the specific circuit of the building, the listener is made more aware of motor co-ordination experiences and of the communication between the conscious and the subconscious mind.

2. An architecture student was also concerned with journeys, more specifically how an individual reconnects with their urban journeys or urban 'labyrinths', which he said *'have been adapted by citizens as empty transitional space, lacking any sort of meaning and event, only used to connect relevant destinations'*. The state of mindfulness this student experienced when walking the labyrinth forced him to become more aware of his surroundings; he proposed 'Mindfulness pop-up kiosks', temporary meditation rooms spread around London streets, that enable you to stop and reconsider your journey.

3. A ceramics and glass student and a jewellery student chose to focus on a comparison between the psychological and physical nature of

journeys/labyrinths that we encounter in our everyday lives. They decided to document and then compare the journeys from their houses to college. The resulting PowerPoint presentation was fascinating; it highlighted the fact that within our urban journeys there are so many similarities in terms of loss and self-discovery. As we all go through our personal labyrinth, getting from point A to point B, we might need to learn to unlearn things in order to find our own centres.

4. Another jewellery student provided the group with guidelines for a mind-set designed to help you find stillness when walking to or from a place. His instructions included advice on how to prepare for the walk and then when walking; how to stay focused by concentrating on the path and pace; how to deal with obstacles; and how to relate to other people that you might encounter. He promotes this as a way of decreasing stress, clearing your mind and being aware of your surroundings without actually thinking about them.

5. Clearly, routines serve a purpose and allow us to intuitively deal with the everyday mundane rituals, whilst freeing up our consciousness to work on other things. But what happens when we examine our own routines and then force ourselves to adopt someone else's? This was the question posed by a group of jewellery, animation and visual communication students, who decided to write down a manifesto of their own routines and then swap them, entering into each other's recorded lives. They found that despite at first resisting the challenge, the experience had been quite freeing and had enabled them to consider what they might want to change about their own routines in the future. They produced a library or archive system to enable an individual to consider rituals and habits and how they can affect thinking, thus enabling conscious choice of alternative ways of being.

6. A textile student was interested in the notion of the labyrinth as a holder of memories. This led her to consider how a labyrinth could be worn and how that, in turn, could be used to work with dementia patients. Her other ideas related to therapeutic applications for patients in the National Health Service, in both Baby and Renal Units. This student will be continuing to develop these ideas as part of her MPhil degree.

Some of the groups were keen to continue working together in the future. The three students who worked alone nevertheless noted the benefits of times of collaboration during the week; in particular the group progress sessions and crit had proved to be very helpful. As a bonus, three Spanish-speaking students from different programmes were delighted to have met for the first time; two who were from Mexico discovered their family homes were only 50 miles apart! It would seem appropriate to give the final words to the students:

I enjoyed the project very much and it has informed my research and current thinking.

It was not until after I bought a book about Zen that I realised that this week's project must have unconsciously inspired me to do so. Thank you for this week!

Thank you so much for such an inspiring week and also for the books that you showed me: this is a new resource for me, full of possibilities, I'm so excited! Really looking forward to meeting you soon and talk about more branching potentialities.

18 Finger labyrinth research: Tracing a path to resilience, concentration and creativity

Nina Johnson

Nina Johnson is a Literature and Creative Writing instructor in the English and Modern Languages Department at Thompson Rivers University, Kamloops, BC, Canada. She is a certified Veriditas labyrinth facilitator and a member of The Labyrinth Society Research Committee. As a Senior Lecturer and TRU Teaching and Learning Scholar, she researches the contemplative effects of the finger labyrinth on student anxiety, concentration and creativity.

▶ Anxiety and academic achievement

After many years as a composition and literature instructor at a small Canadian university, I am increasingly concerned by my students' collective struggle to cope with university life. Instances of depression, exhaustion, stress and exam anxiety seem to be more frequent. My role places me in a privileged position to observe this shift: the nature of literary discussion invites students to share personal analogies of experience, and the study of written expression fosters an exploration of personal voice. Consequently, the students' literary development is often closely intertwined with their personal narratives, and I, as their facilitator, hear many courageous stories. Nevertheless, these observations of suffering have been merely anecdotal, and, although outside my area of expertise, require investigation.

In 2013, the American College Health Association (ACHA) published a report of a survey of over 34,000 students enrolled at 32 Canadian post-secondary institutions, concerning student health on campus. In the previous 12 months, students reported that they had felt: overwhelmed (89 per cent); exhausted, though not from physical activity (87 per cent); overwhelmingly anxious (57 per cent); hopeless (54 per cent) and so depressed it was difficult to function (38 per cent) (ACHA, pp. 13–14; percentages in the present chapter have been rounded to the nearest whole number). The parlous state of student mental health is therefore no longer anecdotal. Their suffering is affecting their achievement at university: participants reported (ACHA, p. 5) that their academic success had been affected in the past year by anxiety (28 per cent), depression (17 per cent) and stress (37 per cent). Compelling personal stories, and now compelling statistics, would seem to indicate the need for a compelling response. What sort of response might be appropriate? Is it possible to learn mental and emotional resilience for the sake of personal well-being and enhanced student learning? Certainly, as a teacher, this must be my business.

▷ Mindfulness: Cultivating mental focus to reduce anxiety

Mindfulness practices, including tai chi, yoga, breath meditation, walking meditation and labyrinth walking, suggest potential pathways to resilience. Each of these traditions offers a means to practise either seated or moving meditation which cultivates a heightened awareness of the present moment. By training the mind and body to perceive sensations fully in each moment, the interior mental chatter that often plagues the mind becomes quiet. If we are present, the mind is not ruminating on thoughts or emotions from the past; nor is it rehearsing thoughts or emotions for the future.

The physical, mental and emotional benefits of mindfulness practices have been well documented. Jon Kabat-Zinn, founder of the Mindfulness-Based Stress Reduction (MBSR) Program at The Center for Mindfulness in Medicine, Health Care, and Society (University of Massachusetts Medical Center), has been researching and writing about the mental and physical effects of mindfulness practices for over 30 years (Kabat-Zinn, 1991, 1994, 2003, 2005; Kabat-Zinn and Davidson, 2011). Kabat-Zinn states, *'It's not anything exotic. Meditation just has to do with paying attention in a particular way. That's something we're all capable of doing'* (Moyers, 1993, p. 116). Kabat-Zinn's patients are referred to his clinic because of stress and stress-related illness, and find relief by training the mind to concentrate on the present moment. Perhaps a similar practice would be beneficial to students. The labyrinth pattern, for example, may provide a strong point of mental focus to cultivate concentration on the present moment. As an alternative to walking, Figure 18.1 shows a wooden finger labyrinth in use.

Figure 18.1 Walking the path by hand: following the pattern of a classical finger labyrinth.

Photograph courtesy Jan Sellers.

▶ Labyrinths and learning

In an effort to educate myself about the history, theory and potential applications of the labyrinth as a mindfulness practice, I trained with Veriditas, becoming a certified labyrinth facilitator. I then approached my university's Landscape Advisory Committee to find out if there might be an available space on campus to create a walking labyrinth. Although possible sites existed, the question of campus real estate was not one to be taken lightly. Not surprisingly, colleagues and administrators first wanted evidence that labyrinths support student learning.

Dr John Rhodes, founder of the Labyrinth Society, notes that labyrinth walkers report a reduction in agitation, anxiety and stress, as well as increased experiences of calm, clarity, openness and reflection (2008, pp. 31–5). I hypothesised that the state of Canadian student mental health and the reported benefits of MBSR research indicated that a systematic study of the 'labyrinth effects' on student learning was timely. The challenge is to design a rigorous, evidence-based inquiry to demonstrate the relationships between labyrinths and learning. Three fields of educational research support the values, methods and goals of such an inquiry: the Scholarship of Teaching and Learning (SoTL); Contemplative Pedagogy; and Transformational Learning.

SoTL is *'a cross-disciplinary field of study that encourages the exploration and public discussion of issues and questions about teaching and learning in postsecondary education'* (Elgie, 2014, p. vii). Ernest Boyer, author of *Scholarship Reconsidered* (1990), and former Carnegie Foundation President, first articulated the concept of SoTL as *'work that examines teaching and learning in a scholarly fashion'* (Boyer cited in Elgie, 2014, p. 45). More recent definitions emphasise the importance of systematic evidence-based inquiry related to the assessment of teaching and learning initiatives (Elgie, 2014, p. viii). Studies are usually classroom based and often rely on evidence drawn from surveys, questionnaires and focus groups (Society for Teaching and Learning in Higher Education, 2014).

Contemplative Pedagogy also demands academic rigour. The Center for Contemplative Mind in Society (CCMS) describes its vision in relation to research:

> Though powerful and vitally important, the conventional methods of scientific research, pedagogy, and critical scholarship need to be broadened. The experiential methods developed within the contemplative traditions offer a rich set of tools for exploring the mind, the heart, and the world. When they are combined with conventional practices, an enriched research methodology and pedagogy become available for deepening and enlarging perspectives, leading to lasting solutions to the problems we confront. (CCMS, 2014)

A study which investigates the labyrinth as a contemplative practice and aspires to promote student well-being in addition to effective learning, situates itself within the expansive vision of Contemplative Pedagogy in which the researcher acknowledges a compassionate intention, a holistic appreciation for the student and broad goals of education as citizenship.

The shared goals of SoTL and Contemplative Pedagogy include:

▶ Systematic exploration of the learning process in higher education.
▶ Emphasis on methods of inquiry critical to learning, demonstration of the effectiveness of these methods and public dissemination of such effectiveness.
▶ Common rhetoric: 'reflection', 'inquiry', 'insight' and 'awareness'.
▶ Emphasis on engaged, experiential and deep learning (Owen-Smith, 2012).

Transformational Learning also seeks to facilitate personal growth and shares the SoTL and Contemplative Learning discourse of individual experience, reflection and insight (Mezirow, 1981). Julia Christenson-Hughes and Joy Mighty link the fields of SoTL and Transformational Learning together:

> It is without question our bias that effective teaching and learning go beyond the traditional lecture and rote learning. Rather, they are trans-formative in nature; providing students with opportunities to become self-directed as well as to examine critically their assumptions and views of themselves, their subjects, their contexts, and the world in general, helping them to develop new habits of perceiving, thinking and acting. (Christenson-Hughes and Mighty, 2010, p. 4)

With these issues in mind, I designed a SoTL study to explore the potential for transformational learning using the finger labyrinth as a contemplative practice for re-shaping habits of anxiety, concentration and creativity.

▶ A Scholarship of Teaching and Learning pilot project

Research context

I chose to run the SoTL pilot project, 'Labyrinths and Learning', in a Crea-tive Writing class where previous students had reported feeling anxious, distracted or uninspired. Three patterns of comments had emerged:

1. **'Writing causes me a lot of stress'**
   Many students are inexperienced creative writers, yet tend to be highly motivated and personally committed to creative writing. An unfortu-nate tension between low skill and high expectations may cause anxi-ety leading to writer's block.

2. **'I can't find a topic'**
   Students may be unaware of the rich experience of their own lives. We live in a distracted culture of Facebook, email and Twitter where our mental focus, observations and verbal fluency are limited to sound-bites, rather than sustained reflection. Our attempts to multi-task do not seem to enhance the mind's ability to observe or recall experience.

3. **'I'm not very creative'**
   Myths about the nature of inspiration may lead students mistakenly to believe that creativity is a matter of luck (through external agency, i.e. the Muse), or that it manifests unpredictably (under unknown conditions).

SoTL research question

The study set out to explore three ways in which contemplative practice using finger labyrinths might foster a deeper learning experience. First, a contemplative practice such as the labyrinth may help to reduce anxiety and the consequences of feeling blocked. Second, by practising habits of mind which induce a sense of physical and mental calm, students may observe an increased ability to concentrate, to observe their external environment and to trace their own mental and emotional activity. These observed experiences may then be more easily verbalised and crafted as fiction. The abilities to concentrate and observe external circumstances, as well as internal emotional nuance, are central to the writer of literary fiction. Third, the circular pattern of the labyrinth, while enhancing a state of relaxation, may also enable metaphorical and associative thinking – commonly labelled as 'creativity'. Through the practice of focused attention on the present moment, cultivated habits of non-judgemental awareness may also sustain a sense of creative play.

Method

The 'Labyrinths and Learning' pilot project ran in a Creative Writing class, English 2060: Introduction to Short Fiction (32 students) in the Fall 2013 semester (13 weeks). There were four components of the study: preliminary self-assessment survey, Labyrinth Journal, test survey and focus group.

1. In the first week of classes, participants completed a short self-assessment survey to establish a baseline for perceived levels of anxiety, concentration and creativity.
2. Daily journaling was a required component of the course. Each student was supplied with a 'Labyrinth Journal' with tear-out surveys and a fold-out finger labyrinth. Participating students were invited to trace the finger labyrinth prior to journaling, and to complete a short survey every two weeks to reflect on their perceived levels of anxiety, concentration and creativity. See Figure 18.2, Labyrinth Journal Survey *(and Kimberly Saward's chapter which offers paper labyrinth templates – eds)*.
3. Participants were invited to use a finger labyrinth during situations testing recall and the application of basic concepts and were asked to complete a short survey reflecting on levels of anxiety and concentration during the test experience.
4. At the end of the semester, participating students were invited to join a focus group discussion.

Research outcomes

In a class of 32 students, the number of participants ranged from 27 in the Preliminary Survey to 18 participants in the Final Journal Survey, indicating gradual attrition over the semester.

Preliminary survey

▶ On a scale reflecting five states of anxiety, ranging from very anxious to very relaxed, 12 of 27 participants reported feeling very anxious or somewhat anxious.
▶ On a scale reflecting five states of concentration, ranging from very distracted to very focussed, 17 of 27 participants reported feeling very distracted or somewhat distracted.

Labyrinth Journal

▶ Journal surveys were completed by students, and collected, at two-week intervals between September and November.
▶ On each successive survey, participants reported reduced anxiety after using the labyrinth: 18 of 25 participants, 13 of 24 participants, 9 of 21 participants, 10 of 19 participants and 8 of 18 participants.
▶ Remaining participants reported no change.
▶ Reduced anxiety was noted by students using the finger labyrinth for as little as one to two minutes on three to four days per week.

Test surveys: Midterm Test

On the Midterm Test, 19 students participated.

▶ Fifteen participants used the finger labyrinth for between one and four minutes; remaining participants used the labyrinth for more than four minutes.
▶ Eleven students reported reduced anxiety, and ten students reported improved concentration, after tracing the finger labyrinth.

Test surveys: Final Test

On the Final Test, 23 students participated.

▶ Nineteen participants used the finger labyrinth for between one and four minutes; remaining participants used the labyrinth for more than four minutes.
▶ Seventeen students reported reduced anxiety, and 19 students reported improved concentration, after tracing the finger labyrinth.

Focus group comments

A representative selection of comments is given below.

Anxiety

▷ I was less physically tense afterwards. Not happier really, but it took away from all the things in my life that were making me upset, frustrating me.
▷ Calmer. Removed the background chatter in your brain telling you [that] you can't do this.
▷ When I had a paper that was worth 30 per cent of my mark, I was freaking out about it, and I did the finger labyrinth and it definitely calmed me physically. I wasn't as tense.

Concentration

▷ Able to focus much more, much more in the present.
▷ When I'm doing the actual assignments I had a lot more focus and concentration.
▷ I had more concentration on writing instead of letting my mind wander off to things I have to do.

Tests

▷ Definitely just being able to disconnect, to focus on it [the labyrinth] is a good way to calm your nerves. Calm your brain.
▷ I liked it a lot for when we had a midterm, because I would write too fast; [I could] calm down, and keep going. I'd say it helped my mark on the midterm.
▷ It improved my performance on exams. I think it had a positive effect. It helps you to centre and to concentrate. It would help in other courses. And it didn't take you long either.

Creativity

▷ I feel more focussed. I'm able to focus my creativity. And so [I'm] able to focus on writing and actually [get] it out on the page.
▷ It doesn't feel like it makes you more creative. It gives you the power to wield [your creativity].
▷ It takes the emotions out of the situation after the labyrinth; you see the bigger picture. You see more depth when you're focussed and calmer.

Beyond the study

▷ There were two weeks there where I had essay after essay. So I used it more, for more lengthy periods of time then. Because it helped.
▷ It's part of the focus toolkit now.
▷ I find if anything, the labyrinth showed you that if you just take the time to take a step back that you could refocus yourself regardless of what's ahead of you. You can do it.

▷ Discussion

Journal Surveys, Test Surveys and Focus Group discussions revealed that students who used the labyrinth for less than five minutes, two or three times per week, felt consistently less anxious and more focussed, present, non-judgmental and open to creative insights. Students found the practice beneficial for assignment completion, test anxiety and exam performance. Having experienced desirable learning outcomes, some participants began using the labyrinth in conjunction with other classes and writing assignments. I am collecting data from another two creative writing classes in 2014–2015 (a total of 72 students, results pending) and have modified the Journal surveys to reflect in more detail, changes in concentration and creativity. I am hopeful that the Students' Union will include a finger labyrinth in the 2015–2016 student agenda (free to all students), and I continue to explore the possibility of designing a walking labyrinth on our campus.

▷ Conclusion

Given the recent statistics on Canadian student mental health and cumulative research on the benefits of mindfulness practices, the positive results from the 'Labyrinths and Learning' pilot project suggest unique pedagogical opportunities for educators. If we embrace the interdisciplinarity, rigour, holistic ethic and long-sighted vision of SoTL, Contemplative Pedagogy and Transformational Learning, we open ourselves and our students to an unprecedented educational experience. Amid a world confronted by political, social and environmental crises, we may impart to our students and our communities skills for equanimity, clarity and insight.

Please tear here and
return to your instructor

Name _____

Date _____

FINGER LABYRINTH STUDY

1. During the previous two-week period, how many days did you use the finger labyrinth before journaling? Circle the response that best reflects your practice.

   1–2 days   3–4 days   5–6 days   7–8 days   9–10 days

2. During the previous two-week period, how many minutes (on average) did you spend tracing the finger labyrinth before journaling? Circle the response that best reflects your practice.

   1–2 minutes   3–4 minutes   5–6 minutes   7–8 minutes   9–10 minutes

3. Circle the picture which best reflects your overall level of anxiety during the previous two-week period.

4. Circle the picture which best reflects your level of anxiety after tracing the finger labyrinth.

5. Circle the description which best reflects your ability to concentrate while journaling during the previous two-week period.

   Very distracted   Somewhat distracted   Neutral   Somewhat focused   Very focused

6. Circle the description which best describes your level of creativity while journaling during the previous two-week period.

   Uncreative   Somewhat uncreative   Neutral   Somewhat creative   Very creative

Additional Comments/Observations:

_____

_____

Figure 18.2 Labyrinth Journal Survey.

19 Case study in imagination: Drawing the labyrinth

Liz Whitney

On leaving school Liz Whitney attended Bradford College of Art, which set the foundation for a creative approach to life. She went on to train as a nurse and midwife where pictorial representation supported her learning. Following considerable clinical practice Liz moved into higher education and is currently a Midwifery Lecturer at the University of Bradford. Highly motivated by student-centred, emancipatory approaches to teaching, learning and assessment, Liz has introduced the creative arts into both her clinical practice and the midwifery curriculum.

Imagination is more important than knowledge. For knowledge is limited to all we now know and understand, while imagination embraces the entire world, and all there ever will be to know and understand.

(Einstein, 1931, p. 97)

▶ Setting the scene

Inspired by my own artistic experience and evidence from the literature on the arts, creativity and professional development in healthcare, I have encouraged students to engage in creative activities, in order to help them explore some of the less tangible aspects of midwifery practice. Reflecting on clinical and personal experience, students produce artwork in the form of drawings, paintings, collage, sculpture, poetry, prose and performance. Positive feedback suggests that the sessions are educational and enjoyable, (Whitney, 2010) although some degree of surprise and reticence is initially evident in comments such as 'what has art got to do with midwifery?' and 'I am not very creative or artistic'.

Art is a means of depicting or viewing our experience of the world. It provides the opportunity to observe life through different perspectives, developing new insight and challenging existing values and beliefs (Newton and Plummer, 2009; Davies, 2013; Powley and Higson, 2013). This in turn supports flexible thinking, empathy and compassion (Wikstrom, 2003), whilst valuing the skills of innovation, creativity and diplomacy (McIntosh, 2010; Pink, 2008). The use of art aims to facilitate a shift from the detached, logical, linear and reductionist position of the science academic, to a more intuitive, sympathetic, multi-dimensional and exploratory stance (Lafferty, 1997; Meakin and Kirklin, 2000; Reilley, Ring and Duke, 2005). Edwards (2008) describes this shift as right brain thinking, in which the logical left brain shuts down as the artist becomes absorbed in right brain creativity. Utilising the labyrinth is one way of facilitating creative engagement, whilst also providing a scaffold by which students can unpack and display their work (England, 2007, 2010).

▶ The midwifery workshop

A brief introduction to the history of labyrinth and its use as a meditative tool sets the scene for the workshop. A range of labyrinth images is displayed and   discussed including contemporary work such as Motoi Yamamoto's salt labyrinths (Hossenally, 2014) and Mark Wallinger's 270 London Underground labyrinths (Wallinger, 2013). Students are also encouraged to share any pre-existing labyrinth experiences. Viewing some examples of childbirth art helps to further set the scene; group discussion of the artwork promotes the concept of interpretation and develops the idea that there is not always a right or a wrong way to see things. It is important to provide sufficient time to prepare the students in order that they feel supported and understand the rationale for the activity.

The workshop usually begins with a guided relaxation focusing on breathing as used in labour preparation sessions; this helps the students to unwind and focus on their inner self. Students are then asked to reflect on an aspect of clinical practice, a value or belief, an ethical dilemma or a philosophical stance, such as 'finding your inner midwife'.

With their topic in mind and using a simple labyrinth picture, students are asked to use their finger to trace the labyrinth path to the centre and out again, allowing their thoughts to flow freely. I suggest that students make full use of their senses, considering aspects such as texture, colour, shape or lack of form, smell, sound, feelings and reflections as they travel the labyrinth. I explain the meditative nature of the workshop and the importance of a quiet environment both when tracing the labyrinth and while completing the artwork. Gentle background music helps to set the scene and I remain present in the room to provide guidance and support.

Students are now ready to begin to produce their own artwork, either incorporating or underpinned by the labyrinth. Instruction on how to draw a basic labyrinth is provided along with a selection of paint, pencils, pastels, charcoal, paper, collage materials/junk and clay. Students choose their own materials, but may need guidance. I remind the group that there is no right or wrong way to tackle the work. There is often discussion at this stage as students start to develop their ideas.

Some students become bewildered or anxious; worried about their perceived lack of artistic talent, they may be reluctant to make a start. A reminder of how painting was a pleasure as a child sometimes helps students to lose their inhibitions (Edwards, 2008). Robertson (1963) discovered that the use of archetypal imagery invoked a deeper level of concentration and centredness in her art students, enabling them to produce more profound and meaningful work. Revisiting the labyrinth seems to help students to unravel their ideas; simply decorating a labyrinth, adding a threshold pattern or centrepiece can bring surprising results (England, 2010). Small group discussion may help to tease out ideas, which can then be developed by the individual. Given space and time, ideas usually begin to emerge. Whilst some students struggle to get started, they are often the ones who get the most out of the session and are frequently surprised by their new-found creative ability (Whitney 2010). As facilitator I move around the room offering feedback and guidance, considering the differing needs within the group (and avoiding the temptation to jump in too soon with my own ideas). Alert to the potential for emotional 'fall out' as students begin to explore inner feelings, I make the group aware of this possibility early on and offer a safe place and the opportunity for private discussion. The group itself, however, generally provides an accepting and supportive environment, which often leads participants to consider the therapeutic nature of the labyrinth activity and how it could be used in the wider clinical context.

Once the art is completed, a critical reflection session, 'the crit', begins. This is an opportunity for students to display their work and to have some meaningful discussion about each piece. Feeding back in small groups, I ask the students not to disclose the meaning or inspiration of their work initially, but rather to listen to others' feedback of their interpretation or understanding. This provides some interesting insights, often unveiling hidden meanings and unintentional messages. The crit can be a moving experience for students as their work takes on new meaning and is appreciated by others. This is particularly the case for those students who initially

Figure 19.1 Example of student artwork.

Painting by Hayley Meadowcroft; photograph courtesy Fiona MacVane Phipps.

believed that they had limited artistic talent. Students are encouraged to keep a record of their artwork by uploading an image to their academic portfolio; in some instances the work is later selected by the student to form part of a summative assessment.

Engaging with the labyrinth through art provides student midwives with a tool for life. Its meditative qualities help the student to focus and tune in to their inner self. Its structure enables the student to explore, unpack and scaffold their experience, the sharing of which reveals diversity, many different perspectives and innovation. In turn this supports the development of empathic understanding and compassion. This is particularly pertinent when working with the public, all of whom have individual needs and expectations, or when functioning in a multi-professional team where the emphasis is constantly shifting. The labyrinth mirrors the student's experience through the many twists and turns of professional development and, perhaps most importantly, offers an opportunity for contemplation and tranquillity in an ever-changing and demanding world.

20 A semester within

Fran Grace

Fran Grace, PhD, serves as Professor of Religious Studies and Steward of the Meditation Room at the University of Redlands, California, where she has pioneered a contemplative-based approach to education. She is the author/creator of many works on meditation, spiritual life and contemplative education. Her dedication is to the 'inner pathway': love, surrender, self-knowledge, compassion, inner peace, joy, humour and beauty. She is founding director of the non-profit organisation Inner Pathway, which seeks to share these timeless values with the public.

▶ Going inward: Contemplative learning

It is common for students to undertake a semester abroad. What about a semester *within*? The labyrinth is an ideal outer setting for an inner journey. This chapter describes how the labyrinth is used in a contemplative-based course at the University of Redlands, California, with particular emphasis on first-hand accounts by students.

In 2007, the University of Redlands opened one of the first contemplative classrooms in the USA (Redden, 2007). We replaced the standard learning equipment – tables and chairs – with meditation cushions and yoga mats. We painted the walls a soft colour and hung flowing curtains to accentuate the spaciousness of the high ceilings.

This unique classroom encourages interior discovery. Self-knowledge is implicit in the dictum 'Know Thyself', often endorsed as a foundation of liberal arts education. Walking across the threshold into the room, students say they 'feel the difference'. It is not an ordinary college space. The posted guidelines ask them to remove their shoes, turn off their mobile devices and place all belongings into the cubbyholes next to the door. It is the difference between ordinary time (*chronos*) and non-ordinary time (*kairos*). In *chronos*, we are counting the passing of seconds and minutes. In *kairos*, we are absorbed in the emergence of a greater meaning. In this way, the classroom is similar to the labyrinth. Stepping onto the labyrinth, a walker enters the timeless *kairos* dimension. Courses offered in the contemplative classroom include Introduction to Meditation; Compassion Seminar; Zen

Meditation; Meditation and Writing; Quest of the Mystics; Intermediate Meditation Practicum; Yoga; Psychology and Religion. Each course integrates contemplative methods into the traditional academic work of a college class (Grace, 2009, 2011b).

Contemplative methods cultivate inner awareness through first-person investigations. The contemplative methods vary: silent sitting meditation; nature observation; mindfulness; walking meditation; deep listening; death meditation; body movement; creative work; centring prayer; walking the labyrinth; compassion practices such as the loving kindness meditation and *tonglen* meditation in Buddhism; story-telling, and more (Simmer-Brown and Grace, 2011).[1]

Qualitative data from the first several years of the programme show that the learning is transformational in a positive way for students' well-being, interpersonal relations, sense of meaning, motivation for academic work and ethical development. Quantitative outcomes from a two-year pilot study on the Compassion class show that the course improved students' tested levels of optimism, empathy, compassion and ability to self–regulate in the face of a lab-induced stressor (Grace, Olson and Ko, 2014). Clearly, contemplative-based courses are beneficial for students.

▷ Labyrinth at the University of Redlands

In 2004, in loving memory of their parents, donors provided the funds to build a high-quality, outdoor labyrinth on campus, an exact replica of the one at Chartres Cathedral. I have used the labyrinth in my teaching ever since its construction. Once students learn how to walk the labyrinth during a class, they often return to it alone; it is open 24 hours a day. They see it as a 'centering place', a 'still point', a 'refuge from the chaos' of their lives and a place for 'clarity'. They often use it when they face a difficult decision or when they feel overwhelmed by life situations.

The labyrinth is an ideal teaching mechanism for many of the topics that I teach: forgiveness, mindfulness, interiority and self-knowledge, wholeness, self-calming, oneness and compassion. Moreover, I use the labyrinth as a ritual or rite of passage in certain classes. For example, when I teach a First Year Seminar with entering students, we walk the labyrinth as an initiation into their college life. They reflect on where they have come from, where they are going.

▷ Use of the labyrinth in a course

In this chapter, I highlight the use of the labyrinth in my upper-division Quest of the Mystics course. The course examines the intense inner quest and culminating realisations of mystics in diverse cultures and religions.

Students explore the topic through three avenues: 1) biographical study of representative mystics; 2) comparative analysis of mystical teachings; 3) first-person investigation of contemplative methods recommended by the mystics studied.

The heart of the course is a 21-day 'Quest' project that begins eight weeks into the 15-week semester. Students are asked to research a particular mystical path to which they are personally drawn. The Quest project gives students an opportunity to integrate analytical, interactive and contemplative learning. They design their own 21-Day Practice Period, inspired by one of the mystical paths we study in the class. Through an in-depth process of consultation with me, peer feedback and their own research, students finalise a 'Quest Practice Contract' that includes four dimensions of studying their chosen path: Ethical Cultivation, Physical Self–Discipline, Mental Cultivation and Contemplative Practice.

An in-class labyrinth walk opens and closes the 21-day Quest assignment. On the opening day of the Quest project, we do a 'launching' ritual in class. Leaving the classroom, we walk silently in a single-file line for five minutes through a grove of oak trees to the labyrinth site. I read aloud the labyrinth inscription by Caroline Adams, 'Walking the Labyrinth' (cited in Grace, 2011a, p. 53). Students enter the labyrinth one by one and are instructed to go at their own pace. It takes about 45 minutes for everyone to finish the labyrinth walk. After students finish their walk, they sit quietly on the grass, writing their reflections.

▷ Student experiences of the labyrinth

Every student who walked the labyrinth found it beneficial, no matter the religious affiliation or personal beliefs. They said that the labyrinth walk had a calming and clarifying effect on them – physically, emotionally and mentally. They saw that they were on a solitary journey but, paradoxically, never alone. They realised that each of them was at a different point on the path, but they were all going in the same direction: inward, to their centre. Walking the labyrinth allowed the shedding of things they no longer wanted. They had 'aha' moments of noetic insight. In sum, it was transformative. Here are some of their first-hand accounts, with names changed for privacy.

▷ Suzanne, although a lifelong Catholic, was not familiar with the labyrinth. Before the labyrinth walk, she felt 'stressed'. Afterwards, she was 'more relaxed' and 'more focused'. Several hours after her walk, Suzanne continued to feel the peacefulness of the experience. She also had an insight about the journey of life, which she emailed to me the next day:

I realized that our spiritual journeys may be long, with many turns. Sometimes it feels like we have walked the same path over and over again, and we don't see ourselves getting any closer to where we want to be. But the truth is that we are always making progress, and we will eventually reach the center. Also, we may sometimes lose sight of our center, but the center will always be there and our journey is always connected to it.

▷ A Buddhist student, Amy, was also nervous before her walk at the labyrinth. She wanted to let go of judgment of self and others. The labyrinth walk not only calmed her nerves but also gave her a new way to see the differences in others without judging them:

> The walk was profound. It sparked new ideas, showed me another perspective about others. Seeing how others approached the walk helped me understand how to interact with people in life. We are all different, on a different path, but we all want to get to the center. It helped to release my judgment.

▷ Elizabeth, a Protestant Christian in her last semester of college, started out the walk in an 'anxious' state of feeling 'off-balance'. The walk helped her to have more courage, confidence and calm: *'I am more focused, steady, calm, able to move forward. Each time I stepped over one of the small cracks in the cement, it was a reminder that "I can do this".'* On the reflection paper, Elizabeth drew a line of how she felt before and after the walk. Before the walk, her line was squiggly and crooked. After the walk, her line was straight and definite. The labyrinth walk had aligned her to her centre.

▷ Nicola, a first-year student hampered by self-doubts, found the labyrinth walk to be *'reassuring and enriching'.* She saw herself as a snake shedding its skin, *'ready to become a new person'.* The walk gave her *'the ability to allow change to happen in my life and to become the best version of myself I can be'.*

▷ Nathan, a junior student who described himself as *'fidgety and anxious'*, enjoyed the labyrinth as a type of moving meditation. During in-class meditation periods, he had difficulty sitting still. Walking the labyrinth worked well for him:

> I feel a calm that radiates throughout my body. I am aware of my anxiety but I don't feel anxious because I have more insight into why it persists. I'm excited to keep this feeling throughout the day.

We walked the labyrinth in silence. As they exited the labyrinth, students sat on the grass by themselves and wrote their reflections. It was a peaceful atmosphere. An hour previous, they had been restless, unsure and nervous about starting their 21-day Quest. As an instructor in observation of their process, the difference was palpable. It was like watching a television channel chaotic with loud static dissolve into a silent solid screen.

Launching their Quest project with the labyrinth walk aligned them with their highest aspirations. They made a symbolic journey into their innermost centre. Having made that symbolic journey, they were empowered to return to the world and carry out their Quest.

▶ **Conclusion: Learning is a path, not a goal**

When they walked the labyrinth again at the end of their 21-day Quest project, the students realised that life is an ongoing journey. Suzanne summarised this lesson well: *'The project period is over, but I don't feel like my 'Quest' is over. In fact, it has just begun.'*

Walking the labyrinth at the beginning and at the end of the Quest project gave students a benchmark for their learning. Nicola, for example, saw a big difference in her confidence level:

When I first walked the labyrinth, I didn't think I could fulfil my Quest. I was nervous about it. Today, I feel relieved and accomplished. I still have work to do on myself, but this walk gave me hope that there can be progress. I just have to believe in myself.

In the labyrinth walk, students saw the power of putting one foot in front of the other – simply taking the next step forward even though they could not see how it would lead them to their goal. They applied this awareness to real life. At the beginning of the Quest project, they could not imagine meeting their goals. But when they took one step at a time, they were amazed at the changes. One student was shocked she had refrained from smoking for 21 days.

Elizabeth noticed a big change in her attitude:

I can't believe how much I saw myself change. Now I can catch myself when I have negative thoughts or attitudes, and I can turn these around to more positive ones. I am much more positive as a person. Because of this, I am much happier.

Many students learned the hard lesson that there are ups and downs, twists and turns, in the inward journey. The labyrinth walk gave them a somatic experience of that spiritual reality. Nathan had wanted to stop biting his nails. He saw the habit as an anxiety-driven behaviour that prevented him from being fully present in his life. As he walked the labyrinth for the closing ritual, he reached acceptance about the twists and turns of his Quest project:

> There will always be disappointment and joy. Some days I adhered to my contract more than others. The good days stand out for me. The bad days were also good in terms of learning. In my Quest and the labyrinth, I concentrated on the step ahead and made sure to follow my path.

The labyrinth served as the students' primary meeting place with their own inner truth. Most of them would not have gone to the labyrinth on their own, as they did not even know of its existence. A class assignment that made use of the labyrinth was of incalculable benefit to them. It not only solidified their learning in this academic course, but also illumined their lifelong learning of a path to peace.

As they uncover the source of peace within themselves, the students become an avenue of peace to others.

Note

1 For a bibliography of resources on contemplative learning in Higher Education, see www.contemplativemind.org/resources/higher–education/recommended–reading. For a discussion of teaching *tonglen* meditation, see Grace (2009).

Part III: Campus and Community

Poems from the Labyrinth

Pilgrim

after Antonio Machado

I walk this path alone
following thousands who came before me
in front of thousands coming after me

I'm heading for the centre
a shrine, an oracle, tomb of a saint
I walk simply for the sake of walking

I am hoping for a miracle
revelation, enlightenment, nirvana
to find the emptiness at the heart of me

The path takes me into myself
and out of myself, the path is walking me
I make this path by walking

Victoria Field

Introduction to Part III: Campus and Community

It will already be clear to you that the sections of this book are not intended to be watertight compartments. It is important in Part III to reflect on some of the wider applications of the labyrinth, both on campus and in the wider community, not least because the contributors to this section are without doubt among some of the most creative leaders in the field. Their stories deserve to be told in this book particularly because they illustrate the ways in which, sometimes against the odds, labyrinth projects have sprung to life. They demonstrate ways in which the labyrinth can soften the (sometimes rigid) boundaries between 'town and gown', to use the famous Oxbridge phrase, where members of the public begin to experience something of the richness of learning in often quite unexpected ways. This happens when creative leadership is brought to bear on the development proposals, and when people begin to catch a vision of what could be possible.

Di Williams' chapter sets the scene for this with an exciting overview not only from her own experience but drawing together some of the work other colleagues have done in Canada, Ireland, Norway, the UK and the USA. There are moments in this section that can only be described as being utterly beautiful, and this is surely something we are delighted to celebrate in the context of teaching and learning. Of course, much of our teaching and learning is at times pedestrian, dealing with the core themes of our professional disciplines. But the labyrinth at its best widens horizons for students and colleagues; it can open up areas of mystery and wonder, awe and stillness that speak to our humanity and remind us of deeper values that education seeks to cherish and celebrate.

So we make no apology for inviting you to approach Part III with a real sense of anticipation, even excitement. Suddenly, teaching and learning can have moments of joyful fun that can enrich us all.

21 Chaplaincies: Labyrinth pioneers

Di Williams

Revd Di Williams, an Anglican priest, was awarded the MBE for Services to Higher Education in 2008 for her leading work in multi-faith and spiritual support. Founder of Still Paths labyrinth consultancy, a Veriditas Master Teacher and formerly chaplain to Lancaster and Edinburgh universities, Di now works with labyrinths in HE, retreat centres, churches, communities and movement-based healing arts. She brings to labyrinth work a deep appreciation of physical, emotional, intellectual and spiritual connection. She is author of *Labyrinth: Landscape of the Soul* (2011) and co-editor of *Working with the Labyrinth: Paths for Exploration* (2012), both published by Wild Goose, Glasgow.

▶ Introduction

This chapter will consider how the labyrinth has been introduced to Higher Education Institutions by Chaplaincy Support Services. It will focus on some of the most significant and rigorous chaplaincy initiatives in Ireland, Canada, Norway, the UK and the USA, with particular reference to the University of Edinburgh's labyrinth initiative in Scotland.

I will explore how these initiatives came about as well as charting their current practice, cross-campus collaborations and future possibilities. I will discuss both the challenges of sustainability and broadening the sense of ownership, look at engagement with the labyrinth across faith, culture and country, and point to the difference the initiatives are making to the institutions, particularly in the area of student experience.

▶ Why chaplaincies?

Internationally, the number of Higher Education (HE) labyrinth initiatives is blossoming. The World-Wide Labyrinth Locator (WWLL, 2014) and internet research suggest that around a third of the current HE initiatives owe their origins specifically to a Chaplaincy, campus ministry or religious and spiritual life provision, with the balance being led by a wide range of academic departments, student support services and university estates and facilities departments.

Chaplains have been extremely well placed to lead the movement to bring labyrinths into our Higher Education Institutions (HEIs). Within the Christian community alone there is a long history reaching back to a fourth century basilica labyrinth in North Africa and encompassing the surge in labyrinth developments in the European churches and cathedrals of the 12th and 13th centuries (Kern, 2000, p. 88; pp. 143–163). The contemporary revival of the practice has found great impetus in the fresh expressions of church and the search for authentic spirituality, which connect with the culture of life today (King, 2009, pp. 110–113). The Revd Dr Lauren Artress has played an exceptional role through her ministry at Grace Cathedral in San Francisco and through the non-profit organisation Veriditas (Veriditas, 2014). The largest growth of labyrinth initiatives worldwide is in churches, cathedrals, retreat and spirituality centres and chaplaincies (WWLL, 2014).

Chaplains of all faiths working in HEIs understand the reflective life. The motivation of their life and work encourages a reflective approach to the life of the inner spirit and human journeying. They seek to share that understanding of learning and development with those they work with and for. They have a strong history of pastoral support for whole communities with a concern for the mental health and general well-being of those they find themselves alongside.

Many Christian Chaplains see their work as being at the forefront of contemporary Christian culture and development. They are often innovators of practice and theology and are well placed to work alongside multi-faith colleagues at the interface between diverse communities of faith and belief in inclusive, collaborative ways. I suggest it is the convergence of a holistic and inclusive sense of call and ministry with the mirrored gifts of the labyrinth that may well have caused chaplains to be at the forefront in developing labyrinth initiatives in our places of work and ministry in HEIs.

▶ **Chaplaincy labyrinth initiatives in the UK and Ireland**

The first known chaplaincy-led initiative in the UK was held at the University of Dundee, in November 1999, when the Chaplaincy and Counselling Service collaborated to lay a replica Chartres canvas labyrinth in the University Chapel. This launched a monthly indoor labyrinth walk hosted by the Chaplaincy and initially facilitated by the Counselling Service (Halpin, 2005).

It was not until 2001 that chaplaincy-led initiatives really took off. Within two years of introducing a canvas indoor labyrinth the Chaplaincy secured funding for a major project at the University of Edinburgh: the first permanent, stone pavement labyrinth at a British university.

The influence of that project has rippled outwards: there are currently around 34 known labyrinth initiatives in UK and Ireland HEIs of which 17 have been initiated by Chaplaincy Services. Of these 17, the Universities of Bedfordshire, Dublin City, Edinburgh, and Stirling have permanent labyrinths; Worcester has a mown lawn labyrinth. Those at Bristol, Derby, Kingston, Leeds Trinity, Lincoln, Northumbria, Queen Mary University of London and Reading use portable canvases. Dundee has a joint Chaplaincy and Counselling initiative using a canvas; Imperial College London and the Royal College of Art, working together, have a joint Chaplaincy and Dyslexia Support initiative using a portable fabric labyrinth; Goldsmiths College London uses finger labyrinths. There are fledgling initiatives emerging as I write.

▶ The University of Edinburgh, Scotland

Interest and beginnings

I have walked labyrinths ever since I encountered my first one along the Welsh coast in 1993. My walk on the St. Martin's College Labyrinth in Lancaster in 1998 was transformative. Chalked (and subsequently painted) on tarmac in 1981 by the Religious Studies Department to promote active learning, it provided a uniquely reflective space in which I was able to connect with a life issue that arose in my mind as I took my first steps along the path. By the time I left the labyrinth I had begun to process the learning that had opened up for me. That walk changed the course of my life. It also led me to consider the potential of bringing labyrinth facilitation into my own work in HE and Chaplaincy.

In 2001 I visited Grace Cathedral in San Francisco, the home of two labyrinths and of Veriditas, a non-profit organisation committed to training facilitators to work with labyrinths across the globe. I was already committed to developing an inclusive, multi-faith Chaplaincy provision across the University with an interest and concern for the whole life of the University. The labyrinth seemed to afford a wonderfully supportive metaphor and practice for that vision.

Introducing the labyrinth to the University

Hopeful of securing funding for a canvas labyrinth from Student Support Services, the Chaplaincy hired a labyrinth facilitator and her 9.75 m (32 ft) Chartres style canvas labyrinth to offer a pre-exam labyrinth walk in the University. The success of that event led to positive press coverage and the funding to go back to Grace Cathedral to undertake facilitator training with Veriditas. The cheque to purchase a canvas labyrinth was on my desk when I returned! Next steps included an open drop-in walk for peace to commemorate 9/11, two days of labyrinth walks in Freshers' Week offering reflection on the transition from school to University and various labyrinth talks with student groups. The inclusive nature of our work attracted further positive publicity in the national press (Wojtas, 2002).

Once our own portable, 11-circuit Chartres style labyrinth arrived, we could offer a weekly drop-in walk in the Chaplaincy Auditorium, supported by the Chaplaincy Administrator and several committed students. One student, a Malayan Buddhist, offered her weekly commitment that year as part of her 'service' requirement for the Duke of Edinburgh's Gold Award. We were able to take the labyrinth to the University's science site for a student-led orientation programme to welcome postgraduates beginning their studies part way through the year. We welcomed University and Edinburgh city residents to an 'all faiths and none' walk to reflect on the theme of life and death; over a hundred people walked that day.

Early challenges in initiating and sustaining the initiative

We began the new academic year with themed walks of transition in Freshers' Week followed by weekly open drop-in walks for students, staff and visitors to the University. There were never huge numbers, but the positive written feedback suggested that walkers experienced an increased sense of well-being and relaxation and of focus in their learning. However, the weekly drop-in commitment was proving costly in Chaplaincy staff and venue time. Initially with Estates and Buildings, and then with other departments, we began to discuss the possibility of building an outdoor pavement labyrinth.

These discussions quickly became serious. A window of opportunity suddenly opened. We were given a week to prepare a full-scale proposal, a bid for the construction of a 12.8 m (42 ft) stone pavement labyrinth (a replica of the Chartres Cathedral Labyrinth), to submit to the University of Edinburgh Development Trust. Despite the inevitable speed of preparation, we hoped for a favourable response as we had addressed the University's current agendas and issues regarding student life. The response came in the form of a gracious £30,000 grant to build the Edinburgh Labyrinth

Figure 21.1 A child races around the Edinburgh Labyrinth, UK.

Photograph courtesy Jan Sellers.

in the beautiful eighteenth-century gardens of George Square, a peaceful space at the heart of the University in Edinburgh's Old Town. The Opening Ceremony and Dedication of the Edinburgh Labyrinth took place in October 2005. The opening walk was supported by the sound of a clàrsach with the labyrinth ringed by flaming torches. The Edinburgh Labyrinth had arrived and we now needed to put it on the map.

Collaborative opportunities

Several collaborative initiatives emerged over the next three years. Now that the outdoor labyrinth was available to all we reduced our weekly indoor drop-in walks to monthly events. A joint Chaplaincy and Student Counselling partnership offered group walks on the more intimate indoor labyrinth followed by a supported reflective process. The outdoor Edinburgh Labyrinth became the venue for workshops and walks for a University staff union meeting, a Staff Development Health and Wellbeing Day (part of the Healthy Universities initiative) and a Student Association Wellness Week.

We led events for the Midlothian Guiding and Scout Associations and the Scottish Episcopal Cathedral and diocese. The Edinburgh Labyrinth linked to Cityspace, a charity helping people to access reflective spaces and events across the city. The Chaplaincy Centre hosted an art installation, 'Reflective Paths – Labyrinth of Light', as part of an art student's final year degree project and exhibited photographs of labyrinths worldwide. Our inclusive approach featured again in the national press, this time in a reflection on innovative, contemplative space in HE (Fox, 2007).

In 2008 further associations between universities and across continents took place. I was invited, first to train staff and students in volunteer labyrinth facilitation at the University of Kent, UK, and then to lead a labyrinth workshop at the Global Higher Education Chaplains' Conference in Finland, a great opportunity to share the labyrinth with chaplains from many continents and traditions. This was followed by a significant visit to Melbourne, Australia for the Parliament of World Religions with a multi-faith group of staff and students. This group, from Buddhist, Christian, Hindu, Muslim and Shamanic communities and practices within the University of Edinburgh, presented their award-winning documentary film with footage of the Edinburgh Labyrinth and facilitated an early morning labyrinth walk together as one of the Parliament's times of spiritual observance (Williams 2010; University of Edinburgh Chaplaincy, 2011).

Figure 21.2 Students from the University of Edinburgh, at the Parliament of World Religions in Australia, prepare a large canvas labyrinth for walking. This labyrinth has been professionally made in three attachable sections, for ease of storage and transport.

Photograph courtesy Di Williams.

Succession and sustainability

I left my post in 2010 having planned for succession and the immediate sustainability of the labyrinth initiative. I had secured funding for the Veriditas training of three people (an Honorary Chaplain, a university administrator and a past student volunteer) to take on the future facilitation and development of the initiative. The Honorary Chaplain was created Labyrinth Chaplain, valuable in ensuring attention to the ongoing labyrinth initiative by someone external to the regular staff of the chaplaincy. This has enabled the initiative to continue to move forward. The University Estates and Buildings department has responsibility for care of the Edinburgh Labyrinth including essential maintenance work to the path.

Current practice and impact

The initiative continues to host and participate in notable events including the world-famous Edinburgh Festival. There are regular facilitated walks on the indoor canvas. Additional walks are held in exam time, and through collaborations with University-wide initiatives. These include Freshers' Week and the Innovative Learning Week, a programme of creative events that brings together staff, students and alumni from across the University. Student Resident Wardens are working to create outdoor grass and sand labyrinths as well as painted classical and medieval calico labyrinths small enough to be laid and walked in residential blocks as part of a Semester 1 health and well-being programme for students living on campus. New work on mindfulness and the labyrinth is beginning (Kendra, 2014). There is clearly considerable ownership of the concept within the University. This has included support from the University Principal, the Director of Student Support Services and many Student Association officers. Professional development for those working most closely with the labyrinth has included facilitator training with Veriditas for four members of staff, and I myself have moved on through advanced facilitator training to become Veriditas' Master Teacher for their work in the UK, Ireland and Europe.

The labyrinth initiative is making a positive contribution to the life of the University. It is a repository of information, skill and expertise in what looks to be a growth area of interest within HEIs. For all of that, perhaps the simplest and deepest success is the impact on the lives of those who have walked the path since 2001. Working with the labyrinth appears to further student engagement in reflective practice; support positive mental health; deepen spiritual journeying; and deliver collaborative, creative opportunities for those of all faiths and none, both home and international students.

▶ University of Bedfordshire, England

Interest and beginnings

The Revd Cassandra Howes at the University of Bedfordshire was first involved in creating a labyrinth at Woodbrooke Quaker Study Centre (Birmingham, England) in the 1980s, and later trained with Veriditas. After taking up her post at Bedfordshire, with encouragement from the Director of Student Services, she borrowed a seven-circuit classical canvas labyrinth and offered a drop-in facilitated walk with a wellbeing focus for a University staff conference.

A year later the labyrinth returned to the Bedford campus Freshers' Fair in the form of tins of baked beans. A group of students worked with Cassandra to create a fascinatingly visual pop-up classical labyrinth providing hundreds of tins for the local food bank. The baked bean labyrinth was sited in the Coffee Hub and drew parents, children and students to walk the path. It seized the imagination and was welcoming to those of all faiths and none, an enjoyable yet reflective space in the lives of those that walked it.

A new labyrinth

After a rejected capital bid to build a permanent labyrinth, the Dean of the Faculty of Education and Sport took up the proposal with senior management. The ensuing successful bid has resulted in the construction of a beautiful seven-circuit classical turf labyrinth at the heart of the campus, at a cost of around £12,000. The labyrinth was launched on 2 October 2014 *(as illustrated in Chapter 27 – eds)*. It offers a reflective space for students of Education: PGCE students walk the labyrinth for personal use but also have the possibility to introduce it into their work in schools. Current plans include team building with MBA students in Business Studies and gentle physical exercise within the Sports Department. Collaboration with stakeholders of Mental Health Awareness Week and other health and wellness initiatives is possible. Collaborations with city groups such as the Bedford Council of Faiths look to be significant developments in support of the multi-faith agenda of the University.

At this early stage, the initiative raises awareness of the Chaplaincy and makes evident its engagement in real and current agendas of the institution including internationalisation. It also promotes the inclusivity of contemporary multi-faith chaplaincy models. The initiative is set to make a difference to well-being and to aspects of teaching and learning in University life; it is already forging key partnerships and offers more for the future.

▷ Dublin City University, Ireland

Interest and beginnings

Fr Joe Jones was the chaplain to Dublin City University until 2014. While mentoring a student, he suggested that the student undertake a reflective practice to enhance his learning. The student did not understand what Joe meant by reflective practice. This prompted a desire in Joe to bring the reflective path of a labyrinth into the life of the University '*because*', he suggested, '*reflective practice is what it does best*'.

Joe first came across a labyrinth during a sabbatical in California in 1996, while on an intentional spiritual journey. He realised that the labyrinth walk helped him to reflect on his past and how he had come to this place in his life, and to be open and attend to what the future might hold.

Introducing the labyrinth to the University

Introducing the labyrinth has been a process of education over six years. Initially, Joe brought in a portable labyrinth for two to three weeks over exam time. It caused some interest within the staff and student bodies, and questioning as to what it was all about. Because Joe is a Catholic priest, assumptions were made that the labyrinth was an entirely religious tool. He has had to work hard to open up that closed and inaccurate sense of ownership. Staff and students now realise that the labyrinth is a welcome path for all and they have begun to understand the benefits of walking. The labyrinth is seen to be supportive for negotiating daily student life and experience as well as offering a path of reflection for the personal and spiritual journeys of staff and visitors to the University.

History and development of the initiative

The Chaplaincy has worked with a canvas labyrinth since 2012. It is open for walking once a week for three hours. Information about the labyrinth in the Interfaith Centre and an initial online video have helped create greater visibility for the initiative on campus (Dublin City University, 2014). The labyrinth is laid in the main foyer of the University Library for two weeks before exams and for the two week exam period. Library staff note that '*its very presence brings a calm atmosphere to the library*'.

The portable labyrinth is used in support of the health and well-being agenda in a striking collaborative venture between the Nursing School, the Counselling Department, the Health Office and the Chaplaincy. The labyrinth is laid out during Mental Health Awareness Weeks, and chaplains offer classes on walking the labyrinth and on wellbeing and spirituality.

In 2012 Joe and a postgraduate student trained as labyrinth facilitators with Veriditas; two more members of staff trained the following year when the University hosted an international Veriditas labyrinth facilitator training programme. In preparation for this event an 11-circuit Chartres style labyrinth was painted on the grass of one of the University gardens. This heightened interest across campus and laid the groundwork for the construction of a beautiful permanent pavement labyrinth on the same site. Funding for construction comprised two donations from the Dublin City University Educational Trust and additional fundraising events, with €37,000 raised over a period of 18 months.

Future development of the initiative

The immediate focus was on introducing the newly constructed permanent labyrinth into the life of the University. The Opening Ceremony in August 2014 was an inspiring launch of that process. The School of Nursing plans to encourage students to carry out their own labyrinth initiatives. Although there is generally much more appreciation of what the labyrinth can offer for those who walk its path, there is still considerable educative work to do and, as staff inevitably move on, succession planning for leadership will be crucial. However, to have a permanent labyrinth needing little maintenance is already a great boost to the longevity of the idea of walking, reflecting and discovering the support most of us need for finding our authentic path in life. This beautiful labyrinth will be '*an icon of welcome and solace for years to come, a path for those of all backgrounds and traditions to walk, and in so doing, discover what is needed for the next step*' (Williams, 2014). For a University Interfaith Centre and Chaplaincy it offers a unique tool for those of all faiths and none to walk alongside each other, a model for our human and community development.

▶ University of Victoria, British Columbia, Canada

Interest and beginnings

Henri Lock is the United Church Chaplain at the University of Victoria. When he arrived at the University his prior interest in the labyrinth fitted the ethos of the Multi-Faith Service. The Director of Student Services supported a labyrinth initiative which began in earnest in 2001 when ten students marked out and painted a 9.1 m diameter (30 ft) Chartres style canvas labyrinth to fit the campus chapel.

Current practice

The labyrinth is available each day for three weeks over exam time. Drop-in walks for de-stressing, meditation workshops and evening candlelit walks are also on offer. A yearly pilgrimage attracts people from the local community. Embedded in the well-being agenda of the institution, departments such as the Counselling Service recommend that students explore the labyrinth.

Succession and sustainability

One of the main challenges is maintaining chapel space to lay the labyrinth in an environment that has many demands on its schedule. To facilitate this, during labyrinth times sheets are laid over the labyrinth to accommodate Muslim prayers; Zen Buddhists move furniture to and fro for their meditation time. However, plans for redevelopment may afford the opportunity to build a classical turf labyrinth in a garden outside the new Chaplaincy Centre. This would greatly enhance accessibility and long-term sustainability for the enterprise. There are also plans for a small committee, perhaps in collaboration with other departments, to sustain the project for the future.

Successes and difference made to the institution

There is interest in walking the Victoria labyrinth each time the canvas is re-laid. The candlelit evenings are popular across the University, as are Advent and Lenten Quiet Days for an external group, the Contemplative Society. A national Symposium in Humanities held at the University requested the canvas labyrinth and encouraged the participants to engage with it. It was a showpiece of affirmation. Nonetheless, Henri suggests the main success is quite simply that walking the labyrinth *can be a transformational experience for people*.

The labyrinth is adding value to the student experience. It is a visible, repeated practice, which is now part of the fabric of the institution. It attracts positive press coverage, thus raising the public profile of the University. Its presence models the inclusive multi-faith agenda and supports the institutional development of internationalisation. It is an imaginative and significant tool for health and wellness.

▶ Gjøvik and Lillehammer University Colleges, Norway

Interest and beginnings

These two colleges, located in central eastern Norway, serve small rural towns. Gjøvik specialises in Health, Informatics, Media, Technology and Economy, and Management. Lillehammer has a social science profile.

The Revd Anne Anker Bolstad was introduced to the labyrinth whilst working as a Norwegian minister in Switzerland where she had previously facilitated walks for children and adults. She now leads the labyrinth initiatives in both institutions where she is Chaplain. Due to the good networks and relationships she had built up over the years it was not difficult to secure the support and interest of both institutions. Her annual chaplaincy budgets from both University Colleges and the Foundation for Student Service (Oppland County) fund the ongoing initiative.

In 2012 Anne commissioned a 9.1 m (30 ft) seven-circuit Chartres style medieval vinyl labyrinth, introducing it at the start of a semester in both colleges to mark the students' transition from school to university. It has been laid in indoor and outdoor venues. During 2013 she began to create colourful classical labyrinths out of scarves. Students who saw her doing this were attracted to the process and helped her finish the labyrinth. Now she is creating more scarf labyrinths and has found that this interactive process helps students over their initial inhibition about walking. Their engagement appears to lead to a more 'owned' and reflective walk.

Current practice

In Gjøvik the vinyl labyrinth and scarf labyrinths are used regularly for workshops, drop-in walks and meditation by staff and students. Anne has introduced the practice to students of Nursing (particularly the BA in Palliative Care) and to counselling students.

At Lillehammer, Anne has used the labyrinth on a regular basis in indoor venues. It is laid at the heart of the campus where almost all students pass by during the day. Here it is visible from four floors and students can 'walk' it with their finger as they look down on it. The labyrinth has been introduced to the Sports Department in a workshop where students learned to make their own scarf labyrinth and then walk it.

Future development of the initiative

This initiative has successfully launched use of the labyrinth in Higher Education in Norway. The creation of a silent space and path in the heart of a busy campus life is making an impact on students and staff. Much of the feedback notes the increased sense of well-being that walkers often experience. There has been positive local and national media coverage for both HEIs, including a national radio broadcast from the first outdoor labyrinth walk, with student interviews. Such publicity has increased appreciation and interest in the labyrinth as an invaluable means of support, reflection and well-being for the University Colleges.

Anne hopes to develop deeper links with the Sports Department in Lillehammer, with scope to build on work in mindfulness and positivity of mind amongst high level athletes. She sees the reflective, mindful, bodily attentive walking of the labyrinth as a valuable experience to offer Sports students. In the longer term there are aspirations for a permanent labyrinth.

Anne suggests the biggest challenge this labyrinth initiative faces is isolation and lack of labyrinth networks but looks to the newly blossoming interest in labyrinths across Norway as a source of future collaboration and support.

▶ University of Maryland, College Park, Maryland, USA

Interest and beginnings

After the tragic events of 9/11 there was a new interest in reflective spaces where students and staff could retreat to process their thoughts and feelings, sorrows and joys, despair and hope. In the spring of 2007 a group of staff and students met to plan how they might bring such a space into the heart of the University of Maryland. This first planning group, including the Lutheran Chaplain, the Revd Beth Platz, received generous funding from the Open Spaces Sacred Places Foundation (whose approach is explored further in Stoner and Rapp, 2008). This funding enabled creation of a Garden of Remembrance and Reflection close by the University Memorial Chapel. The Garden was opened in autumn 2010. It was designed by students of Landscape Architecture and includes an 11-circuit medieval stone labyrinth as well as quiet areas with benches, on-site journals to help people express their emotions and peaceful water features. Described as *'a deeply treasured gem on campus, a place with established ties to the community'*, there is a strong sense that the garden and labyrinth now have *'the potential to change the campus in ways both subtle and profound'* (University of Maryland, 2014a, 2014b).

Introducing the labyrinth to the University

The initiative has been highly collaborative from the start, fostering ownership through diverse areas of University interest and work. It is part of a beautiful garden which is a great asset to the University estate as well as to those students and staff who visit and walk the labyrinth. It offers the type of reflective space that is felt to be a real need on campus. The initiative meets several University agendas. It offers a supportive and creative space for students who might not seek other means of personal support. It is a wonderful wellness resource for the University community and the venue for an annual 9/11 service inclusive of diverse religious and spiritual traditions.

Current practice

The labyrinth is used for open walks and for workshops, quiet days and retreats such as the Dining Staff Wellness Day. It is used by children's groups as part of a summer camp. In common with most outdoor labyrinths, the labyrinth is open to all without a facilitator being present. The Memorial Chapel manages publicity and holds the schedule for organised walks. There are 25 volunteer labyrinth facilitators on the campus who represent many departments including the Health Department and Continuing Education. New volunteers are recruited and trained through the Department of Continuing Education.

Succession and sustainability

Here, as at any university with a constantly changing student population, there is an ongoing cycle of need for education and awareness raising about the labyrinth. A Graduate Assistant post has been secured which delivers programming for the initiative. To date the Department of Student Affairs, in which the Chaplaincy sits, manages sustainability issues. The Manager of the Memorial Chapel and environs ensures that programming continues.

Successes and difference made to the institution

The main success lies in the extent of use of the labyrinth. In the autumn of 2013 the Counseling Center undertook an informal survey of campus assets that most helped reduce stress. The labyrinth featured very highly in the resulting responses. Beth Platz's comment, '*it is in these times apart that you find out who you are*', rings true to the support the labyrinth appears to offer to those who need to 'decompress' and find their centre again. The labyrinth seems well embedded in the culture of the University, with student groups using the labyrinth for memorials and vigils as well as for individual walking.

The Washingtonian magazine featured an article about labyrinths, providing positive publicity for the University (Colbert, 2014). Events held for the tenth anniversary of 9/11 received good attention, while World Labyrinth Day walks offer international links around the globe (Labyrinth Society, 2014). The initiative has always been highly inclusive from first conception. Now many departments and student groups continue to work together to sustain that early sense of collaborative integrity.

▶ Conclusion

Labyrinths add value. They are beautiful and imaginative additions to our campuses; places to release the tensions of the day, to slow down and in the stillness attend to the inner life. They are places for the soul to expand and uncover an authentic path.

Labyrinth initiatives afford a creative contribution to current agendas: internationalisation and multi-faith reality; pastoral and spiritual support; reflective practice and contemplative learning; inter-disciplinary collaboration; and health and wellness.

When initiatives are founded on experienced, committed and inclusive leadership they can deliver unique opportunities in support of the student experience and the well-being of all who walk the path.

22 The Hero's Journey of first-generation and low-income students: On the quest for student success

Michelle Bigard

Michelle Bigard earned her MSW degree at Wilfrid Laurier University in Waterloo, Ontario, Canada. She worked within the Canadian mental health system at an inpatient trauma unit prior to her current position as Associate Director at Central Michigan University Counseling Center. There she provides personal counselling, and has taught in the Bachelor of Social Work programme.

Michelle has incorporated the labyrinth in her practice since the late 1990s. She is a certified Veriditas labyrinth facilitator, trained by Lauren Artress at Grace Cathedral. She continues to explore the use of the labyrinth with students in therapeutic and educational contexts.

▶ Introduction

The labyrinth path as a metaphor for one's life journey has inspired my work for over fifteen years. I was initially introduced to the labyrinth during a workshop with colleagues at the psychiatric facility at which I was employed as a social worker. Together, we created a canvas labyrinth, walked it for our own personal growth, and explored professional applications for our work with psychiatric patients. The labyrinth was embraced as a powerful therapeutic tool in spiritually sensitive clinical practice (Bigard, 2005). When I made a career change and entered the world of higher education as a counsellor, I explored the use of the labyrinth in counselling centre outreach efforts that target the campus community (Bigard, 2009).

Due to a recent organisational change, the Counseling Center where I am currently employed now serves students under the umbrella of the Enrolment and Student Services Division, which has a mandate to address student retention issues. In my search to understand the role counsellors and the labyrinth can play in student retention efforts, I have been gratefully informed by the pioneering and later work of Vincent Tinto (1975, 1993, 2012a, 2012b) and inspired by the current work of Habley, Bloom and Robbins (2012).

Retention generally refers to the student remaining in continuous full-time enrolment from point of matriculation to the completion of a degree at one Institution of Higher Education (IHE). The supporting metrics of re-enrolment and graduation rates reflect persistence and institutional success. Habley et al. (2012, p. 3) view this definition as narrow and institution-centric and propose a new paradigm that focuses on student success rather than institutional success. In the light of this perspective, student success is determined individually by the achievement of educational goals, regardless of the institution where the goals are achieved and the time it takes to achieve them. Student success is viewed not as a problem to be managed but rather the unifying focus that brings the campus community together to assist students in achieving their educational goals.

The shift in perspective to that of individual student success mirrors the unique journey of each walker on the labyrinth's path; it also reflects the student-focused, strength-based approach that informs our Counselling Center's scope of practice. As a social worker, with training grounded in the person-in-environment ecological framework, I appreciate Tinto's evolving Integration Model, which views retention as a complex interplay between individual student characteristics and institutional factors, including the obligation of IHEs to create a campus climate with policies and programmes that support academic achievement (Tinto, 2012b). Interventions designed to support individual student success therefore must be student centred within a supportive institutional framework.

Habley and colleagues present their readers with the following challenge: What would we do (or do differently) if the primary focus of retention initiatives was on individual student success rather than on increased institutional retention rates? (Habley et al. 2012, p. xvi). This question initiated a call to action for me and has influenced my work.

The Hero's Journey Labyrinth Workshop was developed to address the issues confronting first-generation and low-income students, a strength-based approach that fosters the development of student behaviours and characteristics necessary for student success within an institutional retention initiative. The archetype of the Hero within the reflective labyrinth process is a powerful metaphor for students to embrace on their journey to academic success. Campus administrators, faculty and staff are encouraged to view themselves as essential Allies in the Quest to support each student in their Hero's Journey, thus enhancing an institutional culture for student success. The term 'Hero' is understood here as including both male and female heroes.

▶ Student characteristics that contribute to persistence

While student retention is specific to a single IHE, student persistence relates to the individual: those who return to continue or to graduate at any IHE (National Student Clearinghouse, 2014, p. 7). Habley et al. (2012, pp. xiv–xv) identify three student-centred core conditions that are necessary for student success. Students must learn; must be able to identify and commit to a plan of study congruent with their interests and abilities; and must exhibit behaviours and develop personal characteristics that contribute to persistence, such as motivation, social engagement and self-regulation. Others have also stressed self-efficacy as a personal characteristic determinate of academic success. Bandura (1993) defines self-efficacy as one's belief that one is able to reach a goal, thus fostering the performance of tasks to ensure a successful outcome. Self-efficacy has been positively associated with persistence (Wright, Jenkins-Guarinieri and Murdock, 2013), academic adjustment and performance (van Dinther, Dochy and Segers, 2011); coping (Devonport and Lane, 2006); decision making (Petrovich, 2004); and finding meaning and purpose in one's life (Dewitz, Woolsey and Walsh, 2009). Duckworth, Peterson, Matthews and Kelly (2007, p. 1087) identify the long-term effort required to meet personal goals as grit: 'Grit entails working strenuously through challenges and maintaining effort and interest over years despite failure, adversity and plateaus in the process'. It is these characteristics that the Hero's Journey Labyrinth Workshops endeavoured to foster in first-generation and low-income students.

▶ First-generation and low-income student characteristics

At Central Michigan University (CMU), the Hero's Journey Labyrinth Workshops are offered as part of a range of grant-funded initiatives serving first-generation and low-income students and those from communities under-represented in post-secondary education. Student retention initiatives include:

▶ The Student Transition Enrichment Program (for students transferring in from community colleges).
▶ Pathways to Academic Student Success (for first-generation, low-income, first-year students).

▶ The McNair Scholar Program (preparing first-generation and low-income undergraduate students for progression to graduation school and PhD completion).

By promoting systemic change within the educational setting, successful strategies are institutionalised to benefit all students at the institution. First-generation students are those who come from families in which neither parent achieved post-secondary education (Davis, 2010, p. 2). Davis asserts that first-generation status is as important as minority status and should be integrated into the institutional culture (p. 15). In the USA, first-generation students face a number of challenges impeding academic success. They disproportionately come from ethnic and racial minority groups with lower levels of academic preparation. They tend to be older, are less likely to receive familial financial support and have obligations such as family and work that limit academic and social engagement (Engle and Tinto 2008, p. 3).

In a major study of equity in Higher Education in the USA (Cahalan and Perna, 2015), Perna reports (p. 39) that students from low-income families are far less likely to attend college and to successfully graduate. In that context, she highlights that:

> College outcomes are generally lower for Blacks and Hispanics than for Whites and Asians (as a group), lower for students who are the first in their families to attend college than for students whose parents attained a college degree, and lower for older students than for their younger counterparts. (Perna, 2015, p. 40)

Davis (2010, p. 29) observes that first-generation college students are unfamiliar with what it means to be a college student. These are students for whom college attendance was not part of family expectations; they are breaking, rather than continuing, family traditions. College attendance therefore entails a significant and intimidating cultural transition (Irlbeck, Adams, Akers, Burris and Jones, 2014; Housel, 2012). Unlike traditional students, who may view themselves as 'I am an 18 year old American who attends college', first-generation students' identity development is more complicated as the questions 'Who am I?' and 'Why am I going to college?' are seen as two different planes of inquiry. First-generation students are apt to experience the 'imposter phenomenon', believing they do not belong at the institution or that somehow they are taking the place of someone who is more worthy of attendance (Davis, 2010, pp. 48–49). Transition to college for such students tends to be more problematic depending on the degree to which the home environment differs from the college environment (Lippincott and German, 2007, p. 91).

Straddling both home and academic cultures can be difficult. First-generation students require an extended acclimatisation process that provides personal validation for academic goals, and contact with academic and student services that is welcoming in its approach and is actively initiated by faculty and student support staff (Darling and Smith, 2007, pp. 206–209).

▷ Student transition and transformation through rites of passage

The transformational process from a high school senior to a college first-year student and beyond to graduation is under-researched and yet is of critical importance, both for students and for IHEs. Traditional cultures have recognised and responded to this crucial time for youth with rituals of rites of passage. These rites facilitated a successful emergence into adulthood with a clear sense of identity, responsibility and belonging, thus serving the larger community and assuring continuity of the collective purpose. In higher education, faculty and student service personnel are in a position to help students with the transition to the institution and academic life, and to foster self-development as unique individuals. Students in IHEs come from diverse familial, cultural and racial backgrounds and communities. To facilitate student success IHEs must also work to build cultural competency skills and to develop an affirming and inclusive culture on campus (Dumas-Hines, Cochrane and Williams, 2001, p. 439; Habley, Bloom and Robbins, 2012).

The Hero myth

The need for rites of passage may be universal. In the present day, it is still possible to draw on stories from mythology and create relevant and meaningful rituals to facilitate and honour rites of passage, through the language of imagery and through story-telling, which through the ages has served as a primary teaching tool (Oldfield, 1996; Pink, 2006).

In his study of myths from around the world, Joseph Campbell (1949) discovered that the Hero myth is present everywhere, following the same ancient story line, a 'Monomyth' retold in infinite variations. Campbell's thinking is consonant with Jung's (1964) archetypes, universal symbols that reflect the human experience. Christopher Vogler (1992) introduced this template to the film world after its first application to the Star Wars

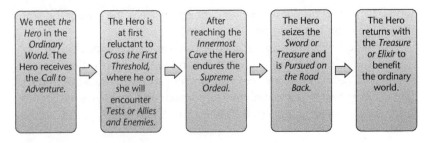

Figure 22.1 Stages of the Hero's Journey.

movie and it has been a guiding principle in movie making ever since: once students have been introduced to the concept, they find it immediately recognisable in popular culture. The stages of the Hero's Journey can be summarised as shown in Figure 22.1.

The Hero's Journey Labyrinth Workshop

The development of the Hero's Journey Labyrinth Workshop was informed and inspired by the universal need for story, meaning and the personal and collective acknowledgement of one's development and experiences. The Hero's Journey provides an imaginary roadmap students can utilise to understand the new landscapes they encounter in college life. Walking the labyrinth provides an opportunity to reflect on and integrate new perspectives. Examples of fictitious heroes (both male and female) are discussed and illustrated with film clips, such as those contained in the montage *The Hero's Journey in Film* (Morgan, 2014). Through identification with the Hero, students are challenged to view life as a Quest and consider how they are currently 'answering the call' in their own lives.

The workshops provide a flexible framework which can be modified to meet the needs of a particular group or time period. At CMU, the workshops were delivered as a single intervention through a half day programme format.

Stages of the Hero's Journey

Students experience the Hero's Journey in a personal way through walking the labyrinth. Both the Hero's Journey and Labyrinth Walk guidelines are presented to the students as five parallel stages (drawing on Oldfield, 1996 and Artress, 2006a) as shown in Table 22.1.

Table 22.1 Stages of the Hero's Journey and Labyrinth Walk

The Hero's Journey	Labyrinth Walk
The Call	Remember
Acceptance of the Call	Release
Trials and Allies	Receive
Return	Return
Ritual	Reflect

Examples are given to parallel the lives of the students.

1. The Call: The student's life changes in some way, for example gradua-tion from high school, and thus change in a new direction is necessary.
2. Acceptance of the Call: The student finds him/herself at university and must decide whether or not to actively choose to answer the call and engage in ways to foster academic success and a positive life transition. Some students have enrolled in university without actually 'answering the call' and are left unmotivated and disengaged.
3. Trials and Allies: Inevitable to academic pursuits and personal growth are challenges along the way that may be predictable and/or surpris-ing, common and/or unique to the individual student. There also will be allies for support, although they may be disguised in new forms to be sought out, accepted and utilised. Student success and character development depends on how the student perceives these challenges and utilises resources to face them. When the institution does not pro-vide the allies and supports needed, the student is left inadequately equipped to meet challenges.
4. Return: In facing challenges and meeting goals, a shift in identity occurs. Self-efficacy is enhanced and meaning is derived from strug-gles. The student thus emerges anew, with gifts, honed from experi-ence, to contribute to the world.
5. Ritual: In this final stage, others (parents, faculty and staff, peers, soci-ety) recognise and celebrate the growth and mastery of the student and welcome, value and utilise their contributions to the community.

Stages of walking the labyrinth

The labyrinth's reflective path is offered as complementary to, and an embodiment of, the Hero's Journey. The stages of walking the labyrinth, as modified from Artress (2006a) to align with the stages of the Hero's Journey, are presented as follows.

1. Remember: The student enters the labyrinth with an intention, a focus to consider during the walk. This correlates with the call of the Hero's Journey. The student may reflect on what is occurring in their life and what changes might be necessary.
2. Release: The student fully accepts the call to walk the labyrinth and is encouraged to honour their own pace and set their own goals. As the student begins to focus on the present moment, physical sensations, imagery, thoughts and emotions are noted and viewed through the lens of the metaphor.
3. Receive: The student may identify and consider trials and allies along the way and, through the lens of the metaphor, consider insights on how to face challenges or access support. This gives personal meaning to the struggle, enhances self-efficacy and rewards persistence.
4. Return: The student reflects on lessons learned in the labyrinth and how to apply and integrate them in their life. The student is challenged to use this new knowledge in the service of self and others.
5. Reflect: After the walk, students reflect on their experience, give expression through artwork and journaling, and share with other walkers. The discussion facilitates the awareness of the universality of their struggles, and, in helping others face challenges in new ways, develops deeper interpersonal connections. Like the welcoming celebration for the returning hero, students are given a needed audience to validate their transition and accomplishments, and accept the gifts that each individual has to offer.

Labyrinth intentions

Labyrinth 'intentions' are the student's chosen focus for the walk. Such intentions invariably address themes related to the student behaviours and characteristics needed for persistence, identified earlier in this chapter. These include motivation; social engagement and relationships; self-regulation (coping styles, stress management, dealing with feelings); self-efficacy; grit, and meaning and purpose in life. The workshop facilitator may suggest intentions for the walk or the student may choose his or her own intention. Ultimately, the student makes the decision; as each walk is unique, what metaphors emerge and insights reflected on will be individual to each student.

It is a powerful experience for students to address one another before the walk and state their intention. For example: *I am on a Quest to end the semester with good grades and peace of mind. My intention for the walk is to look at how I am dealing with my high level of stress.'* The facilitator may use inquiries or prompts, driven by student need, to facilitate reflection after the walk. These are purely suggestions for the student to consider, as the process is organic in nature, driven by individual and group needs and dynamics. These contributions can be used to explore stages of the journey in relation to the intention theme. For example: *'You identified feeling annoyed when distracted during your walk on the labyrinth. How might that parallel your experience as you prepare for the stress of upcoming exams?'* The student may realise that he or she is distracted by roommates and residence floor activities and decide to study in the library to avoid distractions.

▶ Discussion

Student-centric

The Hero's Journey Labyrinth Workshop is student-centric. It validates the journeys of all students: traditional residential students, first-generation and low-income students, older students, veterans, students who identify as having minority status, the part time, slowed down, transferred, stopped out, re-matriculated and swirling students that grace our campuses.[1] Paralleling the assurance that there is no right or wrong way to walk a labyrinth, student success is determined individually by the meeting of academic and personal goals, not by one universal institutional measure. Just as in walking a labyrinth, where one approaches the centre long before actually entering it, the road to academic achievement is non-linear and has many variations.

Metaphors on the labyrinth

Through walking the labyrinth, students are introduced to the concept of viewing their lives through the lens of metaphor, enabling the development of self-reflection and problem solving. This wide, 'soft focused' view enables the consideration of self and others more objectively and less judgmentally (Artress, 2006a). It also provides a safe context to discuss personal experiences. When students feel too vulnerable to disclose personal information, one can talk metaphorically about attempts to find a pace that feels right on the walk, rather than feel pressured to keep up or to slow down to accommodate others.

Addressing student transition and transformation

The Hero's Journey Labyrinth Workshops address the transition and transformation of first-generation and low-income student transition issues in a way that does not pathologise. Whilst acknowledging the constraints and struggles that one may experience as a first-generation and low-income student, it is powerfully motivating to view one's life as a Quest, on a specific Call to Adventure, that predicts both challenge and support, and promises the reward of personal transformation and contribution to others.

The workshops provide a vehicle to address student transition and transformation. Students reflect on what they have left behind and what they want to take with them. Students often report that their faith is a constant on their journey. Some may identify key family and friends who are supportive and those they may need to leave behind to accomplish their goals. Students also process the issues of straddling different worlds. Families may not understand what the students are engrossed in, and students, experiencing change and growth, worry about the impact of such change in their relationships with their families. When they have not yet made new significant relationships, they feel lonely and in limbo. The context of the labyrinth walk provides safety to process these issues.

Fostering student characteristics necessary for persistence

Viewing oneself as on a Quest and trusting in the process builds self-efficacy. By building on experience, learning from and being encouraged by others along the way and coping with inherent stresses, the student's belief in their ability to accomplish goals is fortified. Grit is encouraged and rewarded as the student overcomes challenges and equips themselves for the long road ahead. It also fosters the seeking of individual purpose in life, identifying reasons for action and striving to find meaning along and for the journey. This strengthens motivation as the student identifies what drives and sustains the Quest. Reflecting on encounters with Allies fosters effective use of support; walking the path with others gives assurance that one is not alone on the journey. This enhances social engagement. Taking the time to walk the labyrinth to reflect, think, feel, problem solve and share, enhances coping and builds self-regulation.

Self as hero on a quest

Themes come to the surface, related to students' understanding of their own Quest. Students may feel they are not sure if they want to be at university, or question if they are enrolled for themselves or for their family's ambitions. They may lack academic focus or struggle with motivation. The labyrinth walk provides a structure to contemplate and discuss these issues. One student discovered a new-found appreciation of the individuality of each Quest and call to adventure. Although she was clear regarding her call to study for a PhD, she judged her sister as 'opting out' for choosing not to attend college. She was able to honour both of their Quests as valid and important. Another felt the family pressure to be the first to earn a college education. As she walked the labyrinth, she was able to shift her perspective and view the achievement of a degree as a gift she can give her family rather than a burden to carry. Still another shared her growing dissatisfaction at college and her loss of sense of self. Through her encounter with the labyrinth, she gained a dynamically different perspective, as shown in this anonymised feedback:

> I thought about all the things I have done to get my third year of undergraduate research and education. I gave myself permission to remember why I'm here and why I need to do this for myself. I owe it to myself to be more confident in my potential and use that to drive me forward to a new level. And I set a goal not to lose myself in the process and never forget who I am and what I need to be happy.

Another salient theme is that of seeking, recognising, accepting and utilising support. Students are encouraged to reflect on their attitude to support: embracing it or hesitating to accept it. They playfully relate to the main character in the movie *Shrek* (Adamson and Jenson, 2001). On his Quest, Shrek was initially annoyed by his chief ally, Donkey, and only reluctantly tolerated him. Donkey proved to be a trusted, loyal and necessary part of Shrek's journey and transformation.

Archetype for campus culture

Habley et al. (2012) advocate the adoption of a new paradigm of student success, an opportunity to unify the campus community through *'a fully student centered approach that seeks to meet the unique needs and goals of individual students'* (p. 366). This approach is also a key strand in Harper's (2012) research that explores the characteristics of Black male student success (pp. 21–22). They remind us that all members of the campus community make up the proverbial village necessary for student success.

The creation of an institutional culture of student success requires the positive commitment of all campus constituencies, and, ideally, each campus member. Habley et al. (2012, p. 105) refer to this as the *'power of one'*. Each person on campus – the professor who teaches a class, the housekeeper who enquires about the most recent exam, the upper-level student who models the discipline of staying up late to study rather than to party, the professional staff person who answers questions about registering for classes or navigating financial aid applications – each has the potential to make a positive impact and support student success.

The Hero's Journey provides a universal template to facilitate an institutional culture of student success. When we view ourselves as an Ally in another's Quest, our work takes on a heroic quality. The embodiment of the Hero's Journey archetype enhances the campus ethos and can thus be incorporated as a unifying theme to inspire the proverbial campus village. Such themes serve as anchors for incoming students, provide consistency to campus experiences, enhance deep bonds between members and *'draw students into their learning experiences by moving beyond activities that engage the body and mind to make connections with the students' spirit and heart'* (Kezar, 2007, p. 14).

▶ Conclusion

My quest to understand student retention issues has been significantly influenced by the work of Habley, Bloom and Robbins, who in turn have built on the many other writers, administrators, professors, researchers, clinicians and student service personnel who preceded them. The shift from student retention to student success, and from a problem focus to an opportunity perspective, provided the paradigm to perceive students' college experience through the lens of the Hero's Journey.

My appreciation for the versatility of the labyrinth in therapeutic and educational settings continues to grow. In the Hero's Journey Labyrinth Workshops, the labyrinth provides a vehicle for students to actively experience themselves as a Hero on their own Quest. Inherently student-focused, the labyrinth acts as a mirror that reflects where students are in their own journey towards personal growth and academic success. Processing these experiences with each other not only anchors insights and new resolves that support persistence behaviours, but also builds a sense of community and illustrates beautifully that their path and inherent struggles are universal and that they are not alone.

I discovered in the development and facilitation of the workshops and in writing this chapter, how powerful the archetype of Hero is for students; how powerful the archetype of Ally is for myself and others. We are all called to be Allies on one another's journey. As I ponder the question 'What will I do differently if the desired outcome was student success?' I find myself with a new quest. How does an institution adopt the Hero's Journey as an overarching construct to inspire its mission? How do all members of the campus community, from administrators, faculty and staff, to volunteers, mentors and students embrace the call to be an Ally in another's quest? Another journey has just begun.

Note

1 The term 'swirling student' denotes those who make strategic use of transferable credits, attending a number of IHEs to achieve their degree. For discussion of this approach and its impact on IHEs, see (for example) Bailey, 2003; Clemetsen, Furbeck and Moore, 2013.

23 Creating a space for play: A counsellor's perspective

Maggie Yaxley Smith

Maggie Yaxley Smith is an accredited Senior Registered Practitioner of the British Association for Counselling and Psychotherapy. She was instrumental in developing the Counselling Service at the University of Kent, retiring recently as Head of Service. In over 30 years as a counsellor, she has worked for Relate, for a women's refuge and in workplaces including prisons. Maggie retired in order to focus on writing about counselling: her first book, *Finding Love in the Looking Glass: A Book of Counselling Case Stories* was published in 2014 (London: Karnac).

▶ A new labyrinth project

In 2007, my colleague Jan Sellers came to see me with a new idea, inspired by the University of Edinburgh's labyrinth project (Fox, 2007): might we introduce this kind of work at the University of Kent? In our roles – myself as Head of the Counselling Service, Jan leading the Student Learning Advisory Service – we had many common values and a shared passion for working with students to support them in developing towards their full potential. Though we were both interested in creativity and innovation, I had initial misgivings: how might such an 'alternative' type of project fit into a conventional higher education establishment? A visit to the University of Edinburgh (including a member of the Counselling team) fired us with enthusiasm. A new project was underway with an informal, cross-campus team convinced of the creative, educational and well-being benefits that a labyrinth would bring to the University. With a new canvas labyrinth, we took part in initial training and offered our first walks. In May 2008, two counsellors and two student learning advisers joined an international group, training as Veriditas labyrinth facilitators with Dr Lauren Artress in Chartres.

The highlight of this experience was an evening with the cathedral to ourselves. We took part in a meditation and then, by candlelight, walked through the ancient crypt and up a flight of steps. We were faced with the spectacle of the medieval labyrinth of worn stone, lit by hundreds of candles flickering with an energy that seemed to fill the cathedral. That walk could not have given us a better experience of how powerful a labyrinth can be; it was a potent beginning to our new role as facilitators. On the last day of our training, we each chose a focus for our labyrinth work. I chose play. At the time, I did not quite know how that would manifest itself in the work I was doing.

In the summer of 2008, the Canterbury Labyrinth was built at the University, set into the beautiful hillside above Canterbury. Since then, two more members of the counselling team, along with other colleagues, have undertaken training; to support this work across two campuses, a second canvas labyrinth was purchased.

▷ Creating a place for reflection and play

Looking back over the past eight years, I can see that for me, the labyrinth's greatest appeal is the opportunity it gives us to take space and time to look within (Smith, 2010). Each person may use it in a variety of different ways and that is its strength. I have enjoyed both reflection and play and have seen others do the same. I recently watched a group of overseas students using the centre of the labyrinth as a focal point for a treasure hunt that was in reality a game of trust. Blind-folded 'contestants' walked alone, taking directions to find the path into the centre. Here they met a 'seeing' student, who led them out of the labyrinth by holding hands. I have seen students and staff meditating beside and inside the labyrinth and groups of students playing music in the centre. It provides a focal point, a meeting place, a community space.

In the labyrinth at Chartres Cathedral, which I visit at least twice a year, I watched two brothers aged about eight and ten, one holding firmly to the other's rucksack. They ran around the labyrinth path, intently focussed on what they were doing, laughing out loud with the joy of it. A young girl danced her way round the labyrinth, stopping at the centre to sit for a while, in a world of her own. In the Canterbury Labyrinth, a small determined boy cycled around the path, round and round until he could do it without veering off. As a child I can remember working to get something 'just right'; I would spend hours perfecting whatever it was that week, that month. These are the challenges that we set ourselves through play; later in our lives they become our way of working effectively, growing skills, to do the best we can (Donaldson, 1990, 1993):

> Play is a drive toward exploration, fantasy, adventure, experimentation, creativity, innovation. This drive might be grouped with mastery,

since play can contribute to mastery by serving as a means of trying out new skills and strategies. Play implies self-expression through exploration, experimentation and invention. In its most developed forms, play merges with mastery to become creative work: the innovation that depends on disciplined technique necessary to express artistic, scientific, and economic intuitions with beauty and elegance. (Donaldson, 1990, p. 59)

Figure 23.1 shows a beach labyrinth created by two playful artists on the east coast of England.[1] Fred Donaldson's reflection on play refers mainly to children and people playing with others but is equally true of our relationship with ourselves. The labyrinth enables us to spend prime time developing that important relationship.

At the beginning of life babies play and discover the wonder and joy of life; they know how to be happy. Each of us carries that secret knowledge, waiting to be rediscovered. What seems to get in our way as adults is the way we interpret and manage our time and how we prioritise our activities, often in a driven way; and what so often drives us as adults is anxiety and stress. A little stress is useful and helpful to us but when it becomes too much we seem to lose the balance of work and play and can lose touch

Figure 23.1 Mablethorpe Labyrinth (outdoor drawing), Lincolnshire, UK.
Art and photograph by GRRR.

with our creativity and our imagination. Play naturally evolves into creativity in adults with the resultant psychological health that comes from the confidence and enjoyment of expressing creative skills. This needs openness, flexibility, commitment and a dynamic energy which can be damaged by performance anxiety. Time in the labyrinth enables us to take time out from being driven. It can restore us to ourselves and ground us to find our own pace through a focus within. Making this connection can enable us to centre ourselves and restore balance.

How often are we truly alive to the sensations of the present moment once we reach adulthood? We can spend too much time reliving the past or planning the future. That ability that we have as children, to be in the moment, can restore our energy. Even the brief time of a walk in a labyrinth can enable us to remember what it is like to be free of attachments, programming, expectations and other things that can drive us further away from our true selves.

I believe it is vital for us to allow that space inside ourselves which fuels our imagination and enables us to grow and develop whatever gifts and skills we have. Perhaps a university campus is an especially good place for a tool to enable us to do this. I once worked with a brilliant research scientist who insisted that his medical discoveries and research were the result of 90 per cent time spent playing piano, golf, reflecting and walking and 10 per cent time spent reading, discussing ideas with colleagues and working in the laboratory.

The idea of opening up a space inside us for reflection is a familiar scenario for a counsellor. One of the most important requirements of counselling is that it provides a relaxing and safe space where we are able to express feelings and thoughts and take time to connect with ourselves in order to develop a higher degree of self-awareness. This, in turn, helps us to make healthier and more positive choices in our lives. In the counselling process, there is a sense of being held, both by the counsellor and by a safe space. In the labyrinth there is a sense of being held by the quiet, the rhythm of walking, the ability to find our own pace, and a comparable sense of being contained and held by a well-defined space. In feedback from a facilitated labyrinth walk, I have heard people comment that they have found answers to questions that have been confusing them; found a way through creative blocks; found a sense of calm and courage to face an exam that they were particularly afraid of. Some people have even imagined walking with loved ones who have died and have found peace in that. One of my clients, encouraged to use a finger labyrinth (printed on paper) to help combat homesickness, found it unusually difficult at first to follow the narrow path by hand. She reported:

My first two or three attempts resulted in frustration because I couldn't complete the entire trail. I followed my counsellor's instructions and thought of something I wanted to give up or get rid of when I entered the labyrinth, and when I got to the middle, I asked for what I needed ... I asked to let go of my fear and to gain confidence and understanding. As hard as I tried, though, I couldn't get through the entire labyrinth in one shot ... It eventually dawned on me that I needed a game plan; the only way I have ever been successful at overcoming challenges both big and small has been when I first developed a proper strategy. For this paper labyrinth I decided the pen was truly mightier than anything else. Instead of simply tracing the path with my finger, I traced it with a pen and got through the entire path in one attempt! My experience with the labyrinth reminded me of who I am, what I want to accomplish and why it is important to me that I see my goals through to the end. It also reminded me that I am not a quitter, but am someone who is capable of adapting to new circumstances and rising to new challenges.

(Anonymised personal communication, reproduced with permission)

▶ Seeing within

At different universities, counselling teams have developed their own approaches to labyrinth work including a growing interest in labyrinth walks for collaborative well-being (Walker, 2011; University of the Arts London, 2013; University of Worcester, 2015). Others offer labyrinth walks before or during the exam period. I outline below some of the ways in which I and other university counsellors have used the labyrinth.

'*Seeing within changes one's outer vision*' (Pearce, 1992, p. xv). I have worked with both students and staff who, after walking in the labyrinth between counselling sessions, came back to the counselling with clarity about what they wanted their priorities to be: in the counselling, in a relationship, in their career path. Taking the time out to have a conversation with yourself is easier in the space and silence of a labyrinth. One client came to a session with a poem written down that had come whole to them in their labyrinth walk. After the walk, they sat beside the labyrinth capturing the poem on paper. This gave them confidence about their abilities to express themselves and was the beginning of many pieces of writing.

At the 'Open Walks' held on the indoor, canvas labyrinth, it was good to see several students who identified themselves as being on the Autism–Asperger spectrum, and who were obviously enjoying the walk. One student found it so calming, because of the unchanging predictability of the 'one path in and one path out', that he brought his mother along to experience it with him.

I facilitated a lunchtime staff relaxation course, which included a walk in the labyrinth; one counsellor used the labyrinth as part of a mindfulness course, a useful part of personal and professional development for staff working on campus. Another counsellor and myself ran a short session for students leaving university, which included a walk in the labyrinth. They spent time reflecting on what they had gained from their university experience. At the end of the workshop, we placed some colourful stones in the centre of the labyrinth. The students walked into the centre and chose a stone that most reflected the strength that they felt they would be taking out into the world with them. Five years on, I still see one of those students, now living and working in Canterbury, walking the labyrinth and using it as part of a meditative practice that she has continued since leaving university.

After a day of counselling, I would occasionally walk in the labyrinth before going home, especially if I was particularly moved by the pain expressed by a client I had been working with. At the centre of the labyrinth, I would imagine holding that client up and simply wish them to be surrounded in a cocoon of love. In this way, I was able to 'let them go' in that space and free myself.

▶ Conclusion

Bringing a labyrinth to the University of Kent worked effectively for a wide variety of people on campus; it has also become an excellent community resource for Canterbury. The interest that has grown and developed from that original article about Di Williams' work (Fox, 2007) has blossomed into books, labyrinths, facilitators and international connections that continue to build on the work of Veriditas and the Labyrinth Society. I end with the words of Heather Walker (p. 23, 2011), who writes about the positive future of the labyrinth at the University for the Creative Arts:

> It is being asked whether health and wellbeing could provide the overarching theme for pastoral services, with more emphasis on preventative interventions, which enable students to develop great resilience ... I have no doubt that the labyrinth, which gives an opportunity to centre ourselves, re-focus, connect with our inner resources, slow ourselves down, meditate or pray – whichever language you choose to use – could be part of a wider approach to student wellbeing.

Note

1 GRRR is a mischievously led art and design collaboration between Glen Robinson and Rebecca Robinson. As part of their practice they draw labyrinths on beaches for personal reflection and relaxation. Making a labyrinth and walking its path is a chance to coalesce with nature and attain coherence with our surroundings, while at the same time resonating with an ancient symbol; a token of the unbounded potential of everything. The ephemeral quality of using materials and building in an environment where nature will 'take back' is an interesting process and working in public creates an opportunity to discuss the symbol's design and origin with passers by, who are encouraged to walk the path and discover its purpose.

Glen Robinson is a senior lecturer in Design for Publishing at Norwich University of the Arts, UK; his scholarly work includes the study of labyrinths. For more on GRRR's work, visit www.grrr.org.uk

24 Moving Memory: A Dance–Theatre collaboration

Jayne Thompson

Jayne Thompson and Sian Stevenson are both Senior Lecturers in Drama at the University of Kent. Having co-founded StevensonThompson and established the Moving Memory female dance group in 2010, they became the Moving Memory Dance Theatre Company in 2015 to celebrate the fifth anniversary producing work with the Moving Memory group. Sian is artistic director, and Jayne is an associate and performer in the new company.

Moving Memory signified the end of a very special journey that took place between October 2009 and June 2010, and which culminated in two unique performances on 14 June at the University of Kent in Canterbury, England. The first took place just after three o'clock on the Canterbury Labyrinth and the second, some six hours later, as dusk was falling, on a specially laid, temporary, sand labyrinth sited outside the School of Arts Jarman Building.

For Sian Stevenson and myself the journey began in the autumn of 2009 when we became aware of an opportunity to participate in the *Slipstream* commission, a Creative Campus Initiative (CCI) sponsored by the University of Kent in 2010. Launched earlier in the same year, CCI was one of the many programmes to make up the Cultural Olympiad taking place throughout the United Kingdom in the four-year period leading up to the London 2012 Olympic Games. Involving thirteen universities in the South East of England the emphasis was on engaging:

> leading artists to collaborate with students, academics and local communities; create and present high quality new artworks and cultural events inspired by the Olympic and Paralympic Games; and raise the aspirations, skills and economic potential of young people by exploring relationships between sport and the arts in innovative ways. (Arts Council England, 2011, p. 32)

Figure 24.1 Sian Stevenson and Jayne Thompson dance on the Canterbury Labyrinth in this publicity photograph for the dance performance, *Moving Memory.*

Photograph by Denise Twomey, courtesy StevensonThompson, Mike Keeling Smith and Jon Bidston.

As academics, we were struck by the very obvious synergy between the CCI brief above and our own teaching practice in 'applied theatre' – a somewhat contentious 'umbrella' term for a theatre form which, broadly speaking, derives from and includes types of community, educational and developmental theatre/performance. At Kent, Applied Theatre was at the time a fourth year specialism in the MDrama programme. As well as drawing on our respective professional interests and teaching experience working with students and local communities, the *Slipstream* commission enabled us to embark on a long discussed artistic collaboration stemming from a shared interest in dance, movement based performance and an eagerness to work with older performers.

   In the light of our own teaching and research interests the term 'applied' sat uneasily with us. We both saw in this commission the perfect opportunity to interrogate some of the assumptions and problems inherent in the 'applied' form. We were, therefore, particularly keen to document and explore our artistic practice as it developed to ensure that we achieved the collaborative and participatory creative approach we were aiming for. At the same time we were looking to address very specifically who, in the final analysis, the work was being made for: the creative artist or the participant? Turning the conventional lecturer/student relationship on its head, innovation came in the form of the collaborative working relationship and 'mutual learning triangle' we hoped to establish with the students who had volunteered to join the project:

> If all participants are part of this triangle then mutual learning can take place and the work can have a profound and positive impact. Because the triangle is mutual, it allows for teacher, artist and pupil to work in different modes, so the artist can work as the teacher, the teacher as pupil and the pupil as artist. The model is an ideal ... (Haddon, 2006, p. 186)

Of particular significance was our decision to establish a formal, professional and contractual working relationship with two final year students who were due to graduate later in the year. This marked a new and exciting development in the existing pre-professional emphasis nurtured in the final year of study and specialism in what was then the four-year MDrama programme.

In our proposal we envisaged a project in which '... *collaboratively, artists, musicians, film makers and participants will develop a short piece of performance*' (Stevenson and Thompson, 2010). Creative inspiration for the underlying concept came initially from images of the torch relay and track events. The notion of a 'relay', in which stories, memories and experiences drawn from a local community of elders might be represented in choreographed movement and passed on, was the central idea shaping the process and structure of the project as a whole.

The Canterbury Labyrinth was in many respects an obvious venue for a performance inspired by the Olympics and Paralympics. An initiative developed by Jan Sellers and designed by Jeff Saward, the labyrinth is situated near Eliot College (one of the University colleges) from where, in the distance, the spectator has a spectacular view of the Cathedral and city roof line. As the University website states (University of Kent, 2015), '*its design is medieval, and unusually for labyrinths it also has a circle path enclosing the space*'. Described as a '*work of art*' and neatly set into the hill leading down to Canterbury, the labyrinth – and its surrounding slopes – provides a natural stage and seating area: an ideal performance venue. The sporting associations which had inspired the initial concept resonated once again as we spent time on the labyrinth exploring the ways in which the paths might inspire, dictate, complement or, indeed, restrict the potential choreography for the performance. The labyrinth offered itself as an evocative performance site where memories, stories and experience represented in physical gesture and movement might be relayed across, around and beyond the space.

Having been commissioned, the first stage in the development of the project involved a series of ballroom dancing 'social occasions' held weekly in a local residential home providing care for older people with dementia. Sue Howell and Adrian Gilmartin were the two final-year students with whom we went on to collaborate closely throughout the project. At this stage, they took the lead as experienced ballroom dancers, teaching basic dance steps to the participants including ourselves and a number of other drama students. In an attempt to transform the 'everyday' space of the rear conservatory and momentarily transport the participants somewhere 'other', a hasty costume change into colourful and flamboyant outfits took place prior to the start of each session.

During these occasions, conversations, stories and recollections started to emerge. Sometimes triggered by particular music, and sometimes by costume, the residents, visiting family members and staff responded in the immediacy of the moment, sharing their thoughts with us. Many of the conversations were recorded at the time, and these have been invaluable, serving as a powerful reminder of all the individuals involved, and the relationships forged during the time we were privileged to have spent dancing together. Of particular significance was the relationship we established with one elderly family visitor who summoned the energy to get up and dance with us, patiently teaching steps and techniques he recalled from his favourite dance, the Valetta Waltz. His recollections of dance halls, learning to dance and meeting his future wife were to become the inspiration for a new performance. Extracts from the recordings would later be edited and incorporated into the accompanying soundscape. Film maker Andrew Palmer attended on two occasions to capture footage of the dancing. Although initially planned purely for evaluation purposes, this footage was later carefully edited into a short film which provided a powerful backdrop to the evening performance in June 2010. The film was subsequently reworked to be used again in the 'sequel' performances of *Moving On* (2011) and *Moving on Moving* (2012 and 2013). The social occasions in the residential home continued until the end of May 2010 when routines changed and the Friday afternoons became occupied with other activities.

Throughout the Spring of 2010 we began to envisage a final performance which would feature a group of older female performers *'for whom the moving body would become the "vessel" through which these earlier stories and memories would be conveyed'* (StevensonThompson, 2010). The project entered the next stage of development when we circulated publicity in the Whitstable and Herne Bay areas of Kent, inviting women aged 50 and upwards to participate. Six women responded, aged between 49 and 77 years. Uncertain of what the work entailed, but interested in the concept, the women committed one evening a week to rehearsals in a studio space at the University, and thus their journey began.

Conscious that the group comprised 'untrained' performers, unfamiliar with the type of creative process we were involved in, a key aspect of our methodology started to emerge as we made the decision that in the workshops Sian would ostensibly become the main artistic director whilst I would integrate myself as one of the group of performers – an 'intermediary'. (Our approach is discussed more fully in 'Dancing With Difference: Moving Towards A New Aesthetics' [Shaughnessy, 2015]). Very quickly the initial tensions and anxieties in the group, few of whom had known each other at the first meeting, began to dissolve. An ensemble of artists, student collaborators and performers started to emerge, three of whom shared their recollections of the experience with me in personal correspondence (cited below with permission).

Sian's delicate choreography drew on the earlier workshops in the residential home. Responding to the memories, physical gestures and dancing movements witnessed over the weeks she translated these into a series of sequences, small steps, touches of the hand and gentle strokes along the arm. The music was carefully chosen for harmony, lyric and choreographic potential: *Have you Met Miss Jones* (Rodgers and Hart, 1937), *They Can't Take That Away From Me* (Gershwin and Gershwin, 1937), *A Nightingale Sang in Berkeley Square* (Sherwin and Maschwitz, 1937) and *Beyond the Sea* (Trenet and Lawrence, 1946).

As the days grew longer and the air became warmer, rehearsals moved outside and the performance started to take shape. Sensitive to the context in which the choreography had emerged, there was a poignancy in the way performers inhabited the labyrinth. Sue Howell recalls being particularly moved by the naturalness of the women's movement the first time she witnessed a rehearsal: '*It was as if their bodies remembered how to move through the labyrinth.*'

Val Sanders, one of the participants in this early performance, and now a stalwart member of what has since become the Moving Memory Company, recalls her first impression of the Canterbury Labyrinth as '*a beautiful structure in a perfect setting*'. Overcoming an initial nervousness about moving beyond the boundaries of the formal structure, Val Sanders' experience of performing on the labyrinth was again a '*beautiful*' one in which she felt the '*circles worked with us, guiding us*' achieving a harmony and balance between celebration, the immediacy of the moment and a reverence for the formal pathways.

The idea to create a second performance on a contrasting, quasi-industrial site, outside the School of Arts building, became a reality after a bespoke labyrinth-making session run by labyrinth designer Jeff Saward. For drama students Adrian Gilmartin and Sue Howell, both specialising in scenic design in their final year of study, learning to create a labyrinth was particularly significant. Already familiar with the site, Adrian had drawn on the labyrinth as a source of inspiration for an earlier assessment. Combining the use of mirrors with film of his journey along the paths, he had created an installation in which he presented 'a continuous, repetitive journey' which conceptually addressed the notion of infinity. Delighted to be working with labyrinths once more, Adrian introduced Sue to the qualities and possibilities offered by the labyrinth, an experience that she recalls '*definitely focused the mind*'. In the final weeks leading up to the performance, we all worked together to create a number of temporary chalk labyrinths on which to rehearse. Adrian and Sue, who had by this stage taken on much of the responsibility for the staging and technical elements, led us in a choreographed movement as, together, we circled the concrete plaza laying our chalked lines.

For Adrian, the creation of the final sand labyrinth left him with: '*... a definite sense of accomplishment at completing the "build" which was similar to how I felt when walking the labyrinth outside Eliot [College]*'. Sue Howell remembers creating the sand labyrinth in performative terms:

> as if the steps we took drawing and creating the labyrinth were part of the dance/performance. I remember a feeling of realisation when the labyrinth was completed, as I suddenly saw how the performance would merge in and blend so well.

The first performance of *Moving Memory* took place at the Canterbury Labyrinth on 14 June, a sunny albeit extremely windy afternoon. In the surrounding grasses were sited eight dressed sculptures whose gowns billowed in the wind. They formed part of the scenography in recognition of the absent participants from the residential home. The audience were seated on the grass verges; there was a celebratory atmosphere as the seven-piece band played forties swing and jazz music. Progressively, from behind the trees in the distance, the performers emerged. Slowly floating past the sculptures, they made their way towards the labyrinth, gently stepping on to the path as jazz musician Peter Cook began to sing.

The second performance was particularly memorable for very different reasons. Earlier in the day it was all hands on deck as the temporary labyrinth was traced out and sand laid. The freestanding sculptures now looked down from the steel encased fire escape. The live band occupied one corner of the plaza. As dusk fell, a delicate back-drop of filmed footage appeared on the side of the building. Hands and feet slowly moved to the tempo of the Valetta Waltz, feet in slippers, feet in ballroom dancing shoes, feet in pink stilettos. A pink ball gown, an image projected on the wall, slowly found its way into the present as performers began their journey down the stairs and on to the labyrinth. The present and presence merged with the absent and absence, movements became motifs, as performers journeyed through and across the sand labyrinth, which by morning had blown away leaving only traces of what had been.

Moving Memory signified the end of one journey and the start of another. Pedagogically, the project informed our practice-led teaching, and, indeed, was instrumental in the development of our teaching methodology and vision for a new third-year module 'Applied Performance', which commenced in the autumn of 2010. The professional collaboration between university lecturer and student established in 2009 still continues in our artistic practice.

StevensonThompson became a performance company in 2010, and to date some 40 undergraduates and returning alumni have been involved in stage management; lighting design; compilation and production of soundscapes; technical operation; creative production; dramaturgy and performance.

Whilst the performances have not since been repeated, the journey continues, and four years later the legacy of these two early performances still echoes in our current work. In *Moving On* (2011) and *Moving On Moving* (2012, 2013), spirals of salt were delicately laid across the stage and performers moved slowly across the space as if treading the paths of the labyrinth once again.

25 Case study: A library labyrinth and reflective garden

Ellen Schultz, Michelle Filkins and Jennifer DeJonghe

Dr Ellen Schultz is Nursing Professor Emerita of Metropolitan State University, Minnesota and is Chair of the Board of Directors for the American Holistic Nurses Credentialing Corporation. Michelle Filkins and Jennifer DeJonghe are Professors and Librarians at the same university: their work to create the David Barton Labyrinth and Reflective Garden was recognised in 2013 by the Minnesota Library Association with the 'Above and Beyond Award' for services to the library community.

The labyrinth at Metropolitan State University was installed to facilitate and encourage wellness, inspire creative thinking, provide opportunities for integration within the curriculum and foster strong community connections. The garden and community labyrinth was named to honour David Barton, the founding Dean of the Library, who passed away in 2012. It is a symbol of his love of gardening and his commitment to the University and community partnerships.

Located next to the Library, the David Barton Labyrinth is surrounded by gardens and trees (Figure 25.1). It was constructed in 2013 using the 'Circle of Peace', a seven-circuit pattern designed by Lisa Gidlow Moriarty. It was inspired by an eleventh-century manuscript drawing from Abingdon Abbey, Oxfordshire, England, but this contemporary design features elements of both the classical and the medieval labyrinth. Its quadrants and circling paths offer a pattern with wide appeal and support our community's spiritual practices and symbols including the cross, medicine wheel and four elements of creation (earth; water; fire; air). The versatility of the pattern is important for the multiple uses of a university labyrinth.

A gently curving brick path leads the way from the sidewalk to the labyrinth, including several engraved pavers that invite the community to walk the path with statements such as 'Welcome. The labyrinth belongs to all who walk it.' It is seen as an extension of the Library building and as another way to enrich the lives and minds of learners.

Figure 25.1 The David Barton Labyrinth.

Photograph by Allison Holdhusen, permission to publish granted by Metropolitan State University, St. Paul, MN, USA.

A resource for the University and community, the labyrinth is used for reflection, health promotion, recreation and self-care activities. Community participation is encouraged and the labyrinth has been walked by school groups, the campus Walkabout programme, St. Paul public library programmes and for World Labyrinth Day. The labyrinth is also used in the university curriculum by disciplines such as Nursing, Psychology and Information Studies. For example, nursing students are encouraged to use the labyrinth as part of their self-care activities and to experience the importance of rituals. Community psychology students study the positive impact of community gardens and green spaces.

The Metropolitan State University Library, working with a university-wide Labyrinth Committee assumes responsibility for labyrinth programmes and maintenance. Two wooden finger labyrinths, for students to 'walk' by hand, are also available within the Library.

Visit: www.metrostate.edu/msweb/resources/library/labyrinth.html

26 Enterprise and Arts: Creative interventions with the labyrinth

Alex Irving

After graduating, Alex Irving worked in professional theatre in UK repertories and on national tours as a stage manager, joining the BBC in 1985. Here she gained extensive experience in a range of production roles in network television, working as a writer and presenter, researcher, director and associate producer on fiction, factual and entertainment programmes.

Alex joined Liverpool John Moores University, UK, in 1998. Her research interest focuses on methodologies, techniques, tools and practices capable of unlocking and enhancing creative competencies.

▶ Introduction

This chapter explores the creative use of labyrinths in a variety of commercial and public sector settings as part of the work of my home university. Since 2008 I have presented and applied labyrinths in a wide range of learning and teaching contexts, both as a media lecturer and as a creative facilitator for external clients. These opportunities and installations have varied from professional development programmes for international businesses, to community-based arts events as part of the University's commitment to public engagement, involving media students in installation and event management.

For a number of years alongside my teaching role, I worked as a creative facilitator in *The Automatic*, the University's innovation laboratory. This operated on a commercial basis from 2006 to 2014 with external clients from private and public sectors, employing a diverse range of creative interventions and teaching methods. Bespoke facilitation sessions were designed to meet the needs of each organisation; it was in this context that I first introduced the labyrinth as a possible addition to *The Automatic's* repertoire of creative tools and techniques. In subsequent years the labyrinth became an increasing focus of what *The Automatic* offered to clients either as part of, or as the defining character of, sessions.

Facilitating the labyrinth in a commercially driven environment in which clients paid substantial sums of money for sessions, and expected tangible outcomes, carried significant reputational risks for me and for the University, not least because there were no labyrinth facilitators in the business environment whom I could consult. I had no prior model on which to base this work, but was convinced that the experience of a labyrinth walk is capable of providing insights for anyone who is open to its possibilities. I am therefore deeply indebted to the business development team at *The Automatic* for their support and encouragement. The subsequent success and popularity of the labyrinth interventions, with clients ranging from small and medium enterprise (SME) business leaders to international corporate high flyers, is a tribute to that team.

▶ Case study 1: Business sector

For several years Liverpool University's Management School delivered a ten-month Creative Leadership course called LEAD (Leading Enterprise and Development) with two annual intakes of up to 25 SME owners. On the final day of the course a whole day of reflection was scheduled for the cohort, in which to evaluate and share their individual learning experiences, and identify next steps in applying their learning to their own business and their lives. The design and delivery of this Reflection Day was contracted out by the Management School to *The Automatic* at the nearby Liverpool John Moores University (LJMU); approximately 150 SME owners took part over a three-year period.

It was when designing this Reflection Day that the idea first emerged to use the labyrinth as part of our repertoire. The key challenge was to present the labyrinth to entrepreneurs expecting outcomes that would justify expenditure and time out from their business. It was all too easy to imagine some resistance when asking participants to remove shoes and walk a medieval pattern on a floor cloth as a way of processing their learning at the end of a course.

We anticipated our entrepreneurs would arrive in a heightened state of mind where brain rhythms are pulsing rapidly, known as 'beta' brainwaves, a state of consciousness which is associated with peak concentration, heightened alertness, visual acuity, cognitive activity and the ability to think more critically (Haas, 2003, p. 9). Yet beta state is out of step with the visceral experience of walking a labyrinth, often likened to a walking meditation and more attuned to slower, relaxed 'alpha' brainwave rhythms that enhance the overall awareness of one's self. A study in 1966 by Dr A. Kasamatsu and Dr T. Hirai of the University of Tokyo used the electroencephalogram (EEG) to measure changes in the electrical activity of the brain during Zen meditation. Their research discovered an increasing predominance of regular alpha waves during meditation by Zen monks (Kasamatsu and Hirai, cited in Benson, 2000). Subsequent studies have confirmed their findings (for example, Lagopoulos et al., 2009); this suggests alpha is a more receptive state of consciousness for walking a labyrinth path.

With this in mind we considered morning activities for the LEAD Reflection Day that would prepare participants for a labyrinth walk at lunchtime; we sought an approach that might be capable of modulating and shifting brainwave frequency from dominant rapid beta brainwaves to the slower alpha brainwaves. However, only guided meditation was documented as capable of such a shift of consciousness, which did not seem appropriate in this commercial context. Instead we employed metaphor-based activities, large-scale sketches representing natural landscapes, including physical challenges in those landscapes, for participants to visualise their ten-month learning journey.

At lunchtime the course group was split into two groups. Each group was given an introduction to the labyrinth and its benefits for reflection, followed by a facilitated walk on our 9.75 m (32 ft) hand-painted canvas labyrinth. The metaphorical theme of the learning journey on the LEAD programme was integrated into the walk. Walking into the centre represented the past ten months of learning. The centre was the 'here and now' on the final day of the course, a time to pause, look back, relish, absorb, celebrate new friends. The journey *out* of the labyrinth became an opportunity to consider 'next steps': what they would be taking back from the LEAD programme into their own business, their own lives.

Over a three-year period, six Reflection Days in *The Automatic* provided a colourful collection of anecdotal data about resistances, breakthroughs, joy, sadness, humanity, friendship and alliances. A few such stories (anonymised) are given below. Collectively these insights inspired us to offer the labyrinth to other business clients.

1. Pauline arrived late for the labyrinth walk after getting lost, and had only ten minutes to walk the labyrinth. She began her walk, but a pre-arranged change in the music, a signal to her colleagues to finish their walk, came as a surprise:

   > I kicked off my shoes and ran on. I walked at a steady pace ... Then the next track of music came on which was very quick tempo ... my walk got faster and faster, my colleagues started to leave to attend the next session.
   >
   > Suddenly I realised that I had surrendered my wish – to walk the labyrinth at my own reflective 'me time' pace – to the demands

of the day's timed schedule, to the fast music and to the pressure of colleagues wanting me to hurry up. So I stopped. It was then I realised that this is how my life is. The demands of my clients, my employees, my children and other family members, my account-ants leave no time for me and I need to address this from now on.

2. Richard, the owner of a large building company, said that he wished he had known about the labyrinth months before when his workforce were struggling to process the death of a colleague in a site accident. He spoke sadly about how he had tried to find ways to help them grieve; he was sure that the labyrinth could have offered them some support and peace.

3. Some participants have ended the day by sharing their intention to close their business and do something different; they cited the laby-rinth walk as the moment of realisation or certainty that the business simply made them unhappy. David announced that he was going to sell his business and use the funds to start a new child poverty initiative. He was overwhelmed by joy at realising this was his next step, which he openly attributed to walking the labyrinth.

These stories show the power of an intervention that enables very deep reflection; the experience may be transformational. Due to the nature of the programme, it is not possible to know if (or to what extent) these par-ticipants acted on their insights, but each of them achieved a clarity of insight that they took very seriously, giving them considerable cause for thought in relation to their working lives.

▷ Case study 2: International manufacturing company

Most clients commissioned bespoke sessions at *The Automatic*, but some requested sessions off-site. One international company asked us to design and deliver a career reflection session at their own conference venue. The conference was organised to foster the career paths of 28 pre-selected international staff from bases all around Europe, identified as potential sen-ior managers of the future. Our brief was to design and facilitate a reflective session on the penultimate evening of the four-day conference to enable delegates to reflect upon and process career opportunities presented dur-ing the conference and identify preferred career options.

We set the scene with brief pictorial explanations of labyrinths from their ancient origins in all of the seven countries from which attendees originated, to demonstrate the international ownership of this remarkable archetype. Activities then enabled individuals to draw labyrinths outside in the venue's lamp-lit grounds where they chalked their own small designs in groups of four on the forecourt. Their many labyrinths were playfully chalked and walked, with experiences shared across the whole cohort on a cold November evening.

Meanwhile, the support team was lighting a large candlelit labyrinth in a spacious conference room ready for the attendees to walk together. This aesthetic finale to the session was a welcome surprise to the attendees who eagerly walked the seven-path labyrinth accompanied by classical music. Many delegates returned to walk the labyrinth again, and we were able to stay overnight to be available for further facilitated walks. We learnt much about facilitating the labyrinth experience in commercial settings and installing labyrinths off-site in different physical spaces.

A subsequent testimonial confirmed that the session had pleased the client, and included an anecdote about participants' closing presentations to company executives. One delegate had presented a career plan in the graphic form of a labyrinth, incorporating many twists and turns to represent elements in their future ambitions and career path.

▶ Stress in the workplace

Having discussed labyrinth initiatives with small and medium business enterprises and with a major international company, I will make brief reference here to a national initiative with the potential for use in many workplaces. In wider recognition of the commercial benefits of the labyrinth, LJMU was involved in a series of business events organised by De-Stress UK and supported by the Stress Management Society and ACAS (the British government's Advisory, Conciliation and Arbitration Service). These events demonstrated various applications of labyrinths in managing stress in the workplace and were held in diverse settings; hosts included a major marketing company, a Chamber of Commerce and two (public) De-Stress Shows. The events were designed to help businesses address their loss of productivity now that the top cause of long-term sickness absence is known to be stress. A short online video about the use of labyrinths in dealing with stress was produced by De-Stress to support these events (Irving, 2012).

▶ Case study 3: Tourism/Heritage sector

Following the growing popularity of the University's labyrinth installations at public festivals in Liverpool (such as Liverpool Light Night), we were invited to install an interactive public labyrinth at the World Museum Liverpool in

May 2012.[1] The University welcomed this as part of its public engagement policy. To attract a family audience we created a weekend labyrinth event, with a Wishing Tree in the centre of the labyrinth on which children could hang their own wish written on a leaf.

The five-path labyrinth was installed using masking tape in a dimly lit space with projected images of nature on the back wall and mood music creating a meditational atmosphere. Families poured in to write wishes, walk the labyrinth and hang leaves on the wishing tree. Many then sat for hours around the space observing others and surrendering to its calm meditational atmosphere.

Testimonials from the management of the World Museum commented on the huge footfall success of this labyrinth installation (1800 people over two days) and its economic impact on the whole Museum over the weekend.

Student volunteers from the Media Production Programme assisted the event by facilitating at the 'wish leaf' craft tables. Students became intrigued and engaged by the labyrinth in ways not witnessed during previous, in-house curriculum activities. The openness of children and parents to experience the 'magic' of a labyrinth awakened the imagination of students. As volunteers, in an extra-curricular activity and playing a guiding and leadership role, they were able to engage and learn the value of creative interventions in a way that many were hesitant to do within the classroom.

This has proved a valuable learning opportunity for me, as well as for the students, in finding new ways to foster and enhance the development of creativity. The students themselves, without further prompting, chose to reflect; to experiment; to play; to learn for themselves; to find for themselves what was meaningful.

▶ Conclusion

It has been illuminating to discover how business people in many different roles have been willing to explore the labyrinth and relate it to their current situation and life journey. The depth of reflection shown has often been profound; for some, the experience has the potential to be life-changing. The University's pioneering initiative, *The Automatic*, has enabled an exciting opportunity to share knowledge and expertise and to contribute to the local and national economy.

Through work with the World Museum we have not only created and shared a beautiful, interactive public artefact, but have also enabled the Museum to benefit through an event that involved very significant levels of public participation, generating both income and positive publicity. The benefit to the University was evident, supporting University policy through enhancing and demonstrating commitment to public engagement.

Through these events, commercial and public, the University has taken creative risks that have been amply rewarded. What of the students? As volunteers and film crew, working alongside me to install large-scale labyrinths for public events, these media students have discovered a joy in informal and extra-curricular learning. Failure and risk-taking became, simply, part of the process of working together and learning something new; curiosity and playfulness became part of their work, illustrating characteristics of the truly creative mind-set that is an essential quality for media students of today and the professionals that they will become. And that, I suggest, is teaching and learning at its best.

Note

1 *The labyrinth created for Liverpool LightNight in 2011 is illustrated in Chapter 3 – eds.*

Part IV: Moving Forward

Poems from the Labyrinth

Leaving

April, 2012

Walking the labyrinth alone,
one last time before leaving.
The path was cream, the pattern a deep green.

Above me on the wall, lilies of light
floated and wavered, as if sunshine drifted
wind–blown, from the high window.

All of the walls ahead were in my mind:
if I could see my way clear
there was nothing I could not do.

Look, said the path, sometimes
it does not have to be difficult.
Sometimes the path is strewn with rose petals,
sometimes the way is easy.

Walking this coil, I unwound myself
out from a steep unending climb
to a garden path, an open gate.
Birdsong.

I walked from kairos back to chronos
feet more firmly planted

Ahead, on any path I take,
the faint scent of wild roses.

Jan Sellers

27 Finding resources for labyrinth projects

Kimberly Lowelle Saward

Kimberly Saward, PhD, has worked as an educator and clinician in the field of psychology. She has been working with labyrinths since 1995, and currently serves as co-director of *Labyrinthos* and associate editor of *Caerdroia*. She is the author of *Ariadne's Thread: Legends of the Labyrinth*, a psycho-spiritual study of labyrinth folk practices worldwide. A founding member of The Labyrinth Society, Kimberly served as its president from 2003–08 and on the board of directors for 13 years. Kimberly travels widely with her husband Jeff Saward, researching labyrinths and leading small tours to sacred sites and labyrinth locations.

▶ Introduction

With technological advances in today's world, the current wave of labyrinth enthusiasm has gained momentum with unexpected and unprecedented speed. The internet has had a dramatic impact on the size and scope of the worldwide labyrinth community, matched by advances in publishing and communications. This is exciting, but can also feel overwhelming to someone seeking a solid foundation in labyrinth history and practices, or who wants to source or create a labyrinth.

A small group of people came together in 1998 to set up a worldwide society for those working with and interested in labyrinths. The Labyrinth Society (TLS) was formed with the explicit goal of providing a way to stay connected and support each other in taking the labyrinth into the wider community. The Labyrinth Society remains a key source for information about all things labyrinthine. Their extensive website provides up-to-date information on all aspects of labyrinth interest and is therefore a logical place to begin any research into the subject.

▷ **Labyrinth facts and history**

It is important to understand that the field of labyrinth history, development and distribution is an evolving one; there are still many questions to be answered. Myths and misinformation abound and are frequently quoted and re-quoted. A critical mind is necessary as you explore the many versions of labyrinth history and origins. Historian Jeff Saward has spent a lifetime researching the history, development and distribution of the labyrinth symbol. In 2000, we founded Labyrinthos together. The Labyrinthos website is another good starting place, a source of accurate information, providing a collection of articles on all manner of labyrinth interests as well as an extensive photo archive.

Other people and organisations also provide websites that present interesting and important information and research. As websites come and go, with maintenance and updates often dictated by the energy and funding that are available, we suggest you peruse the links on the TLS and Labyrinthos websites for up-to-date listings as a way to begin your online research.

Many books on the subject of labyrinths have been published in recent years, but here, too, it is important to find those which contain solid factual information in regard to the story of labyrinths. The following is a shortlist of titles that will provide a solid foundation for further understanding of the labyrinth, its history and its potential for the twenty-first century, and will serve as a source of inspiration and guidance for future projects. Though some are out of print, library and second-hand copies remain available.

Publications

▷ *Mazes and Labyrinths: A General Account of their History and Developments* by W.H. Matthews (1922, reprinted 1970), a charming introduction to the subject even though it was written nearly a century ago.

▷ *Through the Labyrinth* by Hermann Kern, a classic in the field: this is the foundation stone of modern research and interpretation of the subject. Originally published in German in 1982, this revised and updated English edition was published in 2000.

▷ *Magical Paths: Labyrinths and Mazes in the 21st Century* by Jeff Saward (2002), an illustrated study of the modern labyrinth revival.

▷ *Labyrinths and Mazes: The Definitive Guide to Ancient and Modern Traditions,* Jeff Saward (2003a), an extensively illustrated guide to labyrinths worldwide, their history, distribution and usage. (There is also an American (2003b) edition entitled *Labyrinths and Mazes: A Complete Guide to Magical Paths of the World.*)

▷ *The Unending Mystery: A Journey through Labyrinths and Mazes* by David Willis McCullough (2004), an accessible exploration of the history of labyrinths and mazes from prehistory to modern times.

▷ *Caerdroia: The Journal of Mazes and Labyrinths* published annually by Labyrinthos since 1980, presenting current research and theories.

▷ Labyrinth usage

Labyrinth training, workshops, events

Experienced labyrinth teachers and enthusiasts schedule retreats, workshops and special events which may be of interest. There is a general calendar of events on the TLS website, and several Facebook pages and websites list current offerings around the world. TLS also hosts an annual conference each autumn where enthusiasts of all levels of experience, network and share information and ideas. Through their regional network, local events, meetings and walks are organised in some areas.

The California-based organization, Veriditas, has been providing facilitation training for over 20 years, offering in-depth information on how to offer labyrinth walks, workshops and retreats, including both initial and advanced training. Their two-day facilitation training and workshops are now offered in various places around the world, including (on a regular basis) Canada, France, the UK and the USA. These events have also been held (in recent years) in Argentina, Australia and Ireland. In the UK, facilitator training has been held since 2010 and is gathering momentum. With an emphasis on spiritual and community development, they have a holistic and inclusive approach; their short courses are open to people of all faiths and none, and are of increasing interest to those in education, counselling, health and other fields, who wish to use labyrinths in their own professional contexts.

Locating labyrinths

Launched in 2004 as a joint endeavour between Veriditas and TLS, the World-Wide Labyrinth Locator is an online database of labyrinths with (at the time of writing) over 4700 examples from around the world. Categorised by setting and type, labyrinths are uploaded by their owners or interested parties to broaden public knowledge and so that they can (if open to the public) be found, visited and enjoyed by others.

▶ Finding resources

Many individuals and organisations offer labyrinth goods and services. As these, too, come and go, a good start for your search is the Labyrinth Market on the TLS website. The Market contains details and links to the websites of providers conveniently grouped into categories to ease your search.

Finger labyrinths

Many people find that using a finger labyrinth can be as beneficial as walking a larger labyrinth. Finger labyrinths can be as simple as a paper sheet with a printed design, can be made with fabric or can be purchased in plastic or wood. The wooden versions can be a bit weighty, but are often beautiful and extremely tactile. These are particularly popular as an accompaniment to a labyrinth walk (in many contexts) or for use in the study, home or office. For classroom settings and for situations where multiple use at one time is needed, consider laminated paper or plastic versions, which can be easily cleaned and sterilised. The TLS Labyrinth Market lists manufacturers who can supply various types of finger labyrinths; within the UK, two organisations, Pilgrim Paths and Rowan, are both current sources of quality finger labyrinths.

Figures 27.2 to 27.5, at the end of this chapter, can be copied and enlarged for classroom use.

Outdoors, finger labyrinths may be provided in many forms including wood, metal, plastic and stone: here, durability and low maintenance are the key factors.

Canvas labyrinths

Canvas labyrinths have become very popular in recent years, and are a viable way of bringing a walkable labyrinth into a community. These portable labyrinths use robust, sail or backdrop canvas and can be purchased as bespoke art pieces, or can be created by the communities where they will be used. Some labyrinth designers offer a service wherein they will source and prepare the canvas and draw the design which can then be painted by a group of local enthusiasts. See the TLS Labyrinth Market for listings of fabric labyrinth suppliers. Some universities have used lighter weight fabric successfully, with a group hand-painting the design; however, these are suitable only for walking, whereas heavy canvas can accommodate those who wish to run or dance. The lighter the fabric in weight, the more care needs to be taken that it does not crease and offer trip hazards during events.

It is worth bearing in mind that international shipping of expensive or heavy goods can incur considerable freight costs and additional customs charges. The vagaries of differing tax regimes in various countries and states may have a substantial impact on what would appear to be a bargain price. There may be smaller, local service providers nearer to home. An internet search with an appropriate geographic filter will help you to find local sources.

Labyrinth construction

A number of people around the world have specialised in designing and building custom labyrinths suitable for both public and private settings. Labyrinths can vary widely in design, material and cost. For major constructions, it would be wise to consult a professional who has experience with the specific complexities of labyrinth designs. A good labyrinth design utilises geometry that is both elegant and meaningful. Note that there are an amazing number of labyrinth designs to choose from, and that certain designs may be better suited to your project and setting than others – a labyrinth consultant should be able to discuss a variety of options. It is also worth noting that a general architectural degree does not necessarily qualify someone to design a labyrinth, so before hiring a designer you will want to ascertain that a thorough and practical knowledge of labyrinth design and geometry can be demonstrated.

Figure 27.1 Performers celebrate the launch of the University of Bedfordshire's new labyrinth in 2014.

Photograph by David Stubbs, courtesy University of Bedfordshire and Divadlo Theatre.

Opportunities and connections

1. Is there a key university policy or strategy (perhaps more than one) that might be supported by a labyrinth initiative?
2. Is there a significant event that might be celebrated, or commemorated, with a new labyrinth?
3. Is there a new phase of building or new campus landscape initiative, where a labyrinth might be included in the design?
4. Is there a forthcoming funding opportunity, perhaps linked to one of the points above?
5. Look for allies who may have fresh insights into such opportunities – perhaps in different departments, in development teams or beyond your own campus?

From vision to reality

6. Consider options. Some universities have installed permanent, fully paved labyrinths; some have focussed on 'soft' landscape materials; some have combined these two approaches and there is growing interest in use of local/regional/recycled materials (for contrasting examples, see Adelaide (2014), Drew (2014) and Edinburgh (2015)).
7. Is there a suitable location, perhaps an ideal view? Consider access; quietness; sense of privacy; potential multiple uses of space and, above all, the question of sufficient space for your project.
8. Might a permanent indoor labyrinth be appropriate? These are (as yet) rare in universities: see the WWLL for examples in other settings.
9. Budget for accessibility, seating, signage, publicity and launch events as well as initial construction; anticipate questions about ongoing maintenance.
10. If space is an issue, consider partnerships (a labyrinth in a local park; a regeneration initiative [Stoner and Rapp, 2008] or even a roof garden [American Psychological Association, 2008]). A labyrinth as ephemeral as light and shadow is possible, but only suitable for a few people to walk at one time (Buchanan, 2007; deSoto, 2003).

Ideas for interesting, creative and beautiful labyrinths can be found online (as well as in earlier chapters of this book). TLS provides instructions and ideas for creative labyrinth construction; the Labyrinth Market on the same site also provides links to designers and builders. Additionally, labyrinth builder Robert Ferré has generously published detailed instructions for creating labyrinths out of various materials. These publications and a variety of free resources are listed on his website (see below).

Publications on construction of labyrinths

▷ *Canvas Labyrinths: Construction Manual* by Robert Ferré (2014). A step-by-step guide with detailed instructions for making a portable canvas labyrinth, this book also addresses numerous issues to do with all phases of portable labyrinth construction.

▷ *Labyrinths for the Spirit* by Jim Buchanan (2007). Written by a labyrinth builder, this book is full of sound practical advice for creating permanent and temporary labyrinths.

▷ Online, Jan Sellers reflects on critical factors influencing Kent's labyrinth project (2008) and Diane Rudebock and Susan Worden share their labyrinth proposal (2012).

Audio-visual resources

DVDs

▷ The Labyrinth Society, 2011: *Labyrinths for our Time*. A 15-minute, introductory DVD showing labyrinths in many different contexts. www.labyrinthsociety.org

▷ Veriditas, 2001: *Rediscovering the Labyrinth: A walking meditation*. A 30-minute DVD with Lauren Artress (founder of Veriditas), exploring spiritual and personal journeys with the labyrinth, including interviews related to health and well-being, arts and career change. www.veriditas.org

▷ Fran Grace, 2008: *A Semester Within: Exploring meditation*. 50-minute DVD about academic courses based in the University of Redlands' 'contemplative classroom'. www.innerpathway.com.

YouTube

▷ Speech at opening of Dublin City University Labyrinth, Ireland, 2014 (Di Williams).
www.youtube.com/watch?v=m1VqUtHAbWQ (Part 1)
www.youtube.com/watch?v=XNmuvjQLbWQ (Part 2)

▷ Stress management, from the De-Stress Show, Liverpool, UK, 2012 (Alex Irving). www.youtube.com/watch?v=O4erZiuSjAo

▷ Mindfulness and labyrinth walking, at the University of Edinburgh, Scotland, 2014 (Lucy Kendra). www.youtube.com/watch?v=g6ObCu7FoRA

▷ An entertaining few minutes: a student YouTube submission on *why I love the University of Kent*, 2008. www.youtube.com/watch?v=9vSOjOJdwjl.

Other films online

▶ Introduction to the labyrinth, at the University of Kent, Canterbury, UK; use of labyrinth in teaching and learning, accessibility and use of finger labyrinths (James and Brookfield, 2014: two brief film interviews with Jan Sellers). www.engagingimagination.com/labyrinths.

Websites

▶ Engaging Imagination: www.engagingimagination.com/labyrinths
▶ Inner Pathways: www.innerpathways.com
▶ Labyrinth Enterprises: www.labyrinth-enterprises.com
▶ Labyrinth Locator: www.labyrinthlocator.org
▶ Labyrinthos: www.labyrinthos.net
▶ Pilgrim Paths: www.pilgrimpaths.co.uk
▶ Rowan: www.rowanhumberstone.co.uk
▶ The Labyrinth Society: www.labyrinthsociety.org
▶ Veriditas: www.veriditas.org

▶ **The path ahead**

The labyrinth symbol has existed – and evolved – for thousands of years. Its history and distribution illustrate how the basic concept has been continually adopted and adapted as the construction techniques have been learned by subsequent generations of practitioners and applied to new contexts. In this modern day and age, traditional and internet research coupled with networking within existing labyrinth communities can support you in your work. Do not be afraid to experiment and create your own uses. While serious work can and does happen on the labyrinth, most find that its meandering pathways also provide a source for renewal and creativity.

Figure 27.2 Classical labyrinth, the seven-circuit, ancient pattern found around the world.

Drawing by Jeff Saward, Labyrinthos.

Figure 27.3 Medieval labyrinth, the pattern of the Julian's Bower Labyrinth, Alkborough, England.

Drawing by Jeff Saward, Labyrinthos.

Figure 27.4 Medieval labyrinth, the pattern of the Chartres Cathedral Labyrinth, France.

Drawing by Jeff Saward, Labyrinthos.

Figure 27.5 The classical chakra-vyuha labyrinth pattern from India.
Drawing by Jeff Saward, Labyrinthos.

28 Conclusion: Vision and journey

Bernard Moss

To have a formal conclusion to this book about labyrinths seems a contradiction in terms: as this volume so eloquently demonstrates, walking the labyrinth does not have neat and tidy endings. Even when we reach the centre – whatever that central point of reflection means to each walker – the story is only half-told: the journey is only halfway through: what happens afterwards is an essential ingredient in the labyrinth experience. To talk of a conclusion is therefore premature and misleading, and risks 'short-changing' the challenging 'unknowns' of what lies ahead. As a result of what we may receive at the central point, new horizons may open up for us; new bursts of creativity may enthuse and re-energise us, and new perspectives may appear that can re-direct our intellectual, emotional and spiritual searching.

Nevertheless, publishing tradition calls for a book to have a conclusion, and as teachers and learners together we tend to expect it. Perhaps in this instance we can be guided by the wisdom of T.S. Eliot (1944) who suggests that there are times when we need to go back to where we began before we can fully understand the meaning and full potential of the journey on which we have embarked. This profound insight captures the experience to which many labyrinth walkers testify: that having completed a labyrinth walk they have begun to understand for the first time something of what 'all this is about' (the phrase is unavoidably vague and can only be fleshed out by each individual walker's insight). It is worth exploring this insight as we both look back on the book as a whole and reach forward into our future.

Chances are that most of our readers will have dipped in and out of the preceding chapters according to their interest, previous experiences or newly stimulated fascination. Some may have read the book from cover to cover. However you have approached the book and whatever has brought you to be reading this conclusion, one thing may be taken for granted: that it is your passion for teaching and learning that underpins your involvement with this book, and your commitment to finding innovative approaches to make learning both fun and inspiring for you and your students. Having completed your labyrinth walk through this book and found yourself back at the starting point, it is worth spending some time reflecting together on what this 'walk' has meant to you, and to be reminded about what caused you to open the book in the first place.

The three 'R's so familiar to labyrinth walkers – Reflect : Receive : Return – provide a useful framework for this concluding chapter.

Reflect

In many ways the theme of the whole book has been on the value and importance of reflection and the way in which the labyrinth provides creative and stimulating opportunities for this all-important approach. It is a hallmark of excellent teaching and learning that we reflect regularly and insightfully into our professional practice. It is worth revisiting for a moment therefore what brought you to this book; what you hoped to gain from reading it and exploring the rich tapestry of ideas, innovations and insights captured on these pages.

Receive

If this book has worked for you, there will have been moments when you have thought *YES – I'd like to have a go at that – this is something I could use – this is an approach I could adopt – this is an innovation I want to introduce into my teaching and into my HEI – I can draw from these authors' experiences to enrich my own.*

This emphasis upon receiving is central to the labyrinth experience, although, as we hope is clear from the book as a whole, there is nothing guaranteed or immediate about it. Sometimes the impact of our walking and reflection takes time to bear fruit; often we need to walk and walk and walk, and to travel hopefully. But as this book so encouragingly reveals, the labyrinth experience can deliver rich rewards.

Return

Here is the challenge but here also is the excitement. Only you will know how the reading of this book has impacted upon you, but the future lies ahead and as someone committed to best practice and to excellent teaching and learning, you will return to your 'day job' a different person as a result of engaging with this book. Seeds will have been sown; opportunities to walk the labyrinth will emerge, and your passion for your work will risk being deepened! Perhaps, as some have said, it will remind you why you came into teaching in the first place, and the gifts and talents which you can use and develop to make learning an enjoyable rewarding activity.

We make no apology for emphasising the passionate nature of teaching and learning, and for offering the labyrinth as a gentle but powerful tool to enable us to reflect deeply on who we are and what we are doing as teachers and learners. We make no apology for challenging the managerialism and sometimes toxic, disempowering cultures which pervade many of our HEIs as the struggle to survive bites deep, and insecurity takes its toll. This book – and the gift to us all that is the labyrinth – is an invitation to seek a better, more humane way of being and doing, and of allowing the human spirit – however we conceive it – to infuse and enthuse our shared teaching and learning, so that what we seek to offer our students is ultimately life-enhancing.

So, no neat and tidy conclusion – but a vision and a hope and a continuing journey, which we trust will continue to be a privilege and a delight. Travel well.

References

Accreditation Council for Graduate Medical Education (2013), *ACGME Common Program Requirements*, 1 July. Available at: www.acgme.org/acgmeweb/Portals/0/ PFAssets/ProgramRequirements/CPRs2013.pdf

Adams, Reginald C. (2015), *Sacred Sites Quest: International Exchange – France*. Available at: www.reginaldadams.com/#!sacred-site-quest/ckf4

Adamson, Andrew and Jenson, Vicky (2001), *Shrek* [film], Glendale, California: DreamWorks

American College Health Association (2013), *American College Health Association– National College Health Assessment II: Canadian Consortium Reference Group Executive Summary Spring 2013*, Hanover, Maryland: American College Health Association

American Psychological Association (2008), *Nation's First Green Roof and Labyrinth Opens*, 2 October. Available at: www.apa.org/news/press/releases/2008/10/ green-roof.aspx

Anh–Huong, Nguyen and Hanh, Thich Nhat (2006), *Walking Meditation*, Boulder, CO: Sounds True

Artress, Lauren (1995), *Walking a Sacred Path: Rediscovering the Labyrinth as a Spiritual Tool*, New York: Riverhead

Artress, Lauren (2006a), *Walking a Sacred Path: Rediscovering the Labyrinth as a Spiritual Practice*, New York: Riverhead

Artress, Lauren (2006b), *The Sacred Path Companion: A Guide to Walking the Labyrinth to Heal and Transform*, New York: Berkley

Artress, Lauren (2015), *From Canvas to Tapestry to Stone ...* Available at: www. laurenartress.com/grace-cathedral/ (accessed 12 October 2015)

Arts Council England (2011), *Cultural Olympiad in the South East, September 2008 to September 2010*. Available at: www.artscouncil.org.uk/media/uploads/se_ website_images/SouthEastCulturalOlympiadVolumeOne.pdf

Attali, Jacques (1999 [1996]), *The Labyrinth in Culture and Society: Pathways to Wisdom* (trans. Joseph Rowe), Berkeley: North Atlantic Books

Bailey, Deborah S. (2003), 'Swirling' changes to the traditional student path, *Monitor on Psychology*, December, 34(11), 36. Available at: www.apa.org/monitor/dec03/ swirling.aspx

Baird, Benjamin, Smallwood, Jonathan, Mrazek, Michael D., Kam, Julia W. Y., Franklin, Michael S. and Schooler, Jonathan W. (2012), Inspired by distraction: Mind wandering facilitates creative incubation, *Psychological Science*, 23(10), 1117–1122

Bandura, Albert (1993), Perceived self-efficacy in cognitive development and functioning, *Educational Psychologist*, 28(2), 117–148

Barthell, John, Cunliff, Ed, Gage, Kathryn, Radke, William and Steele, Cheryl (2010), 'Transformative learning: Collaborating to enhance student learning', in

Higher Learning Commission Annual Conference, A Collection of Papers on Self-Study and Institutional Improvement 26th edn, USA, Illinois: The Higher Learning Commission, p. 56. Available at: www.uco.edu/academic–affairs/files/TransformLrning-Collaborating.pdf

Bassot, Barbara (2013), *The Reflective Journal,* Basingstoke: Palgrave Macmillan

Beer, Laura E., Rodriguez, Katrina, Taylor, Christina, Martinez-Jones, Naomi, Griffin, Jennifer, Smith, Tony R., Lamar, Margaret and Anaya, Reyna (2015), Awareness, integration and interconnectedness: Contemplative practices, *Journal of Transformative Education,* April, 13(2), 61–185

Benson, Herbert with Klipper, Miriam Z. (2000), *The Relaxation Response* (revised edn), New York: HarperCollins

beyondblue (2013), *National Mental Health Survey of Doctors and Medical Students.* Available at: www.beyondblue.org.au/about-us/programs/workplace-and-workforce-program/programs-resources-and-tools/about-the-doctors-mental-health-program

Bigard, Michelle F. (2005), Walking the labyrinth: Enhancing spiritually sensitive clinical practice, *Reflections: Narratives of Professional Helping. Special Issue: Spiritual Diversity in Social Work,* 11(3), 84–95

Bigard, Michelle F. (2009), Walking the labyrinth: An innovative approach to counseling center outreach, *Journal of College Counseling,* 12(2), 137–148

Boud, David, Keogh, Rosemary and Walker, David (eds) (1985), *Reflection: Turning Experience into Learning,* London: Kogan Page

Boyer, Ernest (1990), *Scholarship Reconsidered: Priorities of the Professoriate,* Princeton, NJ: Princeton University

Bright, Jennifer and Pokorny, Helen (2012), Contemplative practices in higher education: Breathing heart and mindfulness into the staff and student experience, *Educational Developments,* 13(4), December, 22–25. Available at: www.seda.ac.uk/past-issues/13.4

Bristol, Tim J. (2014), Educate, excite, engage, *Teaching and Learning in Nursing,* 9, 43–46

Buchanan, Jim (2007*), Labyrinths for the Spirit: How to Create Your Own Labyrinths for Meditation and Enlightenment,* London: Gaia

Burton, Amanda J. (2000), Reflection: Nursing's practice and education's panacea? *Journal of Advanced Nursing,* 31(5), 1009–1017

Campbell, Joseph (1949), *The Hero with a Thousand Faces,* New York: Bollingen

Campbell, Joseph (1968), *The Hero with a Thousand Faces* (2nd edn), Princeton, NJ: Princeton University Press

Cant, Tony and Holley, Debbie (2011), Labyrinth, *Anglia Ruskin University Staff Bulletin,* 8(6), 23. Available at: http://issuu.com/angliaruskinbulletin/docs/bulletin_vol_8_no_6_medres

Capaldi, Nick and Chadbourn, Deborah (eds) (2001), *Year of the Artist: June 2000–May 2001: Breaking the Barriers,* Sheffield, UK: Arts2000

Careri, Francisco (2002), *Walkscapes: Walking as an Aesthetic Practice,* Barcelona: Gustavo Gili

Center for Contemplative Mind in Society (2014), *Our Vision,* at www.contemplativemind.org/about/vision (accessed 25 August 2014)

Chen, Daniel C. R., Kirshenbaum, Daniel S., Yan, Jun, Kirshenbaum, Elaine and Aseltine, Robert H. (2012), Characterizing changes in student empathy throughout medical school, *Med Teach*, 34(4), 305–311

Children's Hospital at Westmead (2013), 'Introduction – A path to wellbeing', in: *The Children's Hospital at Westmead, Annual Review 2013: A Path to Wellbeing*, 2–4. Available at: www.schn.health.nsw.gov.au/files/attachments/chw_annual_report_2013.pdf

Chippendale, Christopher (2013), *Reflections on Making Ephemeral Artworks* (unpublished BSc essay), Writtle College, Writtle, Essex, UK

Christenson Hughes, Julia and Mighty, Joy (eds) (2010), *Taking Stock: Research on Teaching and Learning in Higher Education*, Montreal and Kingston: McGill–Queen's University

Clemetsen, Bruce, Furbeck, Lee and Moore, Alicia (2013), Enabling student swirl: Understanding the data and best practices for supporting transfer students, *Strategic Enrollment Management Quarterly*, 1(3), 153–165

Cleverly, Dankay (2003), *Implementing Inquiry-based Learning in Nursing*, London: Routledge

Colbert, Judy (2014), Are DC's labyrinths a path to inner peace? *The Washingtonian*, 30 April, 131–132

Cook, Matt and Croft, Janet Brennan (2015), Interactive mindfulness technology: A walking labyrinth in an academic library, *College and Research Libraries News*, 76(6), 318–322, June (online 14 July). Available at: http://crln.acrl.org/content/76/6.toc

Cranton, Patricia (2000), 'Individual differences in transformative learning', in Jack Mezirow and Associates, *Learning as Transformation: Critical Perspectives on a Theory in Progress*, San Francisco: Jossey-Bass, ch.7, pp. 181–204

Cunliff, Ed, Franz, Rochelle and Romano, Tracey (2014), Transforming self to facilitate transformative learning, *International HETL Review*, 4, 29 September. Available at: www.hetl.org/transforming-self-to-facilitate-transformative-learning/

CUNY (2010), A community of justice: City University of New York Law, *CUNY Law*. Available at: www.law.cuny.edu/magazine/archive/10–fall–cunylaw.pdf

Curry, Helen P. (2000), *The Way of the Labyrinth: A Powerful Meditation for Everyday Life*, New York: Penguin Compass

Dalley-Hewer, Jayne (2012), *Does Reflection Improve Physiotherapy Practice?*, paper presented at the *3rd European Congress of Physiotherapy Education*, 8–9 November, Vienna

Danielson, Kim J. (2004), *The Transformative Power of the Labyrinth* (unpublished master's thesis), Sonoma State University, California

Darling, Ruth A. and Smith, Melissa Scandlyn (2007), 'First generation college students: First year challenges' in: Mary Stuart Hunter, Betsy McCalla-Wriggins and Eric R. White (eds), *Academic Advising: New Insights for Teaching and Learning in the First Year*, Columbia, South Carolina, USA: National Resource Center for the First-Year Experience and Students in Transition/National Academic Advising Association (NACADA) (joint pub.) USA, Monograph 46, pp. 203–211. Available at: www.nacada.ksu.edu/portals/0/Clearinghouse/AdvisingIssues/documents/first-gen.pdf

Davies, Lorna (ed.) (2013), *The Art and Soul of Midwifery: Creativity in Practice, Education and Research*, Philadelphia: Churchill Livingstone, Elsevier

Davis, Jeff (2010), *The First-Generation Student Experience: Implications for Campus Practice, and Strategies for Improving Persistence and Success,* Sterling, VA: American College Personnel Association (ACPA): College Student Educators International

Dawson Varughese, Emma (2016), *Genre Fiction of New India: Post-Millennial Receptions of "Weird" Narratives,* London and New York: Routledge

deSoto, Lewis (2003), *Labyrinth Gateway 2003* [public art installation, University of Texas]. Information at: http://lewisdesoto.net/Public_Art/Labyrinth_Gateway.html

DeVito, Kathy J. and Dunlap, Jeanetta W. (2012), *Walking the Labyrinth Mindfully,* poster presented at *The Labyrinth Society Annual Gathering,* Hudson, WI, October

Devonport, Tracey J. and Lane, Andrew M. (2006), Relationships between self-efficacy, coping and student retention, *Social Behavior and Personality,* 34(2), 127–138

Dewey, John (1933), *How We Think,* Chicago: Regnery

Dewitz, S. Joseph, Woolsey, M. Lynn and Walsh, W. Bruce (2009), College student retention: An exploration of the relationship between self-efficacy beliefs and purpose in life among college students, *Journal of College Student Development,* 50(1), 134

Dineen, Ruth (2006), 'Views from the chalk face: Lecturers' and students' perspectives on the development of creativity in art and design', in Norman Jackson, Martin Oliver, Malcolm Shaw and James Wisdom (eds), *Developing Creativity in Higher Education: An Imaginative Curriculum,* Abingdon, Oxon: Routledge, ch. 9, pp. 109–117

Donaldson, O. Fred (1990), 'Play it by heart' [workshop resources], p. 59, South Africa, Johannesburg

Donaldson, O. Fred (1993), *Playing by Heart: The Vision and Practice of Belonging,* Deerfield Beach, Florida: Health Communications

Doob, Penelope Reed (1990), *The Idea of the Labyrinth: From Classical Antiquity through the Middle Ages,* Ithaca, NY: Cornell University

Drew University (2014), *Labyrinth.* Available at: www.drew.edu/labyrinth (accessed 17 September 2015)

Driscoll, John (2000), *Practising Clinical Supervision,* London: Bailliere Tindall

Dublin City University (2014), *DCU Labyrinth iWitness* [film], Kairos, 15 March. Available at: www4.dcu.ie/students/chaplaincy/labyrinth/

Duckworth, Angela L., Peterson, Christopher, Matthews, Michael D. and Kelly, Dennis R. (2007), Grit: Perseverance and passion for long-term goals, *Journal of Personality and Social Psychology,* 92(6), 1087–1101

Dumas-Hines, Frances A., Cochrane, Lessie L. and Williams, Ellen U. (2001), Promoting diversity: Recommendations for recruitment and retention of minorities in higher education, *Journal of College Student Development,* 35(3), 433–439

Edwards, Betty (2008), *The New Drawing on the Right Side of the Brain,* London: HarperCollins

Einstein, Albert (1931), *Cosmic Religion: With Other Opinions and Aphorisms,* New York: Dover

Elgie, Susan (2014), *Researching Teaching and Student Outcomes in Postsecondary Education: An Introduction* (2nd edn), Toronto: Higher Education Quality Council of Ontario

Eliot, Thomas S. (1944), Little Gidding V [poem], in *Four Quartets,* London: Faber and Faber, lines 239–242

England, Pam (2007), 'Birth art as a timeless avenue to a soulful birth', in Lorna Davies (ed.), *The Art and Soul of Midwifery: Creativity in Practice, Education and Research,* Philadelphia: Churchill Livingstone, Elsevier

England, Pam (2010), *Labyrinth of Birth: Creating a Map, Meditations and Rituals for Your Childbearing Year,* Santa Barbara, CA: Birthing From Within Books

Engle, Jennifer and Tinto, Vincent (2008), *Moving Beyond Access: College Success for Low-Income, First-Generation Students,* Washington, DC: Pell Institute for the Study of Opportunity in Higher Education

Fairbloom, Lorraine, (2003), *Walking the Labyrinth: Its Impact on Healthcare Professionals in a Hospital Setting* (unpublished master's thesis), University of Toronto, Canada (ProQuest Digital Dissertations database. Publication No. AAT MQ84321)

Fellmeth, Ulrich, Quast, Kathrin (eds) and Wetzel, Gertrud Angelika (artist) (2004), *Faszination Labyrinth: Eine Kulturegeschichte des Labyrinths und Labyrinth-Modelle von G. Angelica Wetzel; Eine Ausstellung im Museum zur Geschichte Hohenheims Universität Hohenheim,* Hohenheim, Stuttgart: Archive of the University of Hohenheim

Ferré, Robert (2012), *Labyrinths: Spiritual Technology for Inner Healing.* Available at: www.labyrinthproject.com/healing.html (accessed 15 May 2015)

Ferré, Robert (2014), *Canvas Labyrinths: Construction Manual,* San Antonio, TX: Labyrinth Enterprises

Ferré, Robert and Saward, Jeff (2000), 'The labyrinth revival', in Hermann Kern, *Through the Labyrinth: Designs and Meanings over 5,000 Years* (revised English edn, trans. from German by Abigail Clay), Munich and New York: Prestel, ch.19, pp. 311–315

Fook, Jan and Gardener, Fiona (2007), *Practising Critical Reflection: A Resource Handbook,* Maidenhead: Open University Press

Fox, Charlie (2007), Quiet space for retreat if the spirit takes you, *Times Higher Education Supplement,* 2 February, 8–9. Available at: www.timeshighereducation. co.uk/news/quiet-space-for-retreat-if-the-spirit-takes-you/207669.article

Francisco, Janice (2006), *Into the Labyrinth: Excursions and Applications for Creative Process* (unpublished master's thesis), Buffalo, NY: Buffalo State College, State University of New York

Frankl, Victor (2006 [1946]), *Man's Search for Meaning* (trans. Ilse Lasch), Boston, MA: Beacon Press

Geoffrion, Jill Kimberly Hartwell (2003), *Pondering the Labyrinth,* Cleveland, OH: Pilgrim Press

Gershwin, George and Gershwin, Ira (1937), *They Can't Take That Away From Me* [song], iTunes [download] [Frank Sinatra and Natalie Cole]. Available at: www .apple.com/uk/itunes (accessed 11 October 2015)

Goldberger, Ellen (2009), Lost and found in the classroom, *Inside Higher Ed,* 27 February. Available at: www.insidehighered.com/views/2009/02/27/goldberger

Grace, Fran (2008), *A Semester Within: Exploring Meditation* [film], Sedona, Arizona, USA: Inner Pathway. Available at: www.innerpathway.com (accessed 12 October 2015)

Grace, Fran (2009), Breathing in: suffering. Breathing out: compassion, *Spirituality in Higher Education, A National Study of College Students' Meaning and Purpose: Newsletter,* 5(2), 1–10, May. Available at: www.spirituality.ucla.edu/newsletter_new/past_pdf/volume_5/Grace_Final.pdf

Grace, Fran (2011a), 'From content to context to contemplation: One professor's journey' in: Judith Simmer-Brown and Fran Grace (eds), *Meditation and the Classroom: Contemplative Pedagogy for Religious Studies,* Albany, New York: SUNY, ch.5, pp. 47–64

Grace, Fran (2011b), 'Meditation in the classroom: What do students say they learn?' in: Judith Simmer-Brown and Fran Grace (eds), *Meditation and the Classroom: Contemplative Pedagogy for Religious Studies,* Albany, New York: SUNY, ch.26, pp. 237–249

Grace, Fran, Olson, Lisa and Ko, Celine (2014), *Student Learning Under a Microscope,* presentation at the *American Academy of Religion, Annual Meeting,* San Diego, 22 November

Gravois, John (2007), You're not fooling anyone, *Chronicle of Higher Education,* (54)11, A1, November

Griffith, Janith S. (2002), Labyrinths: A pathway to reflection and contemplation, *Clinical Journal of Oncology Nursing,* 6(5), 295–296

Haas, Lindsay F. (2003), Hans Berger (1873–1941), Richard Caton (1842–1926), and electroencephalography, *Journal of Neurology, Neurosurgery and Psychiatry,* 74(1), 9

Habley, Wesley R., Bloom, Jennifer L. and Robbins, Steve (2012), *Increasing Persistence: Research Based Strategies for College Student Persistence,* San Francisco: Jossey-Bass

Haddon, Anthony (2006), A long story with a happy ending, *Research in Drama Education: The Journal of Applied Theatre and Performance,* (11)2, June, 185–199

Halpin, Nick (2005), Journey of discovery: the labyrinth tapestry, *Spirited Scotland,* 4, 4

Hargreaves, Janet and Page, Louise (2013), *Reflective Practice,* Cambridge: Polity Press

Harper, Shaun R. (2012), *Black Male Student Success in Higher Education: A Report from the National Black Male College Achievement Study,* Philadelphia: University of Pennsylvania, Center for the Study of Race and Equity in Education. Available at: www.works.bepress.com/sharper/43

Hassed, Craig and Chambers, Richard (2014), *Mindful Learning,* Wollombi, Australia: Exisle Publishing

Hassed, Craig, de Lisle, Steven, Sullivan, Gavin and Pier, Claran (2008), Enhancing the health of medical students: Outcomes of an integrated mindfulness and lifestyle program, *Advances in Health Sciences Education,* 14(3), 387–398

Health and Care Professions Council (2014), *Standards of Education and Training Guidance,* London: Health and Care Professions Council

Higher Education Academy (2010), *HEA Conference 2010: Delegate Comments* [film, quotation at 2.42 min]. Available at: https://vimeo.com/12910579

Hillis, James M., Perry, William R. G., Carroll, Emily Y., Hibble, Belinda A., Davies, Marion J. and Yousef, Justin (2010), Painting the picture: Australasian medical student views on wellbeing teaching and support services, *Medical Journal of Australia,* 192(4), 188–190

Holford, John, Jarvis, Peter, Milana, Marcella, Waller, Richard and Webb, Sue (2013), Exploration, discovery, learning: Mapping the unknown, *International Journal of Lifelong Education,* 32(6), 22 November, 685

Holloway, Margaret and Moss, Bernard (2010), *Spirituality and Social Work,* Basingstoke: Palgrave Macmillan

Hossenally, Rooksana (2014), *Return to the Sea: Saltworks by Motoi Yamamoto,* Yatzer, Art, 12 October. Available at: www.yatzer.com/return-to-the-sea-motoi-yamamoto

Housel, Teresa (2012), First generation focus, *Inside Higher Ed,* March, 23

Illeris, Knud (2014), Transformative learning redefined: As changes in elements of the identity, *International Journal of Lifelong Education,* 33(5), 573–586

Irlbeck, Erica, Adams, Shylo, Akers, Cindy, Burris, Scott and Jones, Stephanie (2014), First generation college students: Motivations and support systems, *Journal of Agricultural Education,* 55(2), 154–166

Irving, Alex (2012), Alex Irving [YouTube presentation], The De-Stress Show, 15 April. Available at: www.youtube.com/watch?v=O4erZiuSjAo

Iwama, Michael (2006), *The Kawa Model: Culturally Relevant Occupational Therapy,* Edinburgh: Churchill Livingstone Elsevier Press

James, Alison (2014), 'Playing Seriously: Lego and labyrinth', in Alison James and Stephen Brookfield, *Engaging Imagination: Helping Students Become Creative and Reflective Thinkers,* San Francisco: Jossey-Bass, ch.6, pp. 129–132

James, Alison and Brookfield, Stephen D. (2014a), *Engaging Imagination: Helping Students Become Creative and Reflective Thinkers,* San Francisco: Jossey-Bass

James, Alison and Brookfield, Stephen D. (2014b), 'Labyrinths' (web page and film). Available at: http://engagingimagination.com/labyrinths (accessed 12 October 2015)

Johnson, Rick, Artress, Lauren and GraceCom Media Ministry (2001), *Rediscovering the Labyrinth: A Walking Meditation* [DVD], San Francisco: GraceCom Media Ministry

Jones, Janice K. (2013), 'Into the labyrinth: Persephone's journey as metaphor and method for research', in Warren Midgley, Karen Trimmer and Andy Davies (eds), *Metaphors for, in and of Education Research,* Newcastle upon Tyne: Cambridge Scholars, ch. 5, pp. 67–90

Jung, Carl G. (1964), *Man and His Symbols,* New York: Anchor Books, Doubleday

Kabat-Zinn, Jon (1991), *Full Catastrophe Living: Using the Wisdom of Your Body and Mind to Face Stress, Pain, and Illness,* New York: Dell

Kabat-Zinn, Jon (1994), *Wherever You Go There You Are: Mindfulness Meditation in Everyday Life,* New York: Hyperion

Kabat-Zinn, Jon (2003), Mindfulness-based interventions in context: Past, present and future, *Clinical Psychology: Science and Practice,* 10(2), 144–156

Kabat-Zinn, Jon (2005), *Coming to Our Senses: Healing Ourselves and the World through Mindfulness,* New York: Hyperion

Kabat-Zinn, Jon and Davidson, Richard (eds) (2011), *The Mind's Own Physician: A Scientific Dialogue with the Dalai Lama on the Healing Power of Meditation,* Oakland, California: New Harbinger

Kendra, Lucy (2014), *Walking the Labyrinth* [film], Edinburgh: University of Edinburgh, www.youtube.com/watch?v=g6ObCu7FoRA

Kermeen, Debi and Kermeen, Marty (2012), *Miracles Along the Path: Labyrinths in Stone,* Yorkville, Illinois: Labyrinths in Stone. Information at: www.labyrinthsinstone.com (accessed 26 August 2015)

Kern, Hermann (1983), *Labyrinthe* (German language edn), Munich: Prestel

Kern, Hermann (2000), *Through the Labyrinth: Designs and Meanings over 5,000 Years* (revised English edn, trans. from German by Abigail Clay), Munich and New York: Prestel

Kezar, Adrianna (2007), Creating and sustaining a campus ethos encouraging student engagement, *About Campus*, 11(6), 13–18

Kierkegaard, Søren (1978 [1847]), 'Letter 150' [to Henriette Kierkegaard], in *Letters and Documents* (trans. Henrik Rosenmaier), Princeton, NJ: Princeton University, p. 214

King, Ursula (2009), *The Search for Spirituality*, London: Canterbury

Kitchenham, Andrew (2008), The evolution of John Mezirow's transformative learning theory, *Journal of Transformative Education*, 6(2), 104–123

Knight, Sara (2012), Joint project labyrinth planted in Chelmer Valley Nature Reserve, *Anglia Ruskin Staff Bulletin*, 9(5), 29. Available at: http://issuu.com/angliaruskinbulletin/docs/bulletin_vol_9_no_5_medres

Knowles, Sally S. and Grant, Barbara (2014), 'Walking the Labyrinth: The holding embrace of academic writing retreats', in Claire Aitchinson and Cally Guerin (eds), *Writing Groups for Doctoral Education and Beyond: Innovations in Practice and Theory*, Abingdon, Oxford and New York: Routledge, ch.8, pp. 110–127

Kolander, Cheryl A., Ballard, Danny J. and Chandler, Cynthia K. (2005), 'Developing a healthy lifestyle', in *Contemporary Women's Health: Issues for Today and the Future* 2nd edn, Boston, MA: McGraw-Hill, p. 15

The Labyrinth Society (2011), *Labyrinths for our Time: Places of Refuge in a Hectic World* [DVD], Trumansburg, New York: The Labyrinth Society. Available at: www.labyrinthsociety.org (accessed 12 October 2015)

The Labyrinth Society (2015), *World Labyrinth Day*. Available at: www.labyrinthsociety.org/world-labyrinth-day (accessed 12 October 2015)

The Labyrinth Society and Veriditas (2015), *Worldwide Labyrinth Locator*. Available at: www.labyrinthlocator.com (accessed 12 October 2015)

Labyrinthos (2015), *Labyrinthos*. Available at: www.labyrinthos.net/ (accessed 12 October 2015)

Lafferty, Patricia (1997), Balancing the curriculum: promoting aesthetic knowledge in nursing, *Nurse Education Today*, 17(4), 281–286

Lagopoulos, Jim, Xu, Jian, Rasmussen, Inge, Vik, Alexandra, Malhi, Gin S., Eliassen, Carl F., Arntsen, Ingrid E., Sæther, Jardar G., Hollup, Stig, Holen, Are, Davanger, Svend and Ellingsen, Øyvind (2009), Increased theta and alpha EEG activity during nondirective meditation, *Journal of Alternative and Complementary Medicine*, 15(11), 1187–1192

Land, Ray, Meyer, Jan H. F. and Smith, Jan (2008), *Threshold Concepts within the Disciplines* [Series: Educational Futures: Rethinking Theory and Practice, Michael Peters (ed.), v.16], Rotterdam: Sense

Lillyman, Sue, Gutteridge, Robin and Berridge, Pat (2011), Using a storyboarding technique in the classroom to address end of life experiences and engage student nurses in deeper reflection on their practice, *Nurse Education in Practice*, 11, 179–185

Lippincott, Joseph A. and German, Neil (2007), 'From blue collar to ivory tower: Counseling first-generation, working class students', in Joseph A. Lippincott, and Ruth A. Lippincott (eds), *Special Populations in College Counseling: A Handbook* for *Mental Health Professionals*, Alexandria, Virginia, USA: American Counseling Association, pp. 80–98

McCague, Hugh (2007), 'Learning from the medieval master masons: A geometric journey through the labyrinth', in: Amy Shell-Gellasch (ed.), *Hands On History: A Resource for Teaching Mathematics,* Washington DC: Mathematical Association of America

McCarthy, John and Holliday, Ebony (2004), Help-seeking and counseling within a traditional male gender role: An examination from a multi-cultural perspective, *Journal of Counseling and Development,* Winter, 82, 25–30

McCullough, David Willis (2004), *The Unending Mystery: A Journey through Labyrinths and Mazes,* New York: Random House

McDougall, Jenny and Davis, Wendy (2011), Role reversal: Educators in an enabling program embark on a journey of critical self-reflection, *Australian Journal of Adult Learning,* 51(3), 433–455

MacFarlane, Robert (2012), *The Old Ways: A Journey on Foot,* London: Hamish Hamilton, Penguin

McIntosh, Paul (2010), *Action Research and Reflective Practice: Creative and Visual Methods to Facilitate Reflection and Learning,* Oxford: Routledge

Manning, Robert E. (2012), Long walks, deep thoughts, *Chronicle of Higher Education,* 14 December, B12–B13

Mariscotti, Janice and Texter, Lynne (2003), *Using the Labyrinth with Those Experiencing Life-changing Illness: Research and practice,* presentation at *The Labyrinth Society Annual Gathering,* Baltimore, Maryland, October

Mariscotti, Janice and Texter, Lynne (2004), *Do You Have Research to Support That?,* presentation at *The Labyrinth Society Annual Gathering,* Camp Courage, Minnesota, October

Mariscotti, Janice and Texter, Lynne (2014), *The Relaxation Effects of Labyrinth Walking among School-age Children,* presentation at *The Labyrinth Society Annual Gathering,* Duncan Conference Center, Del Ray Beach, Florida, November

Marquart, Katja (2004), *Choice, Experience, and Transformation: Space as Metaphor* (unpublished MSc thesis), University of Wisconsin-Madison, Madison, Wisconsin, USA

Marquart, Katja (2006), *The Labyrinth as Environmental Space for Healing, Resolution, and Renewal,* presentation at *Edra 37: Beyond Conflict* (Environmental Design Research Association Conference), Atlanta, Georgia, USA, 3 May

Marquart, Katja (2007), *The Labyrinth as a Localized Walking Tool for Wellness and Civic Space,* presentation at *Walk21: 8th Annual Conference on Walking and Liveable Communities,* Toronto, Canada, 1 October

Marquart, Katja (2008), 'Thinking in circles? Discover the labyrinth as a problem-solving tool for the design process', in *Proceedings of the Interior Design Educators Council (IDEC) Midwest Regional Conference,* Miami University, Oxford, Ohio, USA, 17 October, pp. 8–9. Available at: www.idec.org/files/2008MidwestConferenceProceedings.pdf

Marquart, Katja (2009), *Inside-out: Communicating through the labyrinth,* presentation at the *Design Communication Association Conference,* Southern Polytechnic State University, Atlanta, Georgia, USA, 25 March

Marquart, Katja (2011), *Walking the Line: Exploring the space of labyrinths*, presentation at the *2011 Popular Culture Association (PCA/ACA) Annual Conference*, San Antonio, Texas, USA, 20 April

Marquart, Katja (2013), *Labyrinths for All: The principles of universal design applied to labyrinth spaces*, presentation at *The Labyrinth Society Annual Gathering*, Vancouver Island, British Columbia, Canada, 17 September

Marquart, Katja (2014), *Designing for Labyrinths: Final survey results of preferred design characteristics of labyrinth spaces*, presentation at *The Labyrinth Society Annual Gathering*, Delray Beach, Florida, USA, 14 November

Matthews, William Henry (1970 [1922]), *Mazes and Labyrinths: A General Account of their History and Developments* [reprint], New York: Dover

Meakin, Richard and Kirklin, Deborah J. (2000), Humanities special studies modules: Making better doctors or just happier ones? *Medical Ethics: Medical Humanities*, 26(1), 49–50

Meyer, Tom and Xu, Yu (2005), Academic and clinical dissonance in nursing education: Are we guilty of failure to rescue? *Nurse Educator*, 30(2), 76–79

Mezirow, Jack (1981), A critical theory of adult learning and education, *Adult Education Quarterly*, 32(1), 3–24

Mezirow, Jack (1997), Transformative learning: Theory to practice, *New Directions for Adult and Continuing Education*, Summer, 74, 5–12

Midgley, Warren, Trimmer, Karen and Davies, Andy (eds) (2013), *Metaphors for, in and of Education Research*, Newcastle upon Tyne: Cambridge Scholars

Moon, Jennifer A. (2004), *A Handbook of Reflective and Experiential Learning: Theory and Practice*, Abingdon: Routledge Falmer

Moore, Thomas (2010), *Care of the Soul in Medicine*, Carlsbad, CA: Hay House

Morgan, John P. (2014), *The Hero's Journey: Star Wars, Harry Potter and the Wizard of Oz* [film], John P. Morgan Coaching, 9 January. Available at: www.youtube.com/watch?v=YkhNBJUQRzI

Moss, Bernard (2011), 'Your skin or mine? A living drama in interprofessional education', in: Iain Hay (ed.), *Inspiring Academics: Learning with the World's Great University Teachers*, Maidenhead, Berkshire: Open University Press, ch. 6, pp. 43–49

Moss, Bernard (2015), *Communication Skills in Health and Social Care* 3rd edn, London: Sage

Moyers, Bill (1993), *Healing and the Mind*, New York: Doubleday

Mullen, Jane, Hatton, Jean and Frankland, Sharon (2011), *Transformative Learning: The start of the journey?*, paper presented at the *6th European Conference on the First Year Experience*, 19–20 June, University of Manchester

Murray, Terry (2012), Self-knowledge development as a cognitive, affective, relational and spiritual journey, *Religion and Education*, 39(1), 76–92

National Student Clearinghouse (2014), *Snapshot Report: Persistence – Retention*, Spring, posted 9 July. Available at: https://nscresearchcenter.org/snapshotreport-persistenceretention14/

Newberg, Andrew B. and Waldman, Mark Robert (2009), *How God Changes your Brain*, New York: Ballantine

Newton, Jenny and Plummer, Virginia (2009), Using creativity to encourage reflection in undergraduate education, *Reflective Practice,* 10(1), February, 67–76

Nicolaides, Aliki and Holt, Dyan (eds) (2014), *Spaces of Transformation and Transformation of Space: Proceedings of the XI International Transformative Learning Conference, 23–26 October,* New York, Teachers College, Columbia University

Nohl, Arnd-Michael (2015), Typical phases of transformative learning: A practice-based model, *Adult Education Quarterly,* 65(1), 35–49

Norton, William Skeet (2008), *Labyrinths in the Landscape: Who is Recommending, Who is Using, and Are There Benefits?* (unpublished master's thesis), The University of Texas at Arlington, Texas (ProQuest Dissertations and Theses. Publication No. AAT 1460796)

Nursing and Midwifery Council (2015), *The Code: Professional Standards of Practice and Behaviour for Nurses and Midwives,* London: Nursing and Midwifery Council

Oldfield, David (1996), 'The journey: An experiential rite of passage for modern adolescents', in: Louise C. Mahdi, Nancy G. Christopher and Michael Meade (eds), *Crossroads: The Quest for Contemporary Rites of Passage,* Chicago: Open Court, pp. 147–166

Opie, Joanne, Cunliffe, Elisabeth, East-O'Keeffe, Rebecca, Grace, Emma and Karlsson, Amanda (2014), *Experiences of Disabled Students within Physiotherapy Education,* paper presented at the *Chartered Society of Physiotherapy Annual Congress,* 10–11 October, Birmingham

Otto-Diniz, Sara (2008), *Through Myth to Meaning in Children's Experiences of Art* (unpublished doctoral dissertation), The University of New Mexico, New Mexico. (ProQuest Dissertations and Theses. Publication No. AAT 3318108)

Outram, Steve (2013), Dimensions of leadership, *Educational Developments,* 14(3), 7–9. Available at: www.seda.ac.uk/past–issues/14.3

Overall, Sonia (2005), *A Likeness,* London: HarperPerennial

Overall, Sonia (2011), *The Realm of Shells,* London: HarperPerennial

Overall, Sonia (2015), *The Art of Walking,* Bristol: Shearsman

Owen-Smith, Patricia (2012), *Contemplative Practices: The heart of the scholarship of teaching and learning,* paper presented at the *International Society for the Scholarship of Teaching and Learning (ISSOTL) Conference,* 24–27 October, Hamilton, Ontario

Palmer, Parker (1998), *The Courage to Teach,* San Francisco, CA: Jossey-Bass

Pearce, Joseph Chilton (1992), *Evolution's End: Claiming the Potential of our Intelligence,* San Francisco: HarperOne

Perna, Laura (2015), 'Improving equity in higher education attainment: A national imperative' in: Margaret Cahalan and Laura Perna (eds), *Indicators of Higher Education Equity in the United States: 45 year trend report 2015,* Washington, DC: Pell Institute for the Study of Opportunity in Higher Education, pp. 39–42

Petrovich, Anne (2004), Using self-efficacy theory in social work teaching, *Journal of Social Work Education,* 40, 429–443

Phillips, Tony (2015), *From Mazes to Mathematics.* Available at: www.math.stonybrook .edu/~tony/index.html (accessed 12 October 2015)

Pink, Daniel H. (2006), *A Whole New Mind: Why Right-Brainers will Rule the Future,* New York: Riverhead Books

Pink, Daniel H. (2008), *A Whole New Mind: Why Right-Brainers will Rule the Future* (new edn), London: Marshall Cavendish

Powley, Elaine and Higson, Roger (2013), *The Arts in Medical Education: A Practical Guide,* Oxford: Radcliffe Publishing

Rechtschaffen, Daniel (2014), *The Way of Mindful Education: Cultivating Well-Being in Teachers and Students,* New York: W. W. Norton

Redden, Elizabeth (2007), Meditative spaces, *InsideHigherEd,* 3 December. Available at: www.insidehighered.com/news/2007/12/03/meditation

Reilley, Jo Marie, Ring, Jeffrey and Duke, Linda (2005), Visual thinking strategies: A new role for art in medical education, *Family Medicine,* 37(4), 250–252

Rhodes, John W. (2006a), *The Labyrinth Walk Questionnaire and Instructions,* The Labyrinth Society, Trumansburg, New York. Available at: http://labyrinthsociety .org/useful–research–resources (accessed 4 April 2015)

Rhodes, John W. (2006b), *Perceived Effects of Labyrinth Walking on a Variety of Physical and Emotional Traits,* presentation at *The Labyrinth Society Annual Gathering,* New Braunfels, Texas, November

Rhodes, John W. (2007), *A Framework for Labyrinth Research,* The Labyrinth Society. Available at: http://labyrinthsociety.org/downloads (accessed 25 August 2014)

Rhodes, John W. (2008), Commonly reported effects of labyrinth walking, *Labyrinth Pathways,* 2, 31–37. Available at: http://labyrinthsociety.org/ useful–research–resources

Rhodes, John W. (2011), *Compilation of Labyrinth Walk Questionnaire Data,* The Labyrinth Society, Trumansburg, New York. Available at: http://labyrinthsociety. org/useful–research–resources (accessed 4 April 2015)

Rhodes, John W. and Rudebock, C. Diane (2015), *Bibliography of Articles and Studies Related to Labyrinth Research* (revised edn, January 2015). Available at: http:// labyrinthsociety.org/useful–research–resources

Rice, Amanda Suzanne (2004), *The Use of the Labyrinth in the Treatment of Alcohol and Substance Abuse Problems* (unpublished master's thesis), California State University, Long Beach, California (ProQuest Digital Dissertations database. Publication No. AAT 1421589)

Richardson, Tina (ed.) (2015), *Walking Inside Out: Contemporary British Psychogeography* (Place, Memory, Affect series), London: Rowman and LIttlefield International

Robertson Seonaid M. (1963), *Rosegarden and Labyrinth: A Study in Art Education,* New York: Barnes and Noble

Rodgers, Richard and Hart, Lorenz (1937), *Have You Met Miss Jones* [song], iTunes [download] [Robbie Williams]. Available at: www.apple.com/uk/itunes (accessed 11 October 2015)

Rudebock, C. Diane (2014), Discovering the labyrinth, *Normal Magazine,* Edmond, Oklahoma, University of Central Oklahoma, College of Education and Professional Studies, v1, August, 20–22. Available at: http://issuu.com/ucouniversityrelations/ docs/uconormalmagazinefall2014

Rudebock, C. Diane and Adair, Susan (2010), *The Path of Transformation: Using the labyrinth as a metaphor for learning,* presentation at the *Transformative Learning Conference,* University of Central Oklahoma, Edmond, Oklahoma, USA, 10 February

Rudebock, C. Diane and Worden, Susan (2012), *The Labyrinth: A Path for Reflection and Transformative Learning. Proposal for a Permanent Labyrinth of The University of Central Oklahoma Campus*, 3 February. Available at: www.uco.edu/academic-affairs/cettl/cettl-files/ucos-labyrinth.pdf

Rudebock, C. Diane, Webster, Kathryn, Kambour, Tina and Gregory, Kristen (2013), *Walking and Learning Using the UCO Labyrinth: Integrating the labyrinth in your curriculum*, presentation at the *University of Central Oklahoma 2013 Fall Collegium*, Edmond, Oklahoma USA

Ruminski, Elesha L. and Holba, Annette M. (2012), 'Afterword', in Elesha L. Ruminski and Annette M. Holba (eds), *Communicative Understandings of Women's Leadership Development: From Ceilings of Glass to Labyrinth Paths*, Lanham, MD: Lexington Books, pp. 209–216

Saffron Walden Maze Festival (2013), *Saffron Walden Maze Festival*. Available at: www.saffronwaldenmazefestival.co.uk/ (accessed 12 May 2014)

Sandor, M. Kay (2005), The labyrinth: A walking meditation for healing and self-care, *Explore: The Journal of Science and Healing* 1(6), 480–483

Sandor, M. Kay and Froman, Robin D. (2006), Exploring the effects of walking the labyrinth, *Journal of Holistic Nursing*, 24(2), 103–110

Santa Cruz Sentinel (1972), 'School maze, school days good old … (unattributed article) in *Santa Cruz Sentinel* [newspaper], Santa Cruz, USA: 117th yr, 12(1), p. 1, 14 January

Saward, Jeff (ed.) (1980–present), *Caerdroia: The Journal of Mazes and Labyrinths*, Thundersley, Essex: Labyrinthos. Available at: www.labyrinthos.net/caerdroia (accessed 30 August 2015)

Saward, Jeff (2002), *Magical Paths: Labyrinths and Mazes in the 21st Century*, London: Mitchell Beazley

Saward, Jeff (2003a), *Labyrinths and Mazes: The Definitive Guide to Ancient and Modern Traditions*, London: Gaia

Saward, Jeff (2003b), *Labyrinths and Mazes: The Complete Guide to Magical Paths of the World*, New York: Lark

Saward, Jeff (2009), *Laying out a Labyrinth* (revised and updated edn), Labyrinthos. Available at: www.labyrinthos.net/layout.html (accessed 12 October 2015)

Saward, Jeff and Saward, Kimberly (2015), *Labyrinthos*. Available at: www.labyrinthos.net/ (accessed 12 October 2015)

Saward, Kimberly (2002), *Ariadne's Thread: Legends of the Labyrinth*, Thundersley, England: Labyrinthos

Schaper, Donna and Camp, Carole Ann (2000), *Labyrinths from the Outside In: Walking to Spiritual Insight, a Beginner's Guide*, Woodstock, Vermont: Skylight Paths

Sellers, Jan (2001), *Constructing a Working Life: The Career Patterns of Contemporary Women Part-time Tutors and Lecturers in Adult and Continuing Education* (unpublished PhD thesis), University of Kent, Canterbury

Sellers, Jan (2008), *Labyrinths in Universities and Colleges*, The Labyrinth Society. Available at: http://labyrinthsociety.org/labyrinths-in-places (accessed 19 September 2015)

Sellers, Jan (2009), Exploring the labyrinth, *Educational Developments*, 10(1), 15–16, February. Available at: www.seda.ac.uk/past-issues/10.1

Sellers, Jan (2011), *The Labyrinth: A Pathway for Our Times* (guest lecture), St. Giles Cripplegate Church, Barbican, London, 20 April

Sellers, Jan (2012), 'Universities and colleges', in Ruth Sewell, Jan Sellers and Di Williams (eds), *Working with the Labyrinth: Paths for Exploration,* Glasgow: Wild Goose, ch. 3, pp. 42–53

Sellers, Jan (2013), 'The labyrinth: A journey of discovery', in Paul McIntosh and Digby Warren (eds), *Creativity in the Classroom: Case Studies in Using the Arts in Teaching and Learning in Higher Education,* Bristol: Intellect and Chicago: Chicago University Press, ch.15, pp. 209–223

Sellers, Jan (2014), *About Labyrinths.* Available at: www.jansellers.com/labyrinths1.html (accessed 4 April 2015)

Sewell, Ruth, Sellers, Jan and Williams, Di (eds) (2012), *Working with the Labyrinth: Paths for Exploration,* Glasgow: Wild Goose

Shaughnessy, Nicola (2015), 'Dancing with difference: Moving towards a new aesthetics', in Gareth White (ed.), *Applied Theatre: Aesthetics,* London and New York: Bloomsbury Methuen Drama, ch.3, pp. 87–122

Shelton-Colangelo, Sharon and Duvall, Mimi, (2007), 'Circles of learning in the Women's Studies class', in Sharon Shelton-Colangelo, Carolina Mancuso and Mimi Duvall (eds), *Teaching with Joy: Educational Practices for the Twenty-First Century,* Lanham, MD: Rowman and Littlefield, pp. 39–44

Sherwin, Manning and Maschwitz, Eric (1937), *A Nightingale Sang in Berkeley Square* [song], iTunes [download] [Glenn Miller and His Orchestra]. Available at: www.apple.com/uk/itunes (accessed 11 October 2015)

Simmer-Brown, Judith and Grace, Fran (eds) (2011), *Meditation and the Classroom: Contemplative Pedagogy for Religious Studies,* Albany, New York: SUNY

Smith, Maggie Yaxley (2010), The Canterbury Labyrinth, *Association for University and College Counselling Journal,* May, 8–11

Smith, Maggie Yaxley (2014), *Finding Love in the Looking Glass: A Book of Counselling Case Stories,* London: Karnac

Society for Teaching and Learning in Higher Education (2014), *What is SoTL? Research Methods.* Available at: www.stlhe.ca/sotl/what–is–sotl/ (accessed 25 August 2014)

Solnit, Rebecca (2002), *Wanderlust: A History of Walking,* Harmondsworth: Penguin

Stevenson, Sian and Thompson, Jayne (2010), 'Moving Memory' [Pecha Kucha presentation, Slipstream project proposal], Canterbury: University of Kent

StevensonThompson (2010), *Moving Memory* [event programme], Canterbury: University of Kent

Stoner, Tom and Rapp, Caroline (2008), *Open Spaces Sacred Places: Stories of How Nature Heals and Unifies,* USA, Annapolis, Maryland: TKF Foundation

Sweet, Melissa (2003), Being a caring doctor may be bad for you, *British Medical Journal,* 326(7385), 355

Taylor, Beverly (2010), *Reflective Practice: A Guide for Nurses and Midwives* 3rd edn, Maidenhead: Open University Press

Taylor, Claire (2013), The value of appreciative inquiry as an educational development tool, *Educational Developments,* 14(3), 23–26. Available at: www.seda.ac.uk/past-issues/14.3

Taylor, Edward, W. and Laros, Anna (2014), Researching the practice of fostering transformative learning, *Journal of Transformative Education*, 12(2), 134–147

Tinto, Vincent (1975), Dropout from higher education: A theoretical synthesis of recent research, *Review of Educational Research*, 45(1), 89–125

Tinto, Vincent (1993), *Leaving College: Rethinking the Causes and Cures of Student Attrition*, Chicago: University of Chicago Press

Tinto, Vincent (2012a), *Completing College: Rethinking Institutional Action*, Chicago: University of Chicago Press

Tinto, Vincent (2012b), 'Moving from Theory to Action: A model of institutional action for student success', in: Alan Seidman (ed.), *College Student Retention: Formula for Student Success*, Lanham, MD: Rowman and Littlefield, pp. 251–266

Trenet, Charles and Lawrence, Jack (1946), *Beyond the Sea* [song], iTunes [download] [Robbie Williams]. Available at: www.apple.com/uk/itunes (accessed 11 October 2015)

Tufnell, Miranda and Crickmay, Chris (2004), *A Widening Field: Journeys in Body and Imagination*, Alton, Hampshire: Dance Books

University of Adelaide (2014), *Waite Historic Precinct: Waite Arboretum Labyrinth*, 14 June. Available at: www.adelaide.edu.au/waite-historic/gardens/labyrinth/

University of the Arts, London (2013), *Mental Health and Wellbeing Day*, 20 February. Available at: http://newsevents.arts.ac.uk/event/university-mental-health-wellbeing-day/

University of Central Oklahoma (2013a), *Living Central Newsletter,* September. Available at: www.uco.edu/ur/files/LivingCentralNewsletterSEPT2013.pdf

University of Central Oklahoma (2013b), 'UCO Invites Community to Celebrate New Labyrinth at Ceremonial Dedication' [Press release], 27 August. Available at: http://broncho2.uco.edu/press/prdetail.asp?NewsID=15971

University of Central Oklahoma (2014a), *Transformative Learning*. Available at: www .uco.edu/central/tl/ (accessed 1 December 2014)

University of Central Oklahoma (2014b), *The Central Six [Tenets of Transformative Learning]*. Available at: www.uco.edu/central/tl/central6/ (accessed 1 December 2014)

University of Central Oklahoma (2015), *About University of Central Oklahoma*. Available at: www.uco.edu/about/index.asp (accessed 21 December 2014)

University of Edinburgh (2015), *Labyrinth,* 29 September. Available at: www.ed.ac .uk/labyrinth

University of Edinburgh Chaplaincy (2011), *All We've Got* [film], 15 February. Part 1: www. youtube.com/watch?v=j1jt1h8brOk&index=1&list=PL2B3FD50900090BA5, Part 2: www.youtube.com/watch?v=lODnVJrdqoQ&index=2&list=PL2B3FD50900090BA5

University of Kent (2015), *Creative Campus*. Available at: www.kent.ac.uk/creativecampus/ projects/learning/labyrinth/ (accessed 28 February 2015)

University of Maryland (2014a), *Garden*. University of Maryland, The Stamp: Division of Student Affairs. Available at: www.thestamp.umd.edu/memorial_chapel/ garden (accessed 10 July 2015)

University of Maryland (2014b), *Journey to the Center* [film], University of Maryland, UDMTV. Available at: http://thestamp.umd.edu/memorial_chapel/garden (accessed 6 January 2015)

University of Melbourne, Melbourne Medical School (2013), *Course Attributes,* Melbourne Medical School, 23 December. Available at: http://medicine.unimelb. edu.au/study-here/doctor_of_medicine/course_information/course_attributes

University of Worcester (2015), *Relax Well.* Available at: www.worcester.ac.uk/ discover/relax-well.html (accessed 10 July 2015)

van Dinther, Mart, Dochy, Filip and Segers, Mien (2011), Factors affecting students' self-efficacy in higher education, *Educational Research Review,* 6(2), 95–108. Available at: www.sciencedirect.com/science/article/pii/S1747938X1000045X

Veriditas (2014), *Veriditas.* Available at: www.veriditas.org/ (accessed 15 September 2015)

Vogler, Christopher (1992), *The Writer's Journey: Mythic Structures for Writers,* Studio City, CA: M. Weiss Productions

Walk21 (2015*), Walk21: International Conference on Walking and Liveable Communities* [conference proceedings, website]. Available at: www.walk21.com (accessed 15 September 2015)

Walker, Heather (2011), Creating a labyrinth: A personal and professional journey, *Association for University and College Counselling Journal,* March, 20–23

Wallinger, Mark (2013), *Labyrinth* [enamel plaques: multi-site art installation], London: Transport for London. Information at: http://art.tfl.gov.uk/labyrinth/ (accessed 12 October 2015)

Wang, Victor and King, Kathleen (2006), Understanding Mezirow's theory of reflectivity from Confucian perspectives: A model and perspective, *Radical Pedagogy,* 8(1), Spring. Available at: www.radicalpedagogy.org/radicalpedagogy.org/ Archives.html

Weigel, Christine, Fanning, Linda, Parker, Gary and Round, Teri (2007), The labyrinth as a stress reduction tool for nurse interns during the journey of their first year in practice, *Healing Ministry,* 14(3), 19

Welch, Sally (2010), *Walking the Labyrinth: A Spiritual and Practical Guide,* Norwich: Canterbury Press

White, Mary Joe and Stafford, Linda (2008), Promoting reflection through the labyrinth walk, *Nurse Educator,* 33(3), 99–100

Whitney, Elizabeth J. (2010), *The Art of Reflection: Using Art to Enhance Reflexivity in Midwifery Education* (unpublished MSc dissertation), University of Bradford

Wikstrom, Britt-Maj (2003), A picture of work of art as an empathy teaching strategy in nursing education complementary to theoretical knowledge, *Journal of Professional Nursing,* 19(1), 49–54

Williams, Di (2014), [Speech at opening of Dublin City University Labyrinth], in Joe Jones, *Labyrinth Opening for DCU* [film], 20 August. Available at: www.youtube.com/ watch?v=m1VqUtHAbWQ [Part 1], www.youtube.com/watch?v=XNmuvjQLbWQ [Part 2], 20 August

Williams, Di (2010), Dialogue down-under, *Interfaith Matters,* 3, 5

Williams, Di (2011), *Labyrinth: Landscape of the Soul,* Glasgow: Wild Goose

Williams, Di (2015), *Still Paths.* Available at: www.diwilliams.com/Home.html (accessed 12 October 2015)

Wirth, Jane (2005), *Labyrinth Stress Reduction Project* (unpublished research study), California, USA

Wood, Debra (2006), Wending toward wellness, *Nursing Spectrum,* 31 July

Wotjas, Olga (2002), We're serving Jesus – without the labels, *Times Higher Educational Supplement,* 20 December, 8–9

Wright, Craig (2001), *The Maze and the Warrior: Symbols in Architecture, Theology and Music,* Cambridge, MA: Harvard

Wright, Stephen G. and Sayre-Adams, Jean (2000), *Sacred Space: Right Relationship and Spirituality in Healthcare,* London: Churchill Livingstone

Wright, Stephen, Jenkins-Guarnieri, Michael and Murdock, Jennifer (2013), Career development among first-year college students: College self-efficacy, student persistence, and academic success, *Journal of Career Development,* 40(4), 292–310

Zucker, Donna M. (2012), Labyrinth walking in corrections, *Journal of Addictions Nursing,* 23, 47–54. Available at: http://works.bepress.com/donna_zucker/19/

Zucker, Donna M., Villemaire, Lorraine, Rigali, Catherine and Callahan, Kathryn (2013), The evolution of a labyrinth walking program in corrections, *Journal of Forensic Nursing,* 9(2), April–June, 101–104. Available at: http://works.bepress.com/donna_zucker/22/

Index of Universities and Other Educational Institutions

Index

Page numbers in **bold** refer to illustrations